Educational Philosophies for Teachers

Morris L. Bigge
California State University, Fresno

Charles E. Merrill Publishing Company
A Bell & Howell Company
Columbus   Toronto   London   Sydney

Published by
Charles E. Merrill Publishing Company
A Bell & Howell Company
Columbus, Ohio 43216

This book was set in Palatino
Production Editor: Gnomi Schrift Gouldin

Library of Congress Catalog Card Number: 81-85268
International Standard Book Number: 0-675-09839-4

1 2 3 4 5 6 7 8 9 10—87 86 85 84 83 82

Printed in the United States of America

To
Ada June Merriam Bigge
cherished lifelong companion

Contents

Preface

The purpose of this book is to provide a one- or two-semester orientation to educational philosophy for college students, many of whom have had no prior introduction to philosophy, and to open the way for students' supplemental reading and advanced study in educational philosophy.

The book introduces seven basic systematic educational philosophies and one analytic philosophy by presenting the position of each in regard to the principal components of an educational philosophy. A chapter is devoted to each of the educational philosophies: idealism, classical realism, dualistic theism, logical empiricism, analytic philosophy, existentialism, behavioral experimentalism, and cognitive-field experimentalism. Each philosophy is examined with regard to the following components: the nature of reality—metaphysics and ontology; the nature of human motivation; the nature and source of truth and knowledge—epistemology; the nature and source of human values—axiology; the purpose of education; the nature of the learning process; the nature of the teaching process; and the subject matter that is emphasized. (Table 1 outlines the eight educational philosophies and their components.)

Although each of the eight educational philosophies originated sometime in the past, it is currently represented or advocated either by educational philosophers or by other experts on educational theory. Each of the philosophies is presented in its best light. Critical evaluation of the concepts and development of the weaknesses of each educational philosophy is largely left to professors and students.

To many educational philosophers, educational philosophy is a philosophical study of education. To analytic philosophers, however, philosophy has a different meaning than it has to the adherents of systematic philosophies. Analytic philosophers, from a neutral stance, examine concepts they find significant to the theory and practice of education. They do not attempt to give a direction to education. Instead, they concern themselves with the logical and linguistic forms of statements involving education. In contrast, adherents of systematic philosophies take an involved stance in seeking the best possible interpretations of the world as we know it.

Students beginning their first course in educational philosophy usually are unclear about what to expect, but they anticipate being confronted, in some way, with broad, significant educational issues. Also, "People are not and do not want schools to be neutral about the life they want for their children as citizens, workers, and persons."[1] Furthermore, although philosophers who center their attention on the analysis of concepts and problems have shifted away from any "ism" approach, each one continues to be committed to an ism of some sort. Hence, a case can be made for the method this book uses to introduce teachers to educational philosophy.

The author's experience in teaching introductory courses in educational philosophy leads him to think that a comparative approach is highly effective. As graduate students in education extend their study of educational philosophy in advanced courses, they very well may shift their emphasis to an analytic approach. Or, as adherents or developers of systematic educational philosophies, they may fruitfully employ analytic procedures in developing their respective systematic approaches and outlooks.

The author's goal in presenting each philosophical position has been to present it as understandably as possible within a limited space. The author recognizes that each presentation is something less than a complete representation of both the historical background and the tenets of a position and that each position has been described more completely in other books.

This book then is not an attempt to develop educational philosophies beyond where they already are, but rather to present them to students in such a way that they may gain an understanding of educational philosophy and whet their appetites for its further study. The bibliography of each chapter has been developed with this goal in mind. Whereas there are excellent reference books on each position, there are few introductory textbooks that acquaint students with the spectrum of educational philosophy. This book develops the psychological implications and implementations of each educational philosophy far more than do other introductory books in educational philosophy. (See Table 2 for an introductory development of this facet of educational philosophy.)

The concept *education*, in its broadest meaning, covers all forms of deliberate enculturation of persons. So, a philosophy of education is a philosophy of both informal and formal education or schooling. However, since this book is a teacher's introduction to educational philosophy, it is necessary from place to place to employ the term *school* to denote the aspect of education that is characterized by teachers and other specialists working with students in institutions especially designed to conduct formal education for the purpose of transmission, and sometimes evaluation, of the culture.

Footnote

[1]Harry S. Broudy, "Philosophy of Education Between Yearbooks," *Teachers College Record* 81, no. 2 (Winter 1979): 136.

Chapter 1
What Are the Nature
and Task
of an Educational
Philosophy?

An educational philosophy is an organized, systematic outlook centered upon educational goals and the means of achieving them. In other words, it is a basic position concerning the nature of growing human beings and their total environments that is taken in relation to the appropriate purposes and operations of educational institutions.

Educational Philosophy as Educational Theory

An educational philosophy is a comprehensive educational theory consisting of a broad pattern of ideas for which there is considerable, but not absolute, supporting evidence. At least eight prevalent categories of educational philosophies may be identified and within each category the philosophic theories take several different forms. Anyone concerned with education would do well to examine carefully and critically the prevalent positions that have been developed by professional educational philosophers. This is an effective step in formulating one's own educational philosophy or theory.

Quite often in our scientific age we erroneously think of *theory* as an indefinite or indefensible conjecture that existed prior to the use of scientific knowledge. Consequently, although we might not object to using the term to describe the historical development of modern educational concepts, we would expect the word fact to be used to describe the current scene. After all, are we not now on solid enough ground for the term theory to be discarded? This, however, is not the case; theory should be emphasized, not abolished.

Any action, whether a part of teaching or some other activity in life, either is linked with theory or is blind and purposeless. Consequently, any purposeful action is governed by theory. Everyone who teaches or professes to teach has a theory of education. A teacher may or may not be able to describe that theory in explicit terms; however, we can usually deduce from the teacher's actions the theory that has not yet been verbalized. So, the important question is not whether a teacher has a theory of education, but rather how tenable it is. Everything a teacher does as a teacher is colored by the educational theory that person holds.

A teacher without a strong theoretical orientation inescapably makes little more than busywork assignments. True, many teachers operate this way and use only a hodgepodge of methods without theoretical orientation. However, this jumbled kind of teaching undoubtedly is responsible for much of the adverse criticism of public education that we hear today.

But a teacher's thinking need not be based on folklore when awareness of the most important theories developed by professional educational philosophers can produce a personal theory of education likely to be quite sophisticated. This is what professional philosophers interested in the education of teachers are trying to induce.

Questions concerning educational theory have no final answers and no theory can be found to be absolutely superior to all others. Nevertheless, a teacher can develop a personal educational philosophy that can be supported because of its internal harmony and educational adequacy. Such a philosophy may turn out to be a replica of one introduced in this book or may be derived from the contributions of several educational philosophies. In either event, the quality of one's teaching is enhanced by having thought through the nature of the educational process that a teacher wants to promote in class. What we think generally influences what we do, and any thought, except the most superficial, involves theory. So, development of a sound theory or philosophy of education is one of the most practical pursuits in which educators may engage.

We suggest that, in the process of their developing an effective educational philosophy, teachers employ the two principal criteria or measuring sticks mentioned above, *adequacy* and *harmony*. *Adequacy* means that the philosophy and its tenets are based on careful consideration of all of the pertinent information available. *Harmony* means that the adopted philosophy integrates all, or at least most, of the pertinent information into a reasonably consistent overall pattern.

In embracing an educational philosophy, an educator has at least three possible choices: to conform rigidly to one systematic philosophy;

to borrow eclectically or selectively from the various outlooks and arrange the ideas into a mosaic or patchwork, available to draw upon as the need arises; or to develop an *emergent synthesis,* a systematic outlook that benefits from knowledge of previously developed philosophies but is not an eclectic compromise amongst them. Although eclecticism has its strengths, it provides no defensible, systematic basis for knowing when to use discrete aspects of respective positions. Thus, the choice of outlook and method for each situation becomes largely a matter of whim or chance. In combining the tenets and principles of several systematic positions, teachers should guard against their slipping into that popular educational philosophy, *confusionism.*

An eclectic compromise is found by selecting aspects of opposing theories and taking a position somewhere between them. Whereas an emergent synthesis is achieved by selecting and modifying knowledge from incompatible positions and adding new thinking as needed, in order to develop a somewhat new position that is internally consistent and still more adequate than its precursors. *Emergent* indicates something novel that appears during the evolution of ideas. It is not an intermediate position, but a genuinely new outlook or concept. When an emergent outlook reflects the results of the interplay among conflicting ideas and arrives at something new, it is a *synthesis.* (See Glossary and Chapter 9, page 171, for further explanation of the meaning of an emergent synthesis.)

The Nature of Educational Philosophy

Philosophy is an activity that is undertaken when people are concerned about just what they are and what everything is about. It is an attempt to perceive, in some degree, the ways in which the various experiences of existence form some meaningful pattern. Philosophers direct their attention to people's efforts to achieve an organized picture of themselves and the universe of which they are a part. In this way, they attempt to establish some coherence throughout the entire realm of human experience.

Philosophy centers on three major questions: namely, what is real or metaphysics; what is true or epistemology; and what is good and beautiful or axiology? Educational philosophy deals with these three questions as they relate to education and also asks what is the basic nature of the educational process?

Table 1, column 1, lists eight components, or problem areas, of educational philosophy. The nature of reality and the nature of human motivation ask the question, "what is real?" The nature and source of truth and knowledge ask, "what is true?" The nature and source of human values cover the question, "what is good and beautiful?" The

Table 1. Representative Educational Philosophies

Components of the Philosophy	Chapter 2 Idealism (rationalistic)	Chapter 3 Classical Realism (rationalistic)	Chapter 4 Dualistic Theism (rationalistic)	Chapter 5 Logical Empiricism (empiricistic)
1. Nature of Reality: Metaphysics and Ontology	An absolute universe of mind or consciousness with purposeful meaning; spirit is ultimately real, not physical objects.	Platonic realism: absolute forms or ideas, not contents, of things are most real; a mental-physical dualism; eternal verities are Truth, Goodness, Beauty.	Dualism: mind and matter both created by God; presupposes the reality and presence of God, Christ, and their created Church	Reality is a physical universe governed by natural laws; existence constitutes reality, and reality exists independent of any knowledge of it.
2. Nature of Human Motivation	Good-active substantive minds (absolutely real selves) endowed with free will; minds have bodies.	People are rational animals whose neutral-active mind substance is developed through being filled and exercised.	Bad-active mind substance continues active until curbed; people are fusions of material, mental, and spiritual reality.	Neutral-passive, environmentally determined biological organisms, which are complex machines conditioned by past physical environments.
3. Nature and Source of Truth and Knowledge: Epistemology	All is God's; truth is God's answer given to people's perceptions; test for truth is unity and coherence of ideas.	Absolute truths can be apprehended, to some degree, by cultivated intellects; test for discovered truths is correspondence with reality.	Truths are available through revelation, intuition, and logical reasoning; test for absolute truth is metaphysical roots; for scientific truth is correspondence to natural laws.	Truth consists of a report on an independent and absolute reality consisting of scientifically ascertained facts; it is correspondence to natural laws; any meaningful statements must be empirically verifiable.

4. Nature and Source of Human Values: Ethics and Aesthetics	Values are real and rooted in the cosmos; persons can realize values through actively relating parts and wholes.	Human life has a form or natural law, which provides goals and standards appropriate for the good life; to achieve the good life, one must grasp this form.	Universal moral law has been established by God; we can understand much of it through reason; naturalistic or humanistic ethics are inadequate.	Values are not amenable to scientific study, they are normative, not existent; they are either subjective emotional wishes or absolutistic, nonempirical pronouncements.
5. Purpose of Education	Foster active self-realization and self-perfection of each student, who is a spiritual being; schools are revealers of ultimate reality.	Development of intellectual discipline and moral character; educational elitism; emphasize transmissions of the good and true aspects of the intellectual heritage.	Develop supernatural persons who judge, think, and act properly so as to achieve grace free from mortal sin; propagation of faith and salvation of souls.	Behavioral engineering; plan society and its members, then change observable behaviors of each organism in the desired direction.
6. Nature of the Learning Process	Vital movement from within a self outward in initiating, creating, intending, and acting; a self receives sensations and directs movements.	Mental discipline plus apperception; form habits of acquiring, using, and enjoying classical knowledge; apprehending the forms of objects and activities.	Mental discipline and faculty psychology; develop substantive wills, intellects, and bodies.	Behaviorism or S-R conditioning theory of learning; stimuli are causes, responses are effects; reinforcement is emphasized.
7. Nature of the Teaching Process	Subject meets subject in character formation; teachers set ideal examples for students to emulate.	Separate general from vocational education; emphasize disciplinary nature of learning within which students' intellects are developed to the point they, to some degree, can gain truth.	Development of good wills, minds, and bodies; catechetical mental discipline for training of intrinsic mental powers; promote awareness of God's presence.	Teaching consists of a combination of operant and reflexive conditioning of biological organisms; it results in changes in either the pattern or likelihood of behaviors.

Table 1. *Representative Educational Philosophies*

Components of the Philosophy	*Chapter 2* *Idealism* *(rationalistic)*	*Chapter 3* *Classical Realism* *(rationalistic)*	*Chapter 4* *Dualistic Theism* *(rationalistic)*	*Chapter 5* *Logical Empiricism* *(empiricistic)*
8. Subject Matter Emphasis	Literature, intellectual history, religious philosophy, and biographies, and works of great, good people.	Basic truths of liberal subjects (mathematics, literature, science, and other academic areas) are given priority over vocational subjects.	Intellectually disciplinary subjects that elevate and regulate both moral and physical aspects of life.	Specific behavioral objectives; emphasizes unity of science and hierarchy of physical and biological sciences; objective and neutral in regard to social sciences.

Table 1. *Representative Educational Philosophies*

Components of the Philosophy	*Chapter 6* *Analytic Philosophy* *(rationalistic)*	*Chapter 7* *Existentialism* *(nonrationalistic)*	*Chapter 8* *Behavioral Experimentalism* *(empiricistic)*	*Chapter 9* *Cognitive-Field Experimentalism* *(empiricistic)*
1. Nature of Reality: Metaphysics and Ontology	Reality is a nonmetaphysical existence: a physical universe governed by natural laws; the world of common sense exists in its own right.	Reality is lived existence in terms of feelings; antirational and antispeculative in regard to reality; existence precedes essence.	Reality is an emergent evolving process, not a substance; it is a nonmetaphysical, nonmaterialistic, naturalistic world of experience.	Metaphysical neutrality; emphasizes secular matters; recognize a supposed, but not posited, existent world; reality is what we *make of* ourselves and our environments, and their interrelationships.

2. *Nature of Human Motivation*	People are rational animals but not body-mind dualistic creatures; their animal nature is susceptible to scientific study; rationality is their capacity to reason, solve problems, and answer questions.	Good-proactive (forwardly active) persons, who create themselves by developing their natural talents; psychedelic humanism.	Neutral-passive biosocial organisms in serial alternating reaction with the physical-social environment; life is a process of adjustment of talking, social animals.	Neutral-interactive, purposive persons in simultaneous mutual interaction (SMI) with their psychological environments, including other persons.
3. *Nature and Source of Truth and Knowledge: Epistemology*	Knowledge consists of true beliefs supported by scientific evidence; it is incompatible with mistakes; truth is absolutely so; nonscientific discourse involves definitions, descriptions, and slogans, not truths.	Truths are personal, not social; they do not happen but are chosen by people; they are a matter of subjective choice, subjective feelings are final authority for truth.	Knowledge or truth consists of hypothesized patterns of facts that work successfully; it is tentative and gained through social experiencing; it is tested through doing and then undergoing results; intelligence is a form of behavior.	Truths may be relatively absolute; they constitute an open-ended system of warranted assertions established through experimental, empirical study; the test for truth is accurate predictability; knowledge consists of tested insights.
4. *Nature and Source of Values: Ethics and Aesthetics*	"Rational morality" consists of sequential stages of forms of moral thought; its essence is reasonings, not acts; the form, but not the content, of moral beliefs is culturally invariant.	Revolt against either public or metaphysical norms of value; anguished freedom; each person must create individual ends or goals.	Values are human made principles measured by the scope and intensity of public consequences in terms of public tastes; they are appraised according to their functional social utility.	Values are instrumental not final, relative to human origin and consequences; the outlook is melioristic rather than optimistic or pessimistic; values are acquired through application of human intelligence.

Table 1. *Representative Educational Philosophies*

Components of the Philosophy	*Chapter 6* *Analytic Philosophy* *(rationalistic)*	*Chapter 7* *Existentialism* *(nonrationalistic)*	*Chapter 8* *Behavioral* *Experimentalism* *(empiricistic)*	*Chapter 9* *Cognitive-Field* *Experimentalism* *(empiricistic)*
5. *Purpose of Education*	Education is a practical art with a scientific basis; it refines students' beliefs toward true knowledge and enhances their capacity to think rationally.	Self-actualization of individuals; development of self-directed intuitive awareness; no teacher leadership or direction.	Education is primarily a social undertaking; it consists of forming fundamental intellectual and moral dispositions (behavior patterns) toward nature and people.	Reconstruction of students' life-spaces through helping them change their insights, outlooks, and thought patterns.
6. *Nature of the Learning Process*	Knowing and believing are cognitive terms, and learning at its best is thinking, using words and concepts as tools; belief, evidence, and truth conditions are necessary to knowing that so and so is true.	Development of self-actualized persons centered on their feelings; student centered education: no coercion, prescription, or imposition.	Social behaviorism: behavioristic psychology is employed to provide social reinforcement of behaviors; learning is a process of growth through reconstruction of existing behaviors and attitudes.	Cognitive-field psychology; learnings are purposively acquired understandings, generalized insights, not changed behaviors; changed behaviors are evidence of learning, not the learning.

7. *Nature of the Teaching Process*	Teaching is an active process of developing belief systems through transmitting knowledge or shaping behavior; learning is a passive-active process, but not a pattern of movements.	Awaken persons to responsibility for themselves; fulfillment of students' needs; teachers are a resource for students in achieving self-directed growth, a gadfly function.	Teachers are directors of learning using group dynamics, they select and direct student experiences through arousing their interest; students learn by doing, by solving social problems; the project method is emphasized.	Reflective teaching including purposive involvement and perplexity; problem raising and solving; teacher-student cooperative inquiry; teacher's role similar to that of a head scientist in a laboratory.
8. *Subject Matter Emphasis*	Verifiable synthetic statements centered upon meanings and uses of words; statements about what is known, what to believe, and what to do.	Students' choice of subject matter primarily in art, moral choices, and religion; minor interest in basic subjects.	Social studies are of primary importance; they are centered on life situations in form of things to find out; students learn by doing.	Prevailing subject matter areas and aspects of the culture not as predetermined answers but as problem areas pointed toward progressive refinement of their answers.

purpose of education, the nature of the learning process, the nature of the teaching process, and what subject matter should be emphasized, all are aspects of the question, "what is the basic nature of the educational process?"

The Task of Educational Philosophy

Educational philosophy is based on the assumption that it is worthwhile for teachers, and people in general, to think clearly about the intellectual orientation of educational procedures. Educational philosophers strive to seek a fundamental formula through which all educational processes can best be understood and developed. With a well thought-out educational philosophy, they are convinced teachers will know what they are doing and why they are doing it. Educational philosophers seek a pattern of ideas, so broadly interpreted, that within it human learning can constantly be understood and promoted.

The most cogent reason to study educational philosophy is to enable educators to understand, explain, and guide their educational procedures within a comprehensive set of consistent ideas. Through the study of educational philosophy, teachers learn to think systematically about educational problems and to assess educational ideas. When a school problem arises, a teacher with a well thought-out educational philosophy has a ready set of guidelines, though not a bag of tricks, upon which to act.

Differences in curricula and teaching methods, administrative policies and procedures, and patterns of control of schools ultimately reflect differing commitments concerning the nature of human beings, knowledge, and a viable society. Such commitments are the groundwork of educational philosophies. So, when discussing educational purposes and procedures, it is highly fruitful to do so in the light of the philosophical issues involved. When discussions are held on superficial, nonphilosophical levels, the true nature and cause of disagreements often are not disclosed.

A reasonably precise use of philosophical language provides a teacher with a highly adequate tool for philosophical study and discussion. Hence, serious students of educational philosophy should give careful attention to the meanings of philosophical terms in order to both understand and correctly use basic philosophical concepts.

It is only through ideological self-criticism that a person or a society finds a better way of doing things. This is especially true in regard to teaching children and youth. Theory provides a means for our checking and evaluating our practices. Teachers who are willing to float with existing educational practices may fare very well without a considered educational philosophy; they may fly by the seat of their pants. But, when teachers want something better than the status quo, they need a considered educational philosophy to guide them in improving the general educative process and their own particular teaching procedures. So, teachers need to think through their principles, values, and purposes with all of their intellect, feeling, and imaginative capacity. When they are immersed in this process, they are being philosophical and the results of such cogitations are aspects of an educational philosophy.

An important function of educational philosophy is for both teachers and students to analyze, compare, and evaluate alternate, and often conflicting, educational outlooks. Students of educational philosophy are challenged to consider various points of view, and through mutual inquiry and consultation, to work toward formulation of their respective positions on philosophic issues.

Typically, education students represent a wide range of opinions, prejudices, convictions, and factual information. The wider this range is, the better it will be; students, most of all, learn from one another. In the pursuit of educational philosophies, statements, assumptions, and commitments are reviewed and compared in such way as to reveal their implications, adequacies and inadequacies, consistencies and inconsistencies. In this endeavor, students should respect each other as individuals and simultaneously feel free to attack each other's ideas; they should practice the art of agreeably disagreeing. When they do disagree, they should know as much as possible about the available options and the implications and consequence of each.

Eight Educational Philosophies

Educational philosophies fall into two categories: *systematic positions* identified as isms, for example *idealism*, and *analytic philosophy*. In this book we develop the various facets of seven *systematic* positions and the *analytic* position. The systematic philosophies are *idealism, classical realism, dualistic theism, logical empiricism, existentialism, behavioral experimentalism*, and *cognitive-field experimentalism* (see Table 1). Each position is presented in a separate chapter.

A systematic educational philosophy is a generalized blueprint for a more adequate and harmonious way of thinking, feeling, and acting in regard to educational matters. For this reason, each consists of a cluster of reasonably harmonious assumptions or presuppositions about educational theory, generalized to apply to every level and degree of educational practice.

Analytic philosophy centers upon rational clarification of the meanings of words, concepts, and ideas. It is a reasoning activity rather than a body of knowledge. Teachers are urged to acquire an understanding of the analytic position as well as the systematic positions.

All eight are major educational philosophies, but they do not exhaust the possibilities. Despite some overlapping among the tenets of the respective positions, there is enough individuality within each position that most educators will find themselves more in agreement with the tenets of one particular position. There are subpositions within each of the eight major educational philosophies, and chapter bibliographies include readings in the various forms of each position. Along with studying this *introduction* to the various positions, readers are urged to examine the various sources of the positions.

Introductory Statements on Each of the Educational Philosophies

Idealism is the philosophic position which asserts that reality consists of ideas, thoughts, mind, or substantive selves, of which matter is only a reflection. There are several types of idealism. The position that we describe in Chapter 2 is often called Christian idealism.

Contemporary *classical realism* stems from ancient Greek philosophies, especially those of Plato and Aristotle. *Classical* refers to something that happened long ago but remains with us. Also, a *classical* epoch marks a high peak of achievement in cultural history. Hence, aspects and achievements of the past are used as sources of models of excellence. A thing or idea is "classical" because it is deemed forever relevant; it involves certain truths and principles that hold for all times and places.

Realism in classical realism pertains to the nature of existent things and ideas. It implies that physical things as well as minds exist in their own right and that named universals such as bookness, perfection, and beauty are genuinely real.

Dualistic theism is the traditional position of Roman Catholics and some Protestants, although others are idealistic. It also has much in common with the Jewish view of education. It recognizes the existence of both a supernatural and a natural order of being. It is both a way of *teaching* about the world and man and the relationship with God and a *way of life* flowing from, informed by, and according with this teaching.

Logical empiricism exalts the methods of naturalistic empirical science and belittles all metaphysical positions, which look beyond science to understand the nature of the universe and life within it. For logical empiricists, all meaningful statements are either empirical or logical ones. *Empirical* means that they can be confirmed by physical observation and experimentation. *Logical* describes the way the statements are expressed and the relationship of propositions and definitions. Since empirically verifiable propositions are the concern of the various sciences, philosophy bears the unique task of analyzing the logical relations between propositions and defining their terms.

Analytic philosophy is the name for a school of thought that has its roots in logical empiricism, but has developed beyond that position. It is concerned with whether propositions or statements are meaningful. Meaningful propositions are ones that either can be scientifically demonstrated or are analyses of the logical relations among terms. Meaningless propositions, for analytic philosophers, are ones that can't be empirically verified and are not statements of logical relationships, for example, the statement that people have nonphysical minds.

Analytic philosophy, then, is the art of discovering truth by criticizing and clarifying the meanings of words, concepts, and ideas. Whereas the speculative philosophers deduce knowledgeable statements from what they take to be self-evident premises or truths and normative philosophers are concerned with constructing and evaluating basic outlooks, analytic philosophy is a method of criticism or clarification instead of a body of knowledge or a generalized outlook. As such it can be exercised on any subject matter, including the problems of educational theory.

Existentialism, a prevalent nonrational twentieth century educational philosophy, stresses the uniqueness and absolute freedom of each individual. Since truth is within ourselves and not in systematic thought, existentialism is a theory in which an individual finds meaning through pondering the reason for one's own existence. Before birth and after death the individual is assumed to be in an ocean of nothingness. Existence is one's encounter with nothingness; essence is one's achievement gained through this encounter.

Experimentalism is a generalized educational philosophy that emphasizes the use of experimental scientific and reflective procedures in gaining knowledge. Depending upon the psychological approach that is employed to implement it, experimentalism falls into two categories: *behavioral experimentalism*, described in Chapter 8, and *cognitive-field experimentalism*, described in Chapter 9.

During the past seventy or eighty years, experimentalism has been emerging as a constructive reaction against the absolutism that has characterized many facets of thinking throughout recorded history. Within an absolutistic system of thinking, facts are asserted to be eternally true; they are considered the direct result of either observation or intuition, and truth is taken to be ultimate and final. Experimentalists reject this as the basic frame of reference from which to approach the study of humankind and human learning.

Experimentalism is basically an epistemological philosophy; that is, it is centered on the nature of knowledge. The goal of experimentalists has been to make philosophy serviceable to mankind in general and the concerns of everyday life.

Concisely stated, experimentalists hold that emphasis should be given to critical intellectual activity as contrasted with metaphysical speculation. Ideas and actions should be tested by their *fruits* rather than by their metaphysical *roots*. The serviceable consequences of ideas are the best standard for determining their truth and value, and the method of experimental inquiry should be extended to all realms of human experience. For experimentalists, the ultimate test of any educational process is its ability to contribute to human growth. Accordingly, democratic values and procedures should be pursued both within and outside schools. The purpose of education is to attain warranted assertibilities, not absolute certainties.

Experimentalism was developed during the early part of the twentieth century by William James (1842–1910), C. S. Peirce (1839–1914), George H. Mead (1863–1931), and especially, John Dewey (1859–1952). It is probably the most truly American philosophy. Some historians think that independent life of the American frontier opened the way for development of this philosophy. However, there have been some European representatives of this position, for example, Arthur Balfour in England and Hans Vaihinger in Germany.

John Dewey's voluminous books and articles were always profound, but usually difficult to comprehend. For this reason, his statements often have been given conflicting interpretations by both his followers and his critics. For example, his often-used concept of *intelligent organisms* has been interpreted by behavioral experimentalists to mean high-order biological organisms and by cognitive-field experimentalists to mean psychological persons.[1]

During his early professional career, Dewey was committed to Hegelian idealism. Hegel studied the historical development of ideas through a dialectical process within which an existing idea *(thesis)* is challenged by an opposing idea *(antithesis)* and there emerges another idea *(synthesis)*. Around 1900, Dewey abandoned idealistic philosophy, but he continued to employ the dialectical method in his thinking. For example, in *Experience and Education,* one of his most readable books, he set "progressive education" over against "traditional education," then drew from their conflict not a compromise but an emergent position. The emergent position is centered upon his interpretation of experience as characterized by the principles of continuity, which means that each experience gains something from experiences that have occurred and influences those experiences that follow it, and interaction between human beings and their environments. (See pages 192–193 for an explanation of these principles.)

Dewey was unique as a philosopher because he thought that the best laboratory for testing any systematic theoretical philosophy was its application to work-a-day educational situations. Accordingly he stated, "If we are willing to conceive education as the process of forming fundamental dispositions, intellectual and emotional, toward nature and fellow men, philosophy may even be defined *as the general theory of education.*"[2]

Although, in recent years, academic philosophers have moved heavily into analytic philosophy, they also are showing a renewed interest in Dewey's experimentalist philosophy and its "naturalistic humanism."[3] So, "Humanism and the problems of humanity that students discussed in courses organized according to isms are once more in the forefront of scholarly attention, albeit the new and the old humanisms do not always sound like variations on the same theme."[4]

In their study of two experimentalisms, teachers should bear in mind that, in the past, "Dewey's educational philosophy seldom was applied, [and] seldom was understood."[5] For example, it often has been confused with the romanticism that characterized the Progressive Education movement.

Both behavioral and cognitive-field experimentalists base much of their thinking on the ideas of Dewey. Hence, they have much in common. For example, they both reject the idea that humankind is equipped with any ready-made instinctive patterns of behavior. Also, they agree that their position that ideas and actions should be evaluated on the basis of their fruits rather than any metaphysical roots has spearheaded redefinitions of humankind, the nature of knowledge, and the learning process. However, they disagree quite sharply about metaphysical positions and in the use of psychology to implement their philosophies. Behavioral experimentalists, in an attempt to escape all forms of dualism, insist that the natural world we live in is the only reality. Cognitive-field experimentalists, in contrast, maintain a neutral position in regard to all metaphysical, nonsecular, or theological beliefs. Also, whereas behavioral experimentalists emphasize *behavior* and *adjustment*, cognitive-field experimentalists emphasize *insight* and *understanding*. This difference becomes most important when psychology is employed as a foundation of the actual teaching-learning procedures of formal education.

Alternate Names for the Educational Philosophies

In other books on the subject, the various educational philosophies often are identified by other titles than the ones used in this book. Having several titles for each position is confusing, but this is just the way things are. Throughout this book, we consistently hold to the same title for each position. But, readers will benefit from a knowledge of these alternate titles as they examine other books on educational philosophy.

Idealism sometimes is called *Christian idealism* or *mentalistic monism*. *Classical realism* is also called *rational realism* or *lay neo-Thomism*. *Dualistic theism* may be called *theistic supernaturalism, ecclesiastical neo-Thomism, religious realism,* or *mind-body dualism. Logical empiricism* sometimes is called *logical positivism,* which was its forerunner. *Analytic philosophy* also goes by the names *linguistic analysis, verbal analysis,* the *new rationalism,* or just simply *analysis. Existentialism* often is identified as *radical existentialism, psychedelic humanism,* or *phenomenological philosophy. Behavioral experimentalism* often is called just *experimentalism.* The radical wing of behavioral experimentalism is called *social reconstructionism. Cognitive-field experimentalism* also is called *positive relativism* and sometimes *moderate existentialism.*

Some Basic Issues in Educational Philosophy

There are three basic issues in educational philosophy that have emerged from its close relationship to "pure" philosophy. These issues may be identified as *monism* vs *dualism, rationalism* vs *empiricism,* and *free will* vs *determinism.* We suggest that, in their study of future chapters, readers observe the position of each of the educational philosophies in regard to these major issues. This process will provide some pivotal concepts around which to build an understanding of each philosophy. We, here, only introduce the issues and name the different educational philosophies that are aligned with each position.

Monism vs Dualism

Monism is the philosophical idea that there is only *one* kind of fundamental reality. It may be called mind, God, matter, or something else. Whereas idealism is a mind-reality monism, logical empiricism and analytic philosophy are matter-reality monisms.

Dualism is the philosophical idea that reality is composed of two basically different kinds of fundamental substance that cannot be reduced to one another. In a broad sense, these substances are mind and matter. Classical realism and dualistic theism are dualistic philosophies. Existentialism and the two experimentalisms do not lend themselves to either a monistic or dualistic categorization.

Rationalism vs Empiricism

A second basic issue in educational philosophy is rationalism vs empiricism. *Rationalism* means that the basic source of knowledge is reason. A philosophy is rationalistic if its adherents think that each person either is or has a mind that has the ability to know truths directly; things need not be perceived by the senses in order to be true. The three traditional rationalistic philosophies are idealism, classical realism, and dualistic theism. These philosophies are also speculative ones. *Speculative* means that their adherents think that the role of philosophers is to make considered guesses or speculations about the absolute nature of the cosmos, or the universe, and the people in it. So, they are primarily concerned with the way matters really are.

Existentialism is an antirationalistic and antispeculative philosophy. Analytic philosophy is a rationalistic, but nonspeculative, philosophy.

Empiricism means that the basic source of knowledge is experience, not reason. A philosophy is empiricistic if its adherents emphasize that human learning centers on perceptual, sensory experience instead of being centered on the mentalistic, speculative reasoning or *rational* process that is emphasized in idealism, classical realism, and dualistic theism. Behavioral experimentalism, logical empiricism, and cognitive-field experimentalism are empiricist educational philosophies. But these three philosophies differ sharply in regard to the meaning of *experience* and therefore in how they interpret the nature of the learning process. These three philosophies all emphasize the nature and achievements of modern science in today's world. But, they differ significantly from one another in regard to how the scientific method and procedures are to be defined and applied.

Free Will vs Determinism

A third basic issue in educational philosophy is free will vs determinism. This issue is closely related to how one views the nature of human motivation. A commitment to free will means that one senses within oneself a genuine power of self-determining choice in regard to absolutistic moral principles. A mentalistic, substantive *will* is the force that guides, molds, and directs the life of a person. The will is endowed with the power to choose among motives and either to act or refrain from action. Commitment to the idea of free will involves the conviction that at a choice point one went one way but could have gone the other. Therefore, in the event that one has made the wrong turn, one should be conscious of guilt. Within idealism and dualistic theism, free will is a person's sovereign faculty, distinct from and superior to any sensory desires, physical impulses, and emotional cravings; it has its source beyond one's world of experience.

Determinism is the view that human behavior is caused and entirely controlled by previous chains of causes and effects; it is determined. Determinism denies the existence of a will that is free of what went before, holding instead that all our acts result from some combination of reflexes, instincts, stimuli, sensations, feelings, associations, and habits, which forms their antecedent cause. Whereas adherents of the substantive free will position make much of personal responsibility for past actions, determinists assert that whatever a person did in a given situation is the only thing which the individual could have done. For a determinist, there is no logical basis for guilt. The free-willer, on the other hand, is convinced that even though a person did act in such and such a way in a given situation, that individual could have willed, and consequently done, otherwise. Behavioral experimentalism, logical empiricism, and analytic philosophy hold deterministic positions in regard to causation and human motivation.

Classical realists, existentialists, and cognitive-field experimentalists also sometimes use the expression *free will*, but they give it different meanings than do idealists and dualistic theists. They simply mean freedom of choice in the sense of freedom to make decisions and carry them out. But, even their respective interpretation of free will contrasts against a complete determinism, which means that all human experiences and behaviors result from prior forces, just as the positions and movements of the parts of an engine result from a prior movement and position.

The Components of Educational Philosophy

In Chapters 2 through 9, we develop the historical background and the concepts of each of the educational philosophies. We employ the same eight basic components of a philosophical position to explain in some detail the tenets of each philosophy (see Table 1). These components are: the nature of reality, the nature of human motivation, the nature and source of truth and knowledge, the nature and source of values, the purpose of education, the nature of the learning process, the nature of the teaching process, and the subject matter emphasis. The first two of these components, because of their involved nature, are introduced in this chapter.

The Nature of Reality
The philosophical problem regarding the nature of reality is called *ontology*. Thus, ontology is "is-ology": What is the nature of the being of Being? In its historical sense, the term *reality* has been an absolutistic one. The presumption back of its use has been that there is a preexistent metaphysical reality, which overrides any and all perceptions of it. Within an absolutistic frame of reference, the ontological pursuit has been, not to question the meaningfulness of *reality*, but to determine the nature of existence as an aspect of metaphysics.

Metaphysics means literally *after* physics, but *beyond* physics gives us a more accurate sense of its current meaning. Metaphysics includes ontology, the problem of being; cosmology, the problem of the nature of the order of being; and teleology, the problem of the purpose of the universe's being. The term metaphysical means of, or relating to, what is conceived to be supersensible, and consequently transcendental to humankind's sensory experience. What this says is that metaphysical reality is an ultimate reality, one which lies beyond the observable world; it is a reality that underlies its physical objects.

The Nature of Human Motivation

Educational philosophy is concerned with just what kind of creatures human beings are and what is the nature and source of their motivation. *Motivation* refers to the mainsprings or instigators of behavior. Because of their contrasting conceptions of the basic nature of human beings, adherents of the different educational philosophies have different positions in regard to the source and nature of human motivation.

Motivation arises from a relationship between people and their respective environments. But what is the nature of this relationship? In other words, what is the basic nature of human beings as it expresses itself through each individual's dealings with his environment? This question may be rephrased as, What would children and youth be like if they should be left entirely on their own? This is the raw material with which teachers must work. Although a teacher may not have thought out a specific answer to this question, the way he or she teaches inevitably implies an answer.

The basic outlook of each educational philosophy, to a large degree, rests upon its adherents' particular conception of the *psychological nature of human beings.* One way to study people's generic psychological nature is to consider the character of their basic innate *moral* and *actional* natures. That is, to think about what general psychological features characterize all people as members of the human race. It is essential to make clear that we are using the word *people* in a generic sense. It applies to all members of the human race, and thus to all students at all levels of education and ability. Furthermore, as used here, *innate* and *basic* both mean original or unlearned.

Conception of people's basic innate *moral* and *actional* nature involves the fundamental way in which the teacher views his students. This has a major influence upon the way that the teacher operates in the classroom and the manner in which the students learn as well as upon the outcomes of their learning. Consideration of the basic nature of people would be quite simple were there only one answer. But, interestingly, several distinctly different and mutually opposed answers to this question each enjoy a good deal of support.

Each of the two aspects of the problem of people's basic nature has at least three possible alternatives. They may be stated as follows: In *basic moral natures,* people are (1) innately *bad;* (2) innately *good;* or (3) their original moral nature is *neutral,* that is, originally neither good nor bad. Then, *actionally* or in relationship to their environments people are (1) innately *active,* (2) innately *passive* or *reactive,* or (3) basically *interactive.*

Three Alternate Assumptions Concerning People's Basic Moral Nature. If we assume people's moral nature to be innately bad, then we can expect nothing good from them, except by outside influence. If left to themselves, their badness will naturally unfold; persons will show no traits other than bad ones. Contrariwise, if we assume that people are innately good, then unless they are corrupted by some outside force, everything that comes from them will be good. Assumed neutrality in people's basic moral nature simply means that by nature they are neither innately bad nor innately good. Notice that people's neutrality, as used here, refers only to their innate goodness or badness; it in no sense means that students by nature are inactive.

Three Alternate Assumptions Concerning People's Actional Nature and Their Environmental Relationships.   If the nature of children and youth is *active* then their underlying characteristics are inborn; their psychological natures come from within them. Environment is only the location in which their nature unfolds. Notice that a person's mere physical movement does not necessarily indicate being psychologically active. In order to be psychologically active, the power of one's personal motives must be inner-directed and originate entirely from within. If individuals are basically *passive* or *reactive* their characteristics are largely a product of environmental influences. Thus, their natures are determined by their environments. This does not mean that people do not move about. But it does mean that they are non-purposive and that their behavior is caused by forces outside themselves.

If people are *interactive,* their psychological characteristics result from making sense of their physical and social environments. So their psychological natures arise from personal-environmental relationships. Hence, each person's reality consists of that which he or she *makes of* what is being gained through that person's own unique experience. These three mutually opposed assumptions in regard to the nature of human beings and their environmental relationships are illustrated in Figure 1.

Figure 1. Models of mutually opposed assumptions in regard to the basic actional nature of people and their respective environmental relationships.

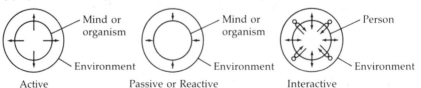

From Morris L. Bigge, *Learning Theories for Teachers,* 3rd ed. (New York: Harper & Row, 1976), p. 16. Reprinted by permission.

Five Alternate Combinations of Assumed Moral Natures With Assumed Actional Natures and Their Implied Environmental Relationships. When we consider the possible, feasible combinations of assumptions concerning people's basic moral nature together with those concerning their actional relationship with their environment, we might reasonably assume the innate natures of students to be either bad-active, neutral-active, good-active, neutral-passive, or neutral-interactive (see Table 2).

There are, then, at least five distinctly different ways in which a teacher may view his students, and each of the ways reflects either one or two specific educational philosophies. A teacher may think that students are (1) innately bad-active individuals in need of direction—dualistic theism; (2) neutral-active rational animals—classical realism; (3) good-active autonomous personalities that develop through expression of their needs, abilities, and talents—idealism and existentialism; (4) neutral-passive organisms whose development depends upon how they are conditioned by outside stimuli—logical empiricism; or (5) neutral-interactive purposive persons, who develop through psychological interaction with their psychological environments—cognitive-field experimentalism. Behavioral experimentalism and analytic philosophy each represent a combination of two views in regard to the psychological nature of students. People consist of neutral-passive organisms accompanied by neutral-active rationalities.

Table 2. Assumptions About People's Basic Moral and Actional Nature and the Educational Philosophies With Which They Harmonize

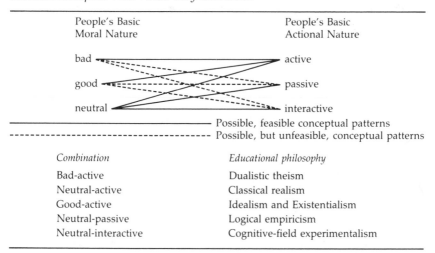

Combination	Educational philosophy
Bad-active	Dualistic theism
Neutral-active	Classical realism
Good-active	Idealism and Existentialism
Neutral-passive	Logical empiricism
Neutral-interactive	Cognitive-field experimentalism

From Morris L. Bigge, *Learning Theories for Teachers*, 3rd ed. (New York: Harper & Row, 1976), p. 17. Reprinted by permission.

Footnotes

[1]See Morris L. Bigge, "Dewey's Relativistic Philosophy, Lewin's Field Psychology, and Learning," in *Philosophy of Education in Cultural Perspective,* ed. James John Jelinek (Tempe, Ariz.: Far Western Philosophy of Education Society, 1977), pp. 399–421.

[2]John Dewey, *Democracy and Education* (New York: Macmillan, 1916), p. 383.

[3]See R. S. Peters, ed., *John Dewey Reconsidered* (London: Routledge & Kegan Paul, 1977).

[4]Harry S. Broudy, "Philosophy of Education Between Yearbooks," *Teachers College Record,* 81, no. 2 (Winter 1979): 137.

[5]Joe R. Burnett, "Whatever Happened to John Dewey?", *Teachers College Record,* 81, no. 2. (Winter 1979): 202.

BIBLIOGRAPHY

Beck, Clive. *Educational Philosophy and Theory.* Boston: Little Brown, 1974.

Belth, Marc. *The New World of Education.* Boston: Allyn and Bacon, 1970.

Brameld, Theodore. *Patterns of Educational Philosophy.* New York: Holt, Rinehart and Winston, 1971.

Butler, J. Donald. *Four Philosophies and Their Practice in Education and Religion,* 3rd ed. New York: Harper & Row, 1968.

Cahn, Steven M. *Education and the Democratic Ideal.* Chicago: Nelson-Hall, 1979.

Eisner, Elliot W., and Vallance, Elizabeth, eds. *Conflicting Concepts of Curriculum.* Berkeley, Calif.: McCutchan Publishing Corporation, 1974.

Green, Maxine. *Landscapes of Learning.* New York: Teachers College Press, 1978.

Gruber, Frederick C. *Historical and Contemporary Philosophies of Education.* New York: Crowell, 1973.

Henry, Nelson B., ed. *Modern Philosophies and Education.* Chicago: The University of Chicago Press, 1955.

Honer, Stanley M., and Hunt, Thomas C. *Invitation to Philosophy.* Belmont, Calif.: Wadsworth, 1969.

Howick, William H. *Philosophies of Education,* 2nd ed. Danville, Ill.: Interstate Printers and Publishers, 1980.

Knape, Carl, and Rosewell, Paul T. "The Philosophically Discerning Classroom Teacher," *Educational Studies,* 11, no. 1 (Spring 1980).

Kneller, George E. *Introduction to the Philosophy of Education,* 2nd ed. New York: Wiley & Sons, 1971.

Morris, Van Cleve, and Pai, Young. *Philosophy and the American School.* Boston: Houghton Mifflin, 1978.

O'Connor, D. J. *An Introduction to the Philosophy of Education.* London: Routledge & Kegan Paul, 1957.

O'Neill, William F. *Educational Ideologies: Contemporary Expressions of Educational Philosophy.* Santa Monica, Calif.: Goodyear, 1981.

Ozmon, Howard, and Craver, Samuel. *Philosophical Foundations of Education.* Columbus, Ohio: Charles E. Merrill, 1976.

Peters, R. S. *Education and the Education of Teachers.* London: Routledge & Kegan Paul, 1977.

Phenix, Philip H., ed. *Philosophies of Education.* New York: Wiley & Sons, 1961.

"Philosophy of Education Since Mid-Century," *Teachers College Record,* 81, no. 2, (Winter 1979): 127–247.

Pratte, Richard. *Contemporary Theories of Education.* Scranton, Pa.: International Textbook Company, 1971.

Titus, Harold H. *Living Issues in Philosophy,* 5th ed. New York: Van Nostrand Reinhold, 1970.

Wirsing, Marie E. *Teaching and Philosophy: A Synthesis.* New York: Houghton Mifflin, 1972.

Chapter 2
Idealism in Education

The heart of idealism is the belief that basic reality consists of ideas, thoughts, minds, or substantive selves, not physical matter. Since priority is given to minds, minds have bodies, but bodies do not have minds. Idealism usually carries with its view the idea of the subsistence (the superexistence) of God, who also is basically mind or self. The universe is an expression of intelligence and will; its order is due to an eternal, spiritual reality. For idealists, people are good-active substantive minds; they are absolutely real selves endowed with free will or genuine moral choice. This philosophy has ancient roots; it dates back to Socrates (469–399 B.C.) and Plato (427–347 B.C.).

Idealism really is idea-ism. The source of this title is based on Platonic thought. For Plato, ideas alone were genuinely real; they consisted of immaterial essences. That which people perceive is a *shadow* of reality; each thing that they perceive gets its existence from its Thingness; an Idea. A book is a book because of its being a more or less imperfect replica of Bookness. A woman is a woman because she is a replica of Womanness. Plato's assumed world of "eternal verities" consisted of the True, the Good, and the Beautiful.

We can trace the development of idealism by listing some of the leading philosophers who have contributed to this position and stating a leading idea that each has contributed to the philosophy. Socrates believed that children are born with knowledge already in their minds, but that they needed help to recall this innate knowledge. Plato contributed the idea of Ideas, which are the universal forms of all existing things and are the essence of reality. Saint Augustine (350–430) held a dualistic (mind-body) theory of humanity within which the mind or soul is the seat of the force of goodness.

René Descartes (1596–1650) was a mind-body dualist who stated, I think, therefore I am. Thus, he was certain of only mental reality. He posited God as the only self-sustaining substance; who transcends and gives meaning to both minds and bodies. A mind, however, has its seat in the pineal gland at the base of the brain, and from there it *controls* the body. George Berkeley (1685–1753) was a subjective idealist. His maxim was *Esse est percipi* (to be is to be perceived). This meant that the existence of anything consisted of its being perceived or thought by some mind: either God's or some human being's.

Immanuel Kant (1724–1804) thought that the real world, independent of human minds (noumena) cannot be known by us as it is in itself. So, the world of experienceable things is made up of the world of appearance (phenomena). But, Kant also thought that it is possible for a person to act purely out of the intention to do good, that is, to fulfill the moral law, which reason, completely free from sensory experience, prescribes as the proper guide to conduct.

Georg Hegel (1770–1831) was an absolute idealist. "For him, the natural order is a finite and temporal aspect of the Absolute Mind, which is infinite and permanent."[1] So, history is God thinking, and the history of the human race consists of recurrence of the ideological triad: *thesis, antithesis,* and *synthesis*. For example, conflict of the antithesis of innocent intention within the thesis (evil) gave rise to the synthesis— conscience. (This Hegelian dialectic was the launching idea upon which John Dewey later developed his emergent position, the underpinning of pragmatic, experimentalist philosophy.)

Some more recent leading idealists were Fredrich Froebel (1782–1852) who taught that everything is in God; Ralph Waldo Emerson (1803–1882), an American essayist and poet who thought that God is above being a person of any kind; Henri Bergson (1859–1941) who equated God with life itself; and Giovanni Gentile (1875–1944) who taught that mind is an activity in an everlasting state of change and who provided a rationalistic background for Mussolini.

Idealistic educational philosophy in the United States has been represented by William T. Harris (1835–1909) who, as superintendent of schools, operated the St. Louis school system according to Hegelian principles; Herman H. Horne (1874–1946), a professor of educational philosophy at New York University, who emphasized that everything is God's; Rupert C. Lodge (1888–1961), whose textbook on realism, idealism, and pragmatism became a classic; and J. Donald Butler (1908–), the leading contemporary idealist educational philosopher.

Idealism: The Nature of Reality

Idealism really is Idea-ism, and an idea is a genuinely real nonphysical essence that is the foundation of every existent thing. Whereas things only *exist*, ideas *subsist*. Mentalistic ideas, minds, or selves are the ultimate reality. So, an active substantive mind or consciousness is the very essence of the universe and its various structures, and human consciousness is a more or less errant variant of this universal mind.[2] To repeat, idealists' substantive minds have bodies, but their nonsubstantive bodies do not have minds.

For idealists, minds are immaterial, yet very real. In fact, they are the most real things of all. What is meant by minds is that which people introspectively know themselves to be. Today's idealists concur with Descartes' seventeenth century statement, I think, therefore I am.

Idealism: The Nature of Human Motivation

The basic tenets of an idealist are that (1) one's origin is within the mind of the deity, (2) one's basic nature is an active substantive mind endowed by the deity with a free will, and (3) one's purpose on earth and eventual destiny are immortality. These three assumptions in regard to the basic nature of human beings epitomize much of the Idealist theory of motivation, within which people consist of good-active substantive minds that are endowed with free will and have bodies to serve them.

People's origin within the mind of the deity means that they are finite, limited beings who come from God and are growing into the image of God, the infinite. Their being endowed by the deity with free will means that they are free in the sense that God is free; they are not determined by their physical and social environment. All-powerful God, by exercising his will, can do anything he desires. People, being a part of God, also have a basic nature that is characterized by freedom. So, a student is essentially a transcendental self, needing assistance in setting himself free from the fetters imposed by the physical and social world. Mind or self is primary and things, including one's biological organism, are secondary. Since people are the only earthly beings that have substantive minds, they are the only educable beings. Lower animals can be trained, but they cannot be educated. Only God and people are actualized, self-active minds.

People's purpose on earth and eventual destiny are immortality. That means as God is immortal, people share the immortality. They are, however, finite beings in the presence of the infinite.

Idealism: The Nature and Source of Truth and Knowledge

Idealistic educational philosophy centers upon epistemology—its theory of knowledge. Since God makes himself evident in the universe, once we understand the nature of knowledge, our understanding will open the way to understanding the nature of reality as a spiritual universal God. God is the self-conscious unity of all reality, and "*to be* is to be experienced by an absolute self."[3]

Since reality is a Universal Mind, which is a logically unified total system, the order of the world is due to the manifestations in space and time of this eternal, spiritual reality. This universal reality is a self, and since nothing can be conceived to exist without its existing in relation to other things, human beings also are selves that are directly experienced as self-evident existents. "From the idealistic point of view the growth and development of knowledge, whether in the individual mind or in the experience of the race, is a matter of extending vision so that individuals and classes are seen in their larger and more complete relationship."[4] The more knowledge is developed, the more analysis and synthesis occur. Through these processes wholes are seen with deeper insight as being constituted of interrelated parts.

Knowledge, then, results from studying the thoughts and purposes of eternal, spiritual reality as embodied in this world of factual experience. It does not relate to objects and events alone, but neither does it relate to persons isolated from external events. "Knowledge only happens when a being who has capacity for knowing crosses paths with entitites external to him about which he does something, such as characterizing or organizing them."[5]

Both idealists and classical realists conceive thinking to be a process discharged by an active, rational, substantive mind. So their interpretations of thinking are quite similar. However, they differ in that, whereas idealists emphasize that one lives one's way into a personal system of thinking, classical realists teach that one should think one's way rationally into a system of living. But, for both idealists and classical realists, thinking is the process whereby an active, subjective mind reads meaning into the universe. This is accomplished through rational development of the universe's coherent conceptual structure. Within the thinking process, a finite mind, or mentalistic self, uses its cognitive faculties to attune itself to an infinite spiritual reality.

Truth is such because it corresponds to the ultimate spiritual reality, and testing its unity and coherence determines whether it is true. Truth happens to persons, not to things. Since everything is a part of God's consciousness, truth is the nature and content of that consciousness. Hence, it is absolute, ultimate, and final. Through contemplation and intuition people may discover original truths. Then, other truths may be derived from these original truths through deduction, using formal logic. So, truth consists of God's answer given to people's intuition and reason.

Idealism: The Nature and Source of Human Values

For idealists, values are genuine, absolute actualities that are rooted in the spiritual Cosmos. The "morality of man has a sanction in the nature, purpose, and will of the Infinite Mind."[6] All human values are temporal expressions of an eternal order, which has value within itself. The object of living and learning is to develop natural people into ideal ones patterned primarily after God, the absolutely greatest personality, and secondarily after the great human personalities of history.

God: The Ultimate Source of Goodness

God or Universal Mind is wholly good. Then, what is the nature and source of evil? Since only perfection is ultimately real, "Evil is nonsubsistent; it is necessary possibly in a world where individuals have the freedom to realize the good."[7] So, evils such as wars, poverty, ignorance, and disease are absence of adequate motives or means for good. Sin, which is commitment to evil, means missing the mark. Sin, then, is a part of the immaturity of the human world. It is a negative concept that is absent in the positive perfection of God, so it is not a characteristic of Ultimate Mind. Goodness, in contrast with evil, is conformity of human wills with the moral administration of the universe.

Human Values

"The origin of man is God, the nature of man is freedom, and the destiny of man is immortality."[8] "God exists, and in Him all value resides, in Him is that perfection in which all possible positive values are fully realized and enjoyed."[9] Students are actualized, self-active minds. Being self-active means that they have free wills. They are self-active in the same way, but not to the same degree, that God is self-active. Each person is a potential that may become either good or bad, depending upon his education and his will. Education nurtures conscience, which directs will. So, with adequate, proper education, each student, who is basically good, exercises his will in such manner as to direct himself to his ultimate destiny—immortality.

Value exists whenever an individual works out the adjustment that gives one personal value and when the individual has the emotional experience which is the enjoyment of that value. Values of human life are what they are largely because there are persons to possess and enjoy them.

People come to realize values through actively relating parts and wholes; the ultimately real relations are those of whole and part, of including and being included. People possess aesthetic values when they understand and appreciate a work of art as a differentiated whole through analyzing and synthesizing its parts. Social values are realized through each person's recognition of his or her place as a part of a total society and when each one is willing to grant others their due privileges. Religious values arise as individuals practice their relations to God, the total Person, in worship, fellowship, and service.

A Hierarchy of Educational Values

Horne listed the following hierarchy of educational values, beginning with the greatest one of all[10]

1. *Worship* is bringing people into conscious relation to the infinite spirit of the universe.

2. *Character and justice* is the bent of the will of people toward eternal right.

3. *Production and enjoyment of the beautiful* is a revelation of infinite perfection.

4. *Knowledge* consists of thinking of the thoughts embodied in the structure of the universe.

5. *Skill* is whatever is requisite to one's economic independence, which is related to both personal character and social justice.

6. *Good health* is a value that is basic to all the others.

Idealism: The Purpose of Education

For idealists, the ultimate real is Spirit, which is absolutely good. Hence, idealists foster active self-realization and self-perfection of each student—a spiritual being. The self-realization or perfection is derived from a connection with, and belief in, a Universal Self. Thus, all education, within idealist intentions, deals in the end with matters of faith not only with morals. Since presently existing people and their society are only transitory in nature, education must conform to the ultimate— God. Idealist-inspired education is *Ideal*-centered as contrasted with its being either *child*- or *subject matter*-centered. It is ideal-centered because "the Ideal, now poorly realized in man and society, is the ultimately real foundation of all things."[11]

For idealists, education is inner spiritual growth of students. This growth consists of development of students' basic spiritual nature toward selfhood, self-consciousness, and self-direction. The purpose of education is to assist the rising generation of people toward achievement of their full growth. So, education should stretch learners to the limits of their abilities and bring them to the edges of their existence where they are forced to ask decisive questions concerning ultimate reality and they are placed in the way of getting echoes of final answers.

For idealists, there are four fundamental reasons for the existence of schools. First of all, schools are one of the revealers of ultimate reality. Then, in addition, schools should bring students to a cultural birth, education should be developed in a social context, and schools, and their teachers, should guide society so as to give it leadership and strive to remake it.

Idealism: The Nature of the Learning Process

Since idealism posits a reality that is mental, learning is centered upon operations of minds. An educable human learner, as distinguished from an animal to be trained, is an actualized, self-active mind. "Pupils and teachers are more than vital mechanisms or behaving organisms; they are living spirits."[12] Learning is a process of mental growth within which a self or personality expands in its development of selfhood, self-consciousness, and self-direction. It takes place through contemplation, imitation, and reasoning. In final analysis, then, learning is the upbuilding of humanity in the image of divinity.

Students as learners are more than responding organisms or social units. They are finite personalities growing into the likeness of an Infinite Ideal; souls capable of genuine initiatives. Their responses are the active struggles of these initiatives germinating and growing into bloom. Thus, selves, personalities, or minds are central in gaining and organizing knowledge. *Experience,* for idealists, *is the active functioning of these mentalistic selves.*

The mind is the source of its own reactions on the world. It interprets sensations and directs movements. Since, *"The development of mind is from within out, not from without in,"*[13] it is only when the self of a person becomes attached to activities by its own initiative that real growth and development occur. Hence, learning "is not so much the stimulus shaping the individual, as the individual responding to the stimulus."[14] Since we live our way into a system of thinking rather than think our way into a system of living, "Living is more influential in determining thinking than thinking is in determining living."[15]

Idealists recognize the existence of behavioristic organic processes in learning. Hence, they speak of relations between biological stimuli and responses. But, stimuli-response relations are not the essence of learning. Although children can learn as animals learn, animals cannot learn as children do; they have no substantive minds to interpret sensations and direct movements.

Idealists define habit formation in terms of sensations, perception, and movements. Whereas sensation is a function of an organism, perception is a function of a mind. Sensation interpreted through perception becomes knowledge, and knowledge directed becomes will. The knowledge (habits) of an educated person is sufficiently general to make him or her feel at home in the universe and yet specific enough to make his work in the world a pleasure to himself and a profit to others.

Idealism: The Nature of the Teaching Process

For idealists, *"Education is the eternal process of superior adjustment of a free, conscious, human being to God."*[16] The primary purpose of education is to foster active self-realization and self-perfection in each student as a spiritual being. Adherents of this educational philosophy are first of all *metaphysical* idealists, then secondarily, they are moral and social ones. For them the ultimate real is the absolutely good Spirit, God.[17]

Teaching, first of all, consists in the teacher setting a proper example for students to imitate; that of an active, mature person living in a creative fashion. The teacher creates the students' educational environment and provides their chief source of inspiration. Accordingly, the teacher constantly inspires those purposive, active responses of learners that are promoted by the learners' inherent interest in their work. Within the teaching-learning process, solid book learning and lecturing are tempered by some slight feeling of suspense in students that is promoted through teacher-led questioning and discussion. Teachers help students live their way into a system of thinking, rather than think their way into a system of living.

Individuals that are encountered in classrooms, as well as in present society, are some distance from the goodness of God in their moral achievements. Since both individuals and society are uncertain and changing, education must conform to an ultimate reality, which is God. So, education, in final analysis, is the upbuilding of humanity in the image of Divinity; a learner is a finite person growing into the image of the infinite Person. Education, then, is inner spiritual growth of persons toward greater selfhood, self-consciousness, and self-direction.

"The educated person is not just a complicated mechanism, not just a set of conditioned reflexes, not just another, though higher, animal, not even a cultivated vocationalist. He is a cultivated personality, ever becoming more cultivated and more of a person."[18] People transcend the realm of nature in their power of conceptual thought, their artistic ideals, and their feeling of obligation to exercise their wills. Whereas matter is indifferent to right and wrong, mind, having a conscience, is sensitive to the difference between the two.

Idealists consider interest an important factor in learning. It is conceived as such a totally positive attraction to the job at hand, that one needs no exertion to perform it; it is an activity pleasurable to the self. Interest, so defined, is developed through *apperception*. Apperception is a process of new ideas relating themselves to a store of old ones within one's mind. In teaching, interest is used to motivate students to a stage where self-effort can be relied upon. The secret of interesting or motivating students is to present their minds with a variety of unity. Unity by itself is tiring, and variety alone is distracting.

What Is the Proper Role of Teachers?
The role of teachers is central in the idealist pattern of education: "the teacher is more the key to the educative process than any other element comprising it."[19] Personalities have supreme worth, and teachers should be personalities or selves more *mature* than those of any of their students. So, teachers as archetypical selves should serve as exemplary mediators between microcosmic selves (students) and the absolute self.

For idealists, an ideal teacher should aim toward being the following:[20]
1. A co-worker with God in perfecting man.
2. The personification of reality for students to emulate.
3. A specialist in knowledge about students.
4. An excellent professional technician.
5. An exemplar of propriety.
6. A personal good friend of each student.
7. One who awakens the desire to learn in students.
8. A master of the art of mature living.
9. One who capably communicates his subjects.
10. One who appreciates—enjoys—the subject he teaches.
11. One who is always learning as he teaches.
12. A conservative apostle of progress.
13. A promoter of democratic living—"a spiritual unity in a social variety."[21]
14. An example of self-elimination—losing oneself in helping one's students grow to a higher life.

What Methods Should Teachers Use?
For idealists, classroom teaching is primarily a meeting of personalities. Less mature selves are stimulated to participate in the experience of a more mature self, and in the process, to become broader, more mature, and more interesting ones. Students are encouraged to imitate worthy models of creative work and a noble teacher's personality. "Idealism says that common habits of life arise because youngsters naturally imitate their elders and by this process grow to maturity,

sometimes attaining levels of achievement above those they imitate."[22]

Through questioning and discussion, supplemented by solid instruction through lecturing and student activities, a teacher should share
experiences with the students, inviting them to seek, in the teacher's
company, progressively deeper insights and thereby develop their personalities to the utmost. "Since it is the self-activity of the pupil in
which genuine education and development take place, he wants the
students to be confronted by decision and selection as much of the
time as practicable."[23] Throughout all teaching activities, the active responses of learners are sought. Real growth and development of selves
occur only when students become attached to activities by their own
initiative.

Professor Butler emphasizes that in leading discussions, teachers
should present thought-provoking questions for the purpose of lend-
ing significance and meaning to the content being studied and confronting students with alternatives, thereby evoking their judgments.
Such questions can open new alternatives of thought and present a
breadth of ideas and opinions to students. Teachers use questions
more to cultivate students' judgments than to find out what they
know. "Teaching methods should be used that create a slight feeling of
suspense for the student—suspense to be resolved only by his own
decision or active effort."[24]

The Subject Matter Emphasis of Idealism

Education is an important adjusting agency that mediates between individual minds and the spiritual environments surrounding them. It
brings students to seek the truth and avoid error, to feel beauty and
transcend ugliness, and to achieve good and conquer evil. In all subject
matter areas, but particularly in art, music, history, and literature, it
sets before students some models of work and personalities of distinct
excellence and directs them in deliberately following their patterns.
Hence, idealists support the "great person" approach to history. Great
personalities are pictured as personification of perfection in such a way
that students are inspired to imitate them.

The objectives of idealist education must be conceived primarily in
religious or theological, not moral, terms; they must relate to the Living and True One, who alone is. Such a relationship is prior to everything else. Apart from it, any "good life," however conceived, is an
anthropocentric (man-centered) fabrication. Idealistic objectives also
should be individual-social objectives, in one piece and at the same
time.

Students should be searchingly exposed to what is noble, generous,
and faith-provoking. Thus, teachers must clearly conceive "the ideal

character of man and the characteristics of an ideal society."[25] If there is to be solidity in education and students are to have a rugged mental diet, they must be given much objective content and much book learning. "But lest education be no more than impartation of knowledge, the curriculum must go beyond books and subject matter to include direct experiential relations with actualities."[26]

Footnotes

[1]J. Donald Butler, *Idealism in Education* (New York: Harper & Row, 1966), p. 32.

[2]See Marie E. Wirsing, *Teaching and Philosophy: A Synthesis* (New York: Houghton Mifflin, 1972), p. 190.

[3]Herman H. Horne, "An Idealistic Philosophy of Education," *Forty-First Yearbook of the National Society for the Study of Education, Part I, Philosophies of Education,* ed. Nelson B. Henry (Chicago: The University of Chicago Press, 1942), p. 139.

[4]Butler, *Idealism in Education,* p. 73.

[5]Ibid., p. 123.

[6]Herman H. Horne, *An Introduction to Modern Education* (Boston: Heath, 1937), p. 452.

[7]Butler, *Idealism in Education,* p. 53.

[8]Horne, *The Philosophy of Education* (New York: Macmillan, 1904), p. 284.

[9]Butler, *Idealism in Education,* p. 76.

[10]Horne, "An Idealistic Philosophy of Education," p. 186.

[11]J. Donald Butler, *Four Philosophies and Their Practice in Education and Religion,* 3rd ed. (New York: Harper & Row, 1968), p. 201.

[12]Horne, *An Introduction to Modern Education,* p. 453.

[13]Herman H. Horne, *The Philosophy of Education,* rev. ed. (New York: Macmillan, 1930), p. 273.

[14]Ibid., p. 275.

[15]Horne, "An Idealistic Philosophy of Education," p. 141.

[16]Butler, *Idealism in Education,* p. 96.

[17]Ibid., p. 97.

[18]Horne, "An Idealistic Philosophy of Education," p. 156.

[19]Butler, *Idealism in Education,* p. 98.

[20]Ibid., pp. 99–102.

[21]Ibid., p. 94.

[22]Ibid., p. 102.

[23]Ibid., pp. 117–118.

[24]Ibid., p. 120.

[25]Herman H. Horne, *This New Education* (New York: The Abingdon Press, 1931), p. 90.

[26]Butler, *Idealism in Education,* p. 120.

BIBLIOGRAPHY

Barrow, Robin. *Plato and Education*. London: Routledge & Kegan Paul, 1976.

Butler, J. Donald. *Four Philosophies and Their Practice in Education and Religion*, 3rd ed. New York: Harper & Row, 1968.

Butler, J. Donald. *Idealism in Education*. New York: Harper & Row, 1966.

Butler, J. Donald. "Idealism as a Contemporary Educational Philosophy," *Bulletin of Information*, The Kansas State Teachers College of Emporia, November 1960, 40:11, Studies in Contemporary Educational Thought, Carlton H. Boyer, Ed. Emporia, Kans.: Kansas State Teachers College.

Froebel, F. W. A. *The Education of Man*. Trans. and annotated by W. N. Hailman. New York: D. Appleton & Company, 1899.

Gentile, Giovanni. *The Reform of Education*. Authorized trans. by Dion Bigoniari. New York: Harcourt, Brace and Company, 1922.

Green, Theodore M. "A Liberal Christian Idealist Philosophy of Education," Chapter IV in John S. Brubacher, ed., *Modern Philosophies and Education*. Chicago: The University of Chicago Press, 1955.

Harris, William T. *Psychologic Foundations of Education*. New York: D. Appleton & Company, 1898.

Hocking, William E. *The Self, Its Body and Freedom*. New Haven, Conn.: Yale University Press, 1928.

Horne, Herman Harrell. *Philosophy of Education*, rev. ed. New York: The Macmillan Company, 1930.

Horne, Herman Harrell. *This New Education*. New York: The Abingdon Press, 1931.

Horne, Herman Harrell. "An Idealistic Philosophy of Education." In Nelson B. Henry, ed., *Forty-First Yearbook of the National Society for the Study of Education, Part I, Philosophies of Education*. Chicago: The University of Chicago Press, 1942.

Lodge, Rupert C. *Philosophy of Education*, rev. ed. New York: Harper & Row, 1947.

Morris, Van Cleve and Pai, Young. *Philosophy and the American School*, 2nd ed. Boston: Houghton Mifflin, 1976. Pages 44–49, 122–130, 172–174, 194–195, 233–237, and 271–273.

Thompson, Merritt Moore. *The Educational Philosophy of Giovanni Gentile*. Los Angeles, Calif.: University of Southern California Press, 1954.

Chapter 3
Classical Realism,
a Rationalistic
Philosophy of Education

Current classical realism is a modernized version of an ancient, classical, way of thinking. The ancient pattern was largely developed by the Greek philosphers Plato (427–347 B.C.) and Aristotle (384–322 B.C.). Classical realists are "literary intellectuals." Their major emphasis is upon thinking ideas and putting them into words. They recognize the value of the sciences in human life, but they make the sciences subservient to a higher level of intellectual literary development.

Classical realists think that we inhabit a universe characterized by genuinely real structures, which exist independent of either human knowledge about them or human desires in relation to them. These structures of reality can be known as they exist, at least in part, by human minds. They consist of both the patterns that are revealed by science and the more fundamental ontological patterns, which require philosophical description and analysis for us to know them. Classical realists rely upon empirical (scientific) data collected by research experts only up to the point where the rational intellects can take over and find what unequivocally is *out there* as universal truth.[1]

Standards of value also are considered not to be created by people. Instead, they are actually based on the metaphysical moral nature of humankind. However, they are accessible to human cognition.

Therefore, classic realism is anchored in a theory about the basic nature of reality, truth, and goodness, and the source of this theory is human reason and logic. Using Aristotle's system of formal reasoning, classical realists seek knowledge about the nature of reality and humankind and interpret people's destiny based on that nature.

Aristotle taught that, "knowledge ultimately rests upon an indubitable intellectual apprehension; yet for the proper employment of the intuitive reason a wide empirical acquaintance with the subject-matter is indispensable."[2] To Aristotle reason meant the ability to know, intuitively, the universal *forms* of things and then to deduct from those forms the characteristics of the things themselves.

Aristotle developed the formal laws of classical logic and invented the *syllogism* as a deductive reasoning device. The syllogism is a process of deducing conclusions from given premises. It involves logic alone and tests how valid is an argument or how proper was the reasoning used. To use a syllogism, one analyzes each related proposition or statement into a subject or predicate and then applies the three basic laws of thought to the proposition. The syllogism then forms the pattern of a formal argument. It consists of a major premise (proposition), a minor premise (proposition), and a conclusion.

The three basic *laws of thought* are *identity* (A is A); *contradiction* (everything but A is non-A); and *excluded middle* (nothing is both A and non-A). These laws give an either-or quality to every issue and situation. A *syllogism* takes the form of: "All men are Mortal" (the major premise); "Socrates is a man" (the minor premise); therefore "Socrates is mortal" (the conclusion). In the major premise, men is the *subject* and mortal is the *predicate*.

Classical realist philosophers infer what humankind is by nature tending to become, and study the forces and factors that either promote or hinder that development. From the very nature of human rationality, they recognize an everlasting obligation to seek the best that their reason discloses. Their fundamental ideas about the structure of human personality, its goals, and its destiny owe much to the ideas of Plato and Aristotle.

Classical realism is deeply concerned with established tradition, and moves in the direction of cultural conservatism. Accordingly, Broudy states that, "It is to the cultural heritage that we must turn for the goals of cultivation as well as the process. The heritage has preserved many styles of the good life and the judgments of men and history upon them. The heritage has models for imitation and the apparatus for the criticism of them."[3] He further states that, "Part of the cultural heritage of the group are the systems of thought and feeling that have crystallized out of the centuries of critical reflection about what is real, true, good, and beautiful."[4] So, according to classical realism, the kind of education that would be adequate for a rapidly changing world involves a *pattern* that does not change at all; a fixed pattern of the human good that abides amid changes and makes sense of those changes.

A "model of excellence" is always relevant in our or any other time.

In a sense, classical realism consists of sophisticated common sense realism. It has always kept in close contact with the common sense of current society, which is radically, ontologically realistic. Its adherents make their point by noting that the sun rises and sets and the seasons follow in order regardless of human knowledge of how these processes occur.

Some leading contemporary classical realists are Mortimer J. Adler (who thinks that people by nature tend toward development as rational animals and who, in 1952, edited Great Books of the Western World), Harry S. Broudy, Robert M. Hutchins, Oliver Martin, and John Wild. Since Professor Broudy has been greatly concerned with integrating the basic position of classical realism with modern educational thought, this chapter draws heavily from his various books and essays. A second highly used source is the writing of John Wild.

Classical Realism: The Nature of Reality

Whereas idealists contend that the only genuine reality has the nature of minds, classical realists think that physical things also exist in their own right. So, whereas idealism is an ontological *mental monism* and logical empiricism is an ontological *physical monism,* classical realism is an ontological *mental-physical dualism.* But, for classical realists, reality in its deepest sense consists of the absolute forms or ideas of things, not the contents. *Forms* are the *essence* of things, and the characteristics of things that we experience are their *accidents.*

The *realism* of classical realism has a two-faceted meaning depending upon the concept with which it is contrasted. *Realism* vs *idealism* involves the basic nature of things; *realism* vs *nominalism* involves the nature of universals. Realism as opposed to idealism means that objects that we experience through our senses really exist "out there." Realism as opposed to nominalism means that the universal forms designated by class names have a genuine, absolute existence quite independent of the particular representative things that appear to the senses. For example, a chair is more or less an imperfect replica of chairness, which is something genuinely real. A nominalist, in contrast, would say that *chair* is merely a name for all of the objects that we call chairs. For classical realists, most objects have a form and a content, but their forms (Platonic ideas) are the genuinely real and most important parts. So, there is a Natural Law of forms back of all things.

Plato is a leading historical source of both idealism and classical realism. In regard to realism vs idealism he was an idealist. He thought that the essence of all things was their mentalistic or idealogical nature.

But, in regard to realism vs nominalism he was a realist. He emphasized that everything gets its reality from real *forms,* which have always prevailed. Idealists, then, emphasize idealism as opposed to realism. Classical realists emphasize realism as opposed to nominalism and also identify with realism as opposed to idealism. Hence classical realists are realists in both senses.

Classical realists, then, hold the conviction that universals as described by general terms genuinely exist and that particular things are more or less imperfect replicas of perfect universals. For example: A given person is a replica of humanity. Thus, the realism of classical realism contrasts sharply with *nominalism. Nominalism,* name-ism, is the theory that only particular things exist, and that general terms, such as book, human, and vegetable, are only composite names, and do not represent genuinely *real* classes of object.

Classical realism is based upon three ontological commitments: (1) The universe consists of real, substantive entities, which exist whether they are known or not. (2) The human mind can know, in part, these real entities and relations as they are in themselves. (3) There is a *moral, natural law* consisting of an invariable, universal pattern of individual and social action that is required for the completion of human nature. This *natural law* may be grasped and clarified by disciplined study of both human nature and the events of history.

Classical Realism: The Nature of Human Motivation

For classical realists, people are *neutral-active rational animals.* They are human biological organisms endowed with substantive (genuinely real) minds, which are to be developed through being filled and exercised. So, the essence of human nature is its rational character. Reason is the essence of human nature as contrasted with lower vegetable and animal natures. However, reality is both physical and mental—both human bodies and human minds are real. Hence, the human intellect and will cannot be adequately understood in terms of either purely physical or purely mental categories.

To say that people are rational animals means that they are endowed with a complex, delicate faculty of apprehension or cognition whose basic aspects are *sense* and *reason.* Hence, they may rationally understand their essential needs and freely determine their conduct in accordance with this understanding. But also, people are endowed with other flexible tendencies (but no instincts) of a nonrational character. However, their *reason* alone is capable of understanding these tendencies and bringing them to ordered realization.

Human beings are born with insight and free self-direction, which distinguish them from all lower animals. These faculties are the active source of truth, freedom, and other characteristics of humanity. However, at birth they are pure capacities or vague tendencies devoid of any actual content. A natural order of human life obtains when all human activities are guided by an end rationally apprehended and willed. Existence, for a human being, is first of all to be a source of decision and commitment. Common to all people, as a part of human nature, are the powers to acquire knowledge, use it, and enjoy it.

In perfecting their conception of humankind, classical realists constantly attempt to distinguish what is *essential* to being human from humanity's *accidents;* what can vary without changing its *substantial form.* They are convinced that all human life has a *form* that, if understood, will give us insight into the standards appropriate for *the good life.* (Both form and the good life, as used here, are absolutistic concepts. Their meanings are expanded on pages 43 and 45.)

According to classical realism, four major principles characterize the essential operations of human personalities. These reflect the strivings of human beings as they try to fulfill their essential nature. They are general features that characterize all people regardless of their individual variations. These basic principles are: the appetitive (or appetite) principle; the principle of self-determination; the principle of self-realization; and the principle of self-integration. All but the appetite principle are aspects of a comprehensive principle, *self-perfection.*[5]

The Meaning of Self
Selfhood relates to individuality within the invariant structure of human nature. A self, within classical realism, is a peculiar tension between what we are at a given moment and the possibilities that we envision for ourselves in the future. One's self, then, is what one's mind envisions as one's possibilities.

In our minds, each of us is the center from which stream our purposes and actions and into which stream the effects of the actions of other people and the forces of nature. So, our self also involves our freedom of choice in carrying out deliberated decisions. A self is an "I" who has desires, makes decisions and choices, suffers, thinks, and acts.

The Appetite Principle
This principle provides the power that moves all life. It consists of innate physiological drives or tissue needs and acquired drives, which are the desires, wants, lacks, and needs that initiate and maintain life. The most general feature of human life is that it is agitated by a set of desires that originate in natural physical and psychic needs, but which, through memory and imagination, develop into a veritable jungle of acquired human wants, needs, and aspirations.

The Principle of Self-Determination

This principle involves the discovery of one's self and others. It entails a freedom that is a natural and essential goal of a human being. The human freedom involved in self-determination is the possibility for persons to vary their responses to forces that they do not control and to choose, on rational grounds, among alternative values using symbols and intelligent discriminations. It enables a life to be fashioned from within by the person who is living it. In self-determination, one becomes aware that one's world is divided into two parts; the self and the other. A person as an actual self is the result of that person's total history. But, through frustration of desires, one becomes aware of an otherness outside one's self.

The Principle of Self-Realization

This principle means that one builds a self through the realization of values. Although self-realization is a characteristic of every human personality, it gets its particular content from the culture of each individual. Only the generic forms of human activity and powers are given at birth. Self-realization means that individuals exploit their capacities for value-realization to the fullest degree. The range and diversity of values possible for an individual are limited by innate capacities, the richness of the culture in which the individual lives, and the education to exploit these capacities. Life is good to the point that the power to realize values is developed and exercised.

The Principle of Self-Integration

Self-integration consists of organizing one's energies for self-realization. Integration means either unifying one's many selves within one personality or unifying one's actions or values so that they blend rather than conflict. A *self* is what unites diverse experience with the flavor of "mineness," it both constructs valuational possibilities and strives to realize those possibilities.

Classical Realism: The Nature and Source of Truth and Knowledge

For classical realists, to say that people are rational animals means that they are biological organisms in the same way the lower animals are. But, in addition, they are endowed with a unique rational or reasoning faculty, which is the principal characteristic of their substantive minds. No other animals have this faculty or trait. Within classical realism, knowledge consists of a body of principles that have been reasoned out by scholars throughout time and set down in the great books. Hence, scholarship consists of a rational investigation of the nature of absolute Reality, Truth, Beauty, and Goodness. So, the appropriate method of acquiring true knowledge is in its highest form rational, instead of experimental as the experimentalists think.

Education, for classical humanists, consists of training students' predominant faculty, reason, along with developing their subordinate faculties such as memory, perception, and imagination. An intelligent person is a highly rational individual with a well developed faculty of reason. An individual's reasoning faculty, when well exercised and thereby developed, qualifies its owner to reason logically and accurately in regard to any matter in almost any situation. So, learning consists of emulating the great intellectuals of history in exercising, and thereby developing, the faculties of one's mind, particularly reason.

Imagination furnishes the raw material for all sorts of reasoning, for the sublimation and idealization of physiological drives, and for the exercise of freedom. Whereas in lower animals strivings are automatic, predetermined struggles, human imaginative, symbolic powers enable people's strivings to take an infinity of forms. Each *concept* is an imaginative, abstract idea or notion about a universal form; a real, substantive entity of the universe, existing in itself.

The Forms or Essence of Things
Is Mendel's law true because it works or can be checked out, or does it work or check out because it is True? Whereas experimentalists accept the first alternative, classical realists emphasize the second. Answers to problems depend upon timeless structures or forms being *revealed* through insight into the form of universal truths. Since the nonmaterial forms of matters are their most important parts, the way to know anything is to grasp its form. Its *form* is genuinely real, and correct comprehension of it is truth.

We understand an object, that is we gain knowledge of it only when our minds by extended abstraction identify themselves with the *essence* of that object, not its matter or *accidents*. However, since real things or processes are formed matter, both form and matter need each other to exist. So, in treating the nature and source of truth, the differences between meaning and process, mind and brain, and form and matter are crucial.

Classical realists think that universal or repeatable natures of objects constitute their essences or forms. Human minds frame a concept of something's form from the concrete thing itself. Since both nature and human nature have constant structures, truth about their structures does not change.

The Role of Knowledge
Broudy states, "The human mind is no more and no less than the operations by which it creates, stores, retrieves, and combines the imagic surrogates of the real world."[6] "Everything I have done, thought,

sensed, remembered, felt, and imagined is registered in me."[7] He further notes that never in the history of humankind have so many people lived so well on the brains of so few. However, he thinks that to live *really well* we need more and more knowledge—the result of intellectual discipline. People can live *pretty well* with little intellectual effort, but for them to live *really well* they need much knowledge gained through intellectual effort. "Knowledge of self, knowledge of society, and knowledge of nature are the *gymnasia* where we practice the skills and perfect the habits needed for self-determination, self-realization, and self-integration."[8] These are the dimensions of the *good life* of self perfection.

Intellectual Elitism
It is knowledge that makes the difference between people's value systems. The more they know about a field, the more high-brow they tend to become, and the higher their brow, the greater is their ultimate satisfaction. Connoisseurs rarely are content to return to the innocence of ignorance. Classical realists appeal to the authority of each discipline, which is lodged in the experts who conduct investigations in that discipline; they are its credentialed members. "The continuity of the credentialing group constitutes what may be called the community or the consensus of the learned as to what is important and true in a given field of inquiry."[9] It is this position that identifies classical realism as an *intellectual elitism.*

Knowledge of Science and Art
Two great human contrivances are recognized as constituting the cultural heritage, science and art. Science controls thinking about actuality so as to give us knowledge about the ways of things. Any proposition that purports to be a factual description must be certified by the method of science. However, through correspondence with reality, *truth is discovered or verified,* but *not determined.* Basic truths remain unaffected by any knowledge about them.

The arts and our system of humanities shape our values, what we prize or desire, and how we judge. They include history, literature, philosophy, theology, and the fine arts. These subjects champion the return to the study of the true, good, and beautiful as Plato had defined them. Here, inability to sense subtle differences makes our lives drab, routinized, and boring. "When science brings us to the point where we cannot dramatize the cosmic story at all, it will have become dehumanized and we with it."[10]

Knowledge and Reflective Freedom
For Broudy and other contemporary classical realists, *freedom of the will* is freedom to carry out our deliberately thought out decisions. "The

self is its freedom."[11] Such freedom is the first good, and whatever
stands in its way is the first evil. However, to be good, a life must not
be fashioned by desire alone, but by desire as weighed and chosen by
a thinking self. Freedom is a necessary, but not sufficient, condition
for conclusive testing and the final discovery of truth. Real freedom
consists of reflective choice.

Reflective freedom relies on dispositions and habits of thought to
inquire into causes, to examine propositions in the light of the evidence
advanced for them, and to remain open to alternative hypotheses.
These dispositions and habits together constitute the liberal or freed
mind. Reflective freedom, as contrasted with natural freedom, evalu-
ates possibilities in terms of their consequences for the *good life* as a
whole. Such goodness is to be established through ascertaining the
grounds for the validity of judgments, not by determining the course
of collective action.

Classical Realism: The Nature and Source of Human Values

Is a rose beautiful because we enjoy it, or do we enjoy it because it is
beautiful? Whereas experimentalists accept the first alternative, classical realists emphasize the second. Classical realists think that human
beings throughout history continue to be the same *form* of human
beings, and that the dynamics of their happiness and their requirements for the good life and good society are generically the same; they
are supported by a metaphysical natural law. Finding this natural law
is a matter of metaphysical speculation. "For metaphysics is simply the
rational attempt to find clues in nature and human experience as to
what the value commitment of the universe might be—if any."[12]

"The invariable, universal pattern of action, individual as well as social, required for the completion of human nature is called the *moral
law* or *natural law*."[13] So, humanity may gain insight into the standards
and goals appropriate for the *good life* through grasp of the natural,
moral law. "One has to turn to metaphysics, epistemology, and ethics
to find a common evaluational scheme that is more than a cultural accident."[14] Although determining values involves a relation between an
organism and an object, neither science nor technology can determine
the significance of things and events for human valuation.

Intrinsic and Instrumental Values

Value is either intrinsic or instrumental. *Intrinsic* value of a thing is the
value it has for itself alone, regardless of its usefulness for anything
else. Instrumental value is the value that something has because of its
individual or social usefulness. "For anything to have *instrumental*
value it must be thought to be able to give rise to a state of affairs not
yet in existence, but which thought can entertain."[15] But, "If there are

instrumental values, there must be intrinsic ones . . .,"[16] which constitute their source.

Whenever we *choose* to perform an act, we do so either because we have decided that it is the *right* thing, so we *ought* to do it (its intrinsic value), or because of all available alternatives, it is the *best* thing to do, it will lead to more satisfying consequences (its instrumental value). The source of value is to be sought not only in results that objects can have as instruments, but also in their basic *structure*, which has the power to make them good instruments. Each area of value—economic, health, social, moral, aesthetic, intellectual, and religious—has an *objective* as well as a subjective aspect.

For a life to be both subjectively and objectively good, one must cultivate one's capacity to achieve value in the intellectual, moral, and aesthetic areas of experience. The *good life* consists of *self-perfection*. It takes the form of self-realization, self-determination, and self-integration. Because of humankind's symbolic power, the means to achieve self-perfection vary widely; potentialities for both successes and failures are enormous. The unique capacity of human beings for self-direction and choice among different alternatives, enhanced by their power to know, presents both opportunity, and dangers.

Our human nature is grounded in the generic drives of our animal nature. But *higher values* are not the material and bodily ones. "Whatever is valued by anyone has grown out of that person's desire for sensory gratification, love, power, self-esteem, glory, self-realization, and self-integration."[17] Higher values are intellectual, aesthetic, moral, religious and sometimes social ones. "Underpinning the common judgement of lower and higher is a metaphysical belief that those activities which exercise the faculties peculiar to man or are most developed in man are more real than the activities which we share with the brutes."[18]

Objective Value Theory
Broudy develops the objective value theory as a means for coming to appreciate values in the various areas of involvement. This theory is based on the presuppositions that things do have an inherent *objective value* to be grasped and that human knowledge can grasp this *value*. "If there is any sense in which goodness, rightness, and beauty are in things and acts, then the more we know of our world the more we know about its value possibilities."[19]

An objective theory of value is one that asserts that value predicates (characteristics) like good and beautiful are qualities that can be immediately known. If objects and acts have certain kinds of structures, they produce certain feelings in those persons who can apprehend the pattern of that structure. One need not be an artist to value or appreciate art. "While some experience with performance helps matters considerably, neither the pupil nor the teacher needs artistic talent to learn to perceive properly."[20]

Objective value theory has several distinct advantages: It locates the source of values in the relation between the structure of things and the structure of human nature. It makes education in values a matter of increasing students' abilities to understand structures in the world that give rise to value experiences. It considers the understanding of value-structures to provide insight into the real nature of things, but also recognizes that it takes experimentation and inquiry for people to discover the *structure* or *form* that underlies value potentialities.[21]

The product of objective value theory is *enlightened cherishing*. This is the love of objects and actions that by intellectual standards are worthy of our love; this love is passionate but not intellectually blind.[22] A good life that is self-determined, realizes its potentialities, and is self-integrated, rests on the belief that human perfection lies in the direction of higher aesthetic, moral, social, and religious values—values that extend well beyond the aspirations of most people. Although the numerous grades of life are differentiated by the forms that the appetite principle takes, the pleasures of intellectual, moral, aesthetic, and religious activity increase with age. The older people become, the less distracting are their bodily appetites.

Aesthetic Values

For classical realists, art has a distinctly unique function. "Art cannot do for us what science or technology or religion or friendship can do, but none of these can do what art can do."[23]

Sensitivity to the structure of aesthetic images is what differentiates an aesthetically developed person from those not so developed. "Sensitivity to aesthetic *form* is at the heart of aesthetic experience and aesthetic education."[24] The goal of art education is to develop the ability to perceive aesthetic images as do persons who, through experience and reflection, have become connoisseurs of art. So, the distinction between experiencing an emotion and contemplating the image of that emotion is important in aesthetic education.

The first step in aesthetic education is to develop the habit of grasping the sensory properties of objects in their fullness and richness. Aesthetic enjoyment is sensual in nature, although not all sensual pleasures are aesthetic. There are three dimensions to aesthetic experience: sensory, formal, and expressive.

Broudy identifies three types of art: serious classical, serious avant-garde, and popular. *Serious classical art* is art that is taken seriously by connoisseurs. It tends to be complex, and it engages life at its deeper levels. It appeals only to that small, cultivated group of persons who are familiar with the tradition of art. *Serious avant-garde art* is highly experimental in form, content, or both; it alienates not only the general public but also many critics. *Serious art* of both kinds requires tuition or instruction for its appreciation and practice. *Popular art*, according to Broudy, does not require tuition of any kind, it is perceived and enjoyed almost spontaneously by those people who live in the milieu in which it is exhibited.

Moral Values

Moral values, for classical realists, are based on *natural law;* they can be established on objective rational grounds. The idea that a natural law exists and is the foundation of moral values is based on the belief in the existence of a permanent universal pattern of human good, which lives in the frail, fickle world of empirical reality.

A moral value system, then, is to be based on reason, not on either scientific experimentation or emotionalism. A life that is committed to the highest values of which human beings are capable requires something more than the various kinds and aspects of scientific activity. But, mere emotional behavior is not the proper supplement. All people have the natural right to think what they please, but they *ought* to think only what, after rational reflection, they believe to be true and valuable. To be human is to imagine what could and ought to be.

Classical realists think that all human beings share certain active traits that determine certain vague tendencies in children. One inherited trait is *free will* which means that "Men are free within limits to act as they choose in the light of what they understand. Thus, they may violate the moral law if they so decide."[25]

As soon as individuals become aware of themselves and develop the ability to reflect and choose, they should regard the freedom of their wills as a fundamental good and its frustration as an evil. But, a completely moral act always aims at some good and chooses it in a certain way. "To make an act fully moral requires correctness in assaying the claims upon us and in carrying out the means to fulfilling it."[26]

The criteria of moral education are the same as those of the good life: self-determination, self-realization, and self-integration. "To determine oneself is to choose on rational grounds; to realize oneself is to choose rationally among our potentialities; to integrate oneself is to remove rationally so far as possible the conflicts among our choices."[27]

Moral values furnish the perspective for all other perspectives. But, even they are not free from such possible aberrations as moral awkwardness, moral rigidity, overconscientiousness, or intellectual smugness. "Without sound and compulsory education in the truth that has been discovered and without nurture in the moral practices founded on knowledge, the human community must be punished by the natural sanctions of ignorance, fanaticism, and practical sterility."[28]

Religious Values

Most classical realists hold a positive attitude toward various religions. However, they often do not identify themselves with any particular religion. Many feel that religion, art, and suffering are the seedbeds of our insights into value. They think that religion, whether or not it is institutionalized, heightens the intensity of people's awareness of what it is to be human in a world that they did not make. It also increases their insight into their simultaneous insignificance and grandeur, and frailty and power.

"The religious values . . . stand on the same footing as all other values. They are real, relevant, and socially important."[29] So, there are connoisseurs and experts in the religious realm, as in others. For its greatest worth religious experience, like other modes of experience, has to be cultivated. But, we need to identify religion and science as two different kinds of processes. "It is when men begin mixing things up—fighting disease with incantations and testing a religious experience with a slide rule—that we have our best examples of both religious and scientific ignorance."[30]

The task for schools in regard to religious values is the same as that for all other values. Students should perfect the habit of acquiring knowledge *about* religion and of using and enjoying that knowledge in reflecting upon religious experience as it intensifies, subtilizes, and enriches immediate experience in that realm. So, schools should disseminate knowledge about religion, but they should *not* promote either the profession or the practice of any one religion.

Classical Realism: The Purpose of Education

Classical realists emphasize the development of intellectual discipline and moral character through students' grasping truths for their own sake. The ultimate goal of education is *self-perfection* in terms of the *good life*. The task of education is to give both students and the community what they need rather than what they want. Classical realists think that we do not so much need more knowledge from scientific research as we need the intelligence and character to use properly the knowledge that we already have.

For classical realists, education is the art of communicating truth. Such communication has both theoretical and practical aspects, but the theoretical aspects are of prior importance and *should not* be intermingled with the practical ones. The essence of education is an intellectual process that emphasizes the importance of symbols, language, and theory. The pattern of such *liberal education* is built around academic excellence.

Education, for classical realists, has four principle aims. It should discern the truth about things as they really are. It should extend and integrate all known truths. It should gain all practical knowledge of life in general and of professional functions in particular that can be theoretically justified. It should transmit both theoretical and practical knowledge in a coherent, convincing manner to children, youth, and adults.[31]

Discernment of Truth
Schools are the home of pure theory. Here, students must learn to become detached from all special needs and interests and to examine things as they really are in themselves. All other aims are secondary and derived from this one. Since the unique function of schools is to cultivate and promote cherishment of pure knowledge, schools must be detached from concrete life and practice.

Extension and Integration of Truths
Education should extend the students' limited visions of the truth in order to gain as complete a view as possible. Schools are the homes of those integrative hypotheses and theories with which people attempt to see things all together as they really are. The process of liberal education is to promote conceptual and theoretical understanding instead of simply the absorption of organized facts and mere development of technical skills. General education should try to form the habits of acquiring, using, and enjoying knowledge to the limits of each person's capacity.

Gaining Theoretically Justified Practical Knowledge
Classical realists emphasize that genuinely new ideas come from students, priests, and scholars, who have time for abstract thoughts. People of practical affairs are too busy to be creative. When educational programs are really detached from practical matters and thereby function in a healthy way, they are ever the source of new ideas and social fermentation in regard to both theoretical and practical matters.

Transmission of Both Theoretical and Practical Knowledge
Since education is the art of communicating truth, it is the duty of educational agencies to teach both theoretical and practical principles and procedures in such a way that they elicit zeal and devotion. This is a matter of instilling the sound habits and convictions that are required for adult learning and practice. At every level of education,

deep conviction, rhetoric, and persuasive force are required of genuine teachers.

A derivative function of education is to interpret and criticize the cultural pattern as a whole so as to enable each student to understand the culture's many functions and to see how and why they fit, or do not fit, into a meaningful social structure.

The real purpose of education, then, is to transmit the *good* and *true* aspects of our intellectual heritage. The ultimate aim of education is to establish student tendencies to choose wisely. Accordingly, education should acquaint students with the *best* literature and arts and *true* science and refine their tastes for these. For rational realists, excellence in aesthetic, intellectual, and religious fields is more to be esteemed than vocational training, physical vigor, or sensual pleasure.

Classical Realism: The Nature of the Learning Process

Within classical realism, cognition or knowing consists of a real interaction between the mind and the world outside the mind. Such interaction involves a brain and sense organs and the energy from surrounding objects. Mental awareness or consciousness of this interaction arises when the mind abstracts the particular qualities of stimuli from the outside objects. But, an object is really understood only when the mind, by a further act of abstraction, identifies itself with the *universal essence*, or *essential form* of the object.[32]

Meanings of Mind, Awareness, and Abstraction

"Mind is the 'form of forms'."[33] It is a processor of data that sorts, classifies, and connects them. Its basic aspect is awareness or consciousness. Awareness is always a process of abstraction, that is, of concentrating on some aspects of things and ignoring others. *Abstraction* is the process of imaginatively extracting certain qualities of a thing without altering its shape and other qualities, for example, taking the color from a piece of cloth or hardness from iron. "In awareness the perceived situation is grasped in both its concrete richness of sound, color, shapes, sizes, and smells and as objects in their relations."[34]

The core of all knowing is sensation, which depends upon energy emanating from external objects, and sensory organs are the only gateway to the external world. So, sense experience is the interaction of our sense organs with the external world. But, human experience is a process that is aware of itself, and by being aware of itself, can extend beyond itself. Human experience has the ability to activate the mind's inherent capacity to apprehend higher levels of knowledge. In awareness, the mind abstracts the forms from individual things. When the mind abstracts, it separates a particular sense quality from the complex sensory process; the more complete is the separation, the more objective is the process of representing the quality of the energy that the object sent out. In other words, in abstracting the brilliance of a diamond, we note the characteristics of the diamond that give it that brilliance.

For classical realists, there are crucial differences between meaning and process, mind and brain, form and matter. Also, in understanding learning, the concepts *meaning, mind,* and *form* outweigh their opposites. Since classical realists regard real things or processes as formed matter, they think that we truly understand or know an object or activity only by grasping its form. They are convinced that we can apprehend real qualities and relations directly and immediately. Since universal forms exist in individual objects and constitute their essence, minds abstract these forms from concrete things, and thereby make the forms of concrete things present to themselves.

The Nature and Function of Concepts

A *concept* is a common meaning that can be abstracted from sense experience by minds. Whereas the forms of things are definite and fixed, concepts of them are somewhat variable. So, the concept of a class of objects (chair) corresponds more or less, to its form (chairness). A concept is rooted in perception. In *perception,* sense, memory, imagination, and the combination of these provide us with a more or less complex image of a particular individual thing, for example, a certain maple tree. In contrast, the concept *maple tree* applies to a universal, all maple trees. So, *concepts are apprehensions of forms.*

Absolute meanings exist in a world of their own; a world of *forms,* which are universal and repeatable natures. However, minds that have the ability to combine images, perceptions, and concepts into patterns may abstract the forms of things from our sensory experience. (The existence of these forms is called *noetic* being.)

Concepts, once formed, are employed in our knowing and thinking to relate real things to each other. Concepts are stated in symbols that take on a life of meaning of their own. There is a conviction that certain combinations of symbols work because they are in accord with the structure of the real world. Symbolization is the essential act of one's mind, and symbolic possibilities are the raw material for choice and decision. "Every man is a potential manufacturer of possibility; to restrict him is to limit possibility; it is to shrink human being."[35]

Formation of Habits

"To know something is to become *relationally* identified with an existent entity as it is."[36] All learning is the means for purifying the aesthetic, ethical, political, and social experience of students by subjecting it to intellectual discipline. The highest and most important learning task consists of synthesizing universal concepts and grasping self-evident truths. This is a process of intellectual self-cultivation, or discipline. "The first step of self-cultivation is mastery of the arts of learning."[37] The next stage is using this mastery to apprehend the knowledge and arts selected by the best minds of every epoch.

The arts of learning are the formation of habits of acquiring, using, and enjoying knowledge through engaging in these acts day after day until students become adept at them. A habit is a unity of content and form; the content is particular and the form is general. Symbolic habits and skills operate in the widest variety of knowledge-seeking and knowledge-using situations, for example, using the three Rs. Habits have a dynamic nature; they are *active* tendencies that seek occasions for their own employment.

Classical Realism: The Nature of the Teaching Process

Although classical realists' ideas are anchored in antiquity, they now may seem to represent a compromise position between idealism, which also goes back to the ancients, and logical empiricism, which has emerged in the present century. This compromise is evidenced most clearly by classical realists' tendency to dichotomize—split in two— many mutually complementary concepts into antinomies or opposites. Examples of some dichotomies are form vs matter, mind vs body, intellectual or liberal education vs vocational education, and theory vs practice. So, in their approach to teaching, rational realists seem to draw upon both idealistic and logical-empiricistic principles. Their primary emphasis on forms, minds, intellects, and theory seems idealistic; but their recognition of a secondary level of reality, which involves matter, bodies, vocations, and practice, reminds one of the position of logical empiricists.

Contemporary classical realists make quite a bit of democracy in education, but their idea of democracy differs distinctly from that of the experimentalists. For classical realists, democracy in education means the opportunity for each person to cultivate the classical ideal, to develop one's mind or intellect first and then prepare oneself for practical matters. Enlightened people are assumed to have the ability and willingness to search for the Common Good and to sustain it in all relevant situations. The Common Good consists in that which is good for all people at all times and in all places simply because they are human beings; it is discovered through enlightened inquiry into the Nature of things. Accordingly, each individual's democratic right to education should be limited only by that individual's capacity to learn and society's ability to provide opportunities to do so.

Classical realists consider teaching to be the art of communicating truth. So, in the broadest sense, *"Education is the process or product of a deliberate attempt to fashion experience by the direction and control of learning."*[38] *Formal* education refers to the process as it .is advanced in schools. Agencies other than schools provide learning opportunities, but their educational functions are only incidental to their primary functions. Hence, they educate informally.

For classical realists, education is theoretical and intellectual; it emphasizes symbols, language, and theory. Except perhaps in advanced technical schools, the major emphasis of education should be placed on theoretical insight and mastery. So, the objectives of teaching are *insight* (the moment of learning) and *mastery* (the perfection of habit). "Realistic methodology is centered in perceptual organization, concept attainment, and insight as basic to the learning process."[39]

Although individual differences in brain and talents are not denied, there still is a *natural* structure or way of living that should characterize all human beings. "In general education, the school would induct every pupil into the vestibules of connoisseurship in all phases of human life."[40] The only viable criterion for the induction of youth is the judgment of experts, the connoisseurs. *Connoisseurship* means the refinement of immediate experience through the use of knowledge. "Life is judged good to the degree that we recognize it as resulting from our own choice and striving; to the degree that it stretches our powers, and to the extent that it unified us as persons."[41] But students' standards are authentic, not simply because the standards are theirs, but because the students accept them through the means of the same sort of perception, analysis, and reflection as that used by experts. The objective of classical realistic teaching is to persuade learners to perceive, classify, and relate matters as do experts in a given domain. Then, once these intellectual processes have been shaped, the students are expected to use this cognitive equipment for solving problems.

Nature of the Teaching-Learning Process
Educators should first examine the nature of reality, knowledge, and goodness, then deduce the kind of curriculum, methodology, and school organization that would seem to follow from it. *"The skill of the teacher lies in eliciting the interests of the child in the right things, especially in grasping the truth for its own sake."*[42] In teaching, *incidental* matters should be clearly distinguished from what is *essential* and really grounded in the nature of things.

"The child is naturally curious and imitative."[43] But, teachers need to lead discussions and ask questions to bring out the eternal verities. They need to guide students to an understanding of independent reality, which they must grasp for themselves. Students are confronted with a range of existence for which they are in no sense responsible. Their duty, as students, is to learn those arduous operations by which this existence may be revealed to them as it really is. The discovery of the nature of the world, social order, and themselves is the material with which students are to perfect the habits or tendencies of acquiring, using, and enjoying truth. Within the teaching-learning process, "Imposition is not bad in itself, only when it cannot be justified by the authority of the intellect itself."[44]

Within the teaching-learning process, the teacher's provide experiences through manipulating the stimuli that students receive. Next, intervening processes of storage and selective recall occur inside the students: perceiving, remembering, imagining, feeling, analyzing, sorting, combining, judging, and choosing. Then, the outcomes of having the experiences occur; there are both school outcomes and life outcomes.

Phases of the Teaching-Learning Process
Broudy distinguishes six phases in the teaching-learning process. They are motivation, presentation, trial response, insight or achievement of the model response, incorporation of learnings into habit or mastery, and testing for outcome.[45]

Motivation. Motivation relates to the promotion of student interests in learning the desired subject matter. The more that learners recognize a situation as relevant to their concerns, the greater will be their attention, effort, and learning. So, teachers need to know what their students interests really are and how these interests vary at different age levels. Interests are symptoms of deeper and more pervasive urges to self-determination, self-realization, and self-integration; the three aspects of self-perfection. To motivate students beyond their intrinsic interests, teachers must both help students see the relevance of academic learning to their urges toward self-perfection and bring the learning tasks within student capabilities.

Presentation. In presentation, the teacher presents a learning task to students. The objective is to prepare students to carry out instructions through understanding the requirements of the learning task. The task may be to read, write, perform an experiment, watch a demonstration, or solve a problem.

Trial Response. The learner must make some kind of trial response. It may be either a motor or muscular act, a verbal-symbolic act, or an act combining muscular and symbolic behavior. The teacher's responsibility is to see that students make enough of the right kind of trials in the right way. So, the teacher either confirms the correctness of, or corrects, trial performances. Trials and needed corrections continue until each student *has within himself* a model of the correct response. Broudy calls students' feeling of rightness *insight*.

Insight—Achievement of the Model Response.   Broudy gives *insight* a somewhat mystical meaning as did the Gestaltists. Gestalt psychology had roots in German idealism, thus it emphasized awareness and the idea of insights being instantaneous. This definition of insight differs significantly from its definition within cognitive-field psychology (See Chapter 9, p. 190).

Insight (the moment of learning) is seeing, feeling, or apprehending a new pattern of experience or attainment of a model response. Regardless of what is learned, the learning moment is the one in which the person achieves insight. A teacher's job is to help learners become aware of the pattern that constitutes the *right* response. In place of immediately felt pleasures or pains resulting from success and failure, which do occur in some situations, the teacher often must supply clues in terms of pleasure or displeasure or verbal responses. Also, the teacher must disclose complex and hidden patterns that are not easily accessible to students. The means of achieving insight is to match the learning readiness of a student with the cognitive demands of a learning task.

Incorporation of Learnings Into Habit or Mastery.   Broudy states that, "All teaching methods are in their various ways preparation for insight."[46] The moment of learning is the moment of insight into a pattern; it is when the learner has incorporated the model response and judges that it is correct. But this is not mastery. Mastery consists of incorporation of new insight patterns into the habits of a learner. It makes successful performance efficient and reliable by being habitual and semiautomatic. It frees the "master" to think about variables in a situation that call for master judgment. The tendency to seek ever more inclusive and more subtle patterns is the habit of acquiring knowledge.

Testing for Outcomes.   Education has both life outcomes and test outcomes. The good life is the ultimate aim of education, but it is not a test outcome of schooling. Since schooling is only one factor in producing the good life, test outcomes may be necessary conditions for the good life, but they are not sufficient ones. The problem, then, is for the school to include within the scope of its instruction deliberative tasks that can be test outcomes and yet be similar enough to life outcomes to give us assurance that success in school will promote success in life.

It is by their tests that the true aims of an educational agency are known. The teaching process is completed by tests in which students are asked to perform their learned tasks without most of the clues and aids that were furnished them during the learning. The "pay-off" in the form of the score on a test is the most potent instrument for the shaping of learning.

The Subject Matter Emphasis of Classical Realism

Classical realists take their norms for education from their view of the nature and destiny of human beings. For them, people have an unchanging human *essence*, which education needs to externalize under conditions that are dictated by the nature of our technologically mature society. But, society does not *determine* the nature of people. "Each self has the power to free itself from the sources of its stimuli insofar as it can deal with the symbols of these stimuli rather than the sources themselves."[47] Yet, there is no natural opposition between the common good of a whole society and the good of an individual within it; any antagonism between the two is a sign of corruption. "The continued existence of the public schools in our country depends on their being able to invoke norms for instruction that transcend ethnic and social differences."[48]

Classical realists reject both subject-centered and problem-centered curricula. In their place, they develop the self-perfection theory of education. They reject a subject-centered curriculum, as conceived by traditional schools, because it does not adequately deal with the problem of motivation, it does not guarantee retention of knowledge, and it does not develop thinking. They reject a problem-centered curriculum because problems need not require any knowledge beyond that furnished by ordinary life experience and not all problems require scientific method for their solution. Furthermore, "An experimental society—one in which everything is open to trial and retrial—cannot exist."[49]

Within *self-perfection* theory, all learning is a means for purifying the aesthetic, ethical, political, and social experiences of students by subjecting them to intellectual discipline. Only the abstract principles of pure theory can free people from slavery to detailed routines such as those practiced by many primitive cultures.

Liberal Education

Within the classical tradition, knowledge as such has a liberating power, thus the term *liberal education*. A liberated person is a highly literate one. Educators should devise studies that everyone can master and which apply to a wide variety of situations due to their theoretical nature. "There is certainly a basic core of knowledge that every human person ought to know in order to live a genuinely human life as a member of the world community, of his own nation, and of the family."[50] Such a core of knowledge should be presented to every student at increasing levels of complexity and discipline. Hence, a simplified, highly generalized curriculum should be pursued through both elementary and secondary levels. However, students will learn such studies at different rates and "If we choose a set of studies that will apply widely, the number of people who can learn them well is relatively small."[51]

Truth may be taught in regard to both incidental matters and essential forms. However, the forms of things are their most important parts. Whereas formal knowledge is theoretical, incidental education is vocationally oriented. The way to teach students something is to help them grasp its real form, which is in the thing itself. Through general education, the most important kind, teachers promote knowledge of classical models of excellence, those forever relevant.

A classical-realistic curriculum, then, sets the habits and skills of acquiring, using, and enjoying knowledge as the immediate objective of general education. Such habits and skills are the universal forms of human activity. So, through general education, students gain symbolic, research, study, deliberative, analytical, imaginative, and evaluative habits and skills.

Aspects of Basic Knowledge

There are five aspects of the basic core of knowledge that should be given to everyone. The goal in all five is to lead students toward an exact, rigorous understanding of prescribed generalizations. Hence, all of the subject matter should be developed in terms of large universal, eternal, and immutable generalizations or abstractions instead of mere facts. (1) Students should learn to use the basic instruments of knowledge including their own and at least one foreign language, the essentials of formal logic, and elementary mathematics. (2) They should become acquainted with the methods and basic facts of the various sciences. (3) They should study the history and science of humankind. (4) They should gain some familiarity with the great classics of literature and art. (5) They should be introduced to the problems of philosophy and to the task of integrating knowledge and practice. Throughout the teaching-learning process, "Language and grammar should be taught as essential phases of the mysterious process of apprehension by which the actual structure of things is mentally reflected and expressed, and by which such knowledge is achieved."[52]

In the early grades, teachers should stress the three Rs and other fundamentals. They should have high regard for subject matter and they should not cater to the whims of each child. Secondary schools should center upon formal study of the key concepts of the humanities and sciences. Students' formal education should be completed here so that it need not be extended into either higher or vocational education. Higher education, then, should center itself on specialized work of a professional or preprofessional nature. Vocational education is not disparaged. It, however, is placed on a lower level of student needs than is intellectual training.

Footnotes

[1]See John Wild, ed., *The Return to Reason: Essays on Realistic Philosophy,* (Chicago: Regnery, 1953), p. v.

[2]Dagobert D. Runes, ed., *The Dictionary of Philosophy,* (Ames, Iowa: Littlefield, Adams, 1959), p. 21.

[3]Harry S. Broudy, *Enlightened Cherishing: An Essay on Aesthetic Education,* (Urbana, Ill.: Kappa Delta Pi, University of Illinois Press, 1972), p. 110.

[4]Ibid., p. 18.

[5]Harry S. Broudy, *Building a Philosophy of Education,* 2nd ed. (Malabar, Fla.: Robert E. Krieger Publishing Co., Inc., 1961), Chapter 3, pp.42–72.

[6]Broudy, *Enlightened Cherishing,* p. 14.

[7]Broudy, Building a Philosophy of Education, *p. 51.*

[8]Ibid., p. 71.

[9]Broudy, *Enlightened Cherishing,* pp. 96–97.

[10]Ibid., p. 38.

[11]Broudy, *Building a Philosophy of Education,* p. 53.

[12]Ibid., p. 261.

[13]John Wild, "Education and Human Society: A Realistic View," in *Modern Philosophies and Education,* ed. Nelson B. Henry, (Chicago: The University of Chicago Press, 1955), p. 18.

[14]Broudy, *Building a Philosophy of Education,* p. 132.

[15]See Broudy, *Enlightened Cherishing,* p. 13.

[16]Broudy, *Building a Philosophy of Education,* p. 135.

[17]Broudy, *Enlightened Cherishing,* p. 21.

[18]Broudy, *Building a Philosophy of Education,* p. 143.

[19]Ibid., p. 138.

[20]Broudy, *Enlightened Cherishing,* p. 89.

[21]See Broudy, *Building a Philosophy of Education,* pp. 139–140.

[22]See Broudy, *Enlightened Cherishing,* p. 6.

[23]Ibid., p. 52.

[24]Ibid., p. 36.

[25]Wild, "Education and Human Society: A Realistic View," p. 23.

[26]Broudy, *Building a Philosophy of Education,* p. 254.

[27]Ibid., pp. 125–126.

[28]Wild, "Education and Human Society: A Realistic View," pp. 39–40.

[29]See Broudy, *Building a Philosophy of Education,* p. 277.

[30]Ibid., p. 276.

[31]Wild, "Education and Human Society: A Realistic View," pp. 28–31.

[32]Broudy, *Building a Philosophy of Education,* p. 120.

[33]Ibid., p. 339.

[34]Ibid., p. 339.

[35]Ibid., p. 57.

[36]Wild, "Education and Human Society: A Realistic View," p. 18.

[37]Harry S. Broudy, "New Problems and Old Solutions," in Joe Parks, *Selected Readings in the Philosophy of Education,* 2nd ed. (New York: Macmillan, 1963), pp. 318–339.

[38]Broudy, *Building a Philosophy of Education,* p. 8.

[39]Ibid., p. 340.

[40]Harry S. Broudy, *The Real World of the Public Schools.* (New York: Harcourt Brace Jovanovich, 1972), p. 230.

[41]Broudy, "New Problems and Old Solutions," p. 320.

[42]Harry S. Broudy, "A Classical Realist's View of Education," in *Philosophies of Education,* ed. Philip H. Phenix. (New York: Wiley, 1961), p. 18.

[43]Wild, "Education and Human Society: A Realistic Way," p. 26.

[44]Broudy, *Enlightened Cherishing,* p. 103.

[45]See Broudy, *Building a Philosophy of Education,* pp. 340–348.

[46]Ibid., p. 353.

[47]Broudy, "New Problems and Old Solutions," p. 329.

[48]Broudy, *"Enlightened Cherishing,* p. 92.

[49]Ibid., p. 115.

[50]Wild, "Education and Human Society: A Realistic View," p. 34.

[51]Broudy, "A Classical Realist's View of Education," p. 20.

[52]Wild, "Education and Human Society: A Realistic View," p. 31.

BIBLIOGRAPHY

Broudy, Harry S., *Building a Philosophy of Education*, 2nd ed. Malabar, Fla.: Robert E. Krieger Publishing Co., Inc., 1961.

Broudy, Harry S., "A Classical Realist's View of Education," in Philip H. Phenix, ed., *Philosophies of Education.* New York: Wiley, 1961, pp. 17–24.

Broudy, Harry S. *Enlightened Cherishing: An Essay on Aesthetic Education.* Urbana, Ill.: Kappa Delta Pi, University of Illinois Press, 1972.

Broudy, Harry S., "New Problems and Old Solutions," in Joe Parks, *Selected Readings in the Philosophy of Education*, 2nd ed. New York: Macmillan, 1963, pp. 318–339.

Broudy, Harry S. *The Real World of the Public Schools.* New York: Harcourt Brace Jovanovich, 1972.

Broudy, Harry S., and Palmer, John R. *Exemplars of Teaching Method.* Chicago: Rand McNally, 1965.

Kneller, George F., *Introduction to the Philosophy of Education*, 2nd ed. New York: Wiley, 1971.

Martin, Wm. Oliver, *Realism In Education.* New York: Harper & Row, 1969.

Morris, Van Cleve, and Pia, Young. *Philosophy and the American School*, 2nd ed. Boston: Houghton Mifflin, 1976.

Neff, Frederick C., *Philosophy and American Education.* New York: Center for Applied Research in Education, 1966, pp. 40–58.

Pratte, Richard, *Contemporary Theories of Education.* Scranton, Pa.: International Textbook Company, 1971.

Wild, John, "Education and Human Society: A Realistic View," in Nelson B. Henry, ed., *Modern Philosophies and Education.* Chicago: The University of Chicago Press, 1955.

Wirsing, Marie E., *Teaching and Philosophy: A Synthesis.* New York: Houghton Mifflin, 1972, pp. 103–107.

Wynne, John P., *Theories of Education.* New York: Harper & Row, 1963, pp. 468–514.

Chapter 4
Dualistic Theism,
a Religion Oriented
Education Philosophy

In general, we may think of most supernatural Christian educational philosophies as being either monistic idealisms or dualistic theisms. (Monism and dualism are explained in Chapter 1, page 16.) The position of dualistic theism is represented by Roman Catholicism and many Protestant sects, although others are monistical idealists in their orientation. (Idealism is treated in Chapter 2.) Traditional Jewish views on education also have much in common with this position. However, since Jewish views center on teachings of the Old Testament along with other sources and Christian views center on those of the New Testament, Jewish and Christian theologies are somewhat different.

Space does not permit our attempting to present the various theistic educational philosophies. Hence, we present the Roman Catholic position as representative of the various positions. We are mindful that there are significant theological differences among the various dualistic theistic positions. So, the following few paragraphs will present the basic difference between the Roman Catholic position and that of Protestant dualistic-theistic educational philosophies; thus enabling the reader to apply much of the content of this chapter to an understanding of either viewpoint.

Because of their shared source, there is much in common between the educational philosophies of various fundamentalist Protestant sects and Roman Catholicism. The greatest difference between Protestant and Roman Catholic religious systems is that, whereas Protestants tend to look directly to the Bible as their major source of authority and inspiration, Roman Catholics are more prone to look to their Church and its priestly hierarchy for authority, which these leaders have received from their contemplation and Bible reading.

Protestants, beginning in the sixteenth century, engaged in a *protest* against what they considered to be abuses within the established church, and they sought either reform or replacement of those abuses. Although the various Protestant sects represent a great divergence of beliefs, there are some principles upon which there has been considerable Protestant consensus through the years. The greatest of these principles is that, in all areas of life, God must be recognized as the ultimate sovereign power. Two other major principles are *the priesthood of all believers* and *the authority of the Bible*. The priesthood of all believers means that each person has direct access to God and may also serve as his neighbor's priest. The authority of the Bible establishes the need for each person to read and understand the Bible for himself as a guide to life.

> Protestants, first of all, are committed to education by virtue of their being protestants. In order to read the Bible, to know the nature of their calling in the world, to understand better their relationship with men and God, the protestant must search diligently, must develop his own capacities as far as possible, must seek to replace ignorance with knowledge, and immaturity with maturity.[1]

The educational philosophy espoused by Roman Catholic leaders is called neo-Thomism after its developer, Saint Thomas Aquinas (1225–1274). In the thirteenth century, St. Thomas developed his theistic philosophy by drawing mainly from the Christian tradition and earlier Aristotelian thought. His philosophy essentially was a synthesis of early Christian beliefs with Aristotelian logic and metaphysics. St. Thomas, by applying Aristotelian teachings to the tenets of the then traditional Christianity, switched the mainstream of Christianity from an early idealistic emphasis to its current dualistic position. In general, this philosophy, even today, is the principal basis for Catholic theistic educational philosophy. Present day neo-Thomistic theism is Thomism updated to the twentieth century by keeping it consistent with the ideas of St. Thomas and simultaneously striving to make it compatible with modern science and by giving greater emphasis to the social dimension of human living.

Theism embraces the fundamental beliefs that God, for a purpose, created humankind with a human nature consisting of a material human body and an immaterial immortal soul, in His own image, and bestowed upon it the power of divine grace; thus the expression *dualistic theism*. Divine grace means that humankind has been destined for a supernatural end, union with God, and has been endowed with a gift, grace, that will enable each person, through faith and works, to attain it.

Because Adam and Eve sinned in the Garden of Eden, people are born into the world deprived of a supernature. Hence, they are deprived of supernatural life. But, the destiny of humankind is to return to the estate of their lost inheritance. Through acceptance of the teachings of the Church, every person can be restored to a divine, supernatural life. The Church has the responsibility of guiding people back to their lost supernatural estates. People regained their supernatural potentiality through the death and resurrection of Christ. So, the destined fulfillment of neo-Thomism is immortal Being in union with God.

The theistic position, that God both transcends nature and is immanent in it, should be distinguished from both deism and pantheism. *Deism* is the position that God transcends nature, but is in no way immanent in nature. God created the natural universe, including natural laws, then withdrew from the doings of nature. *Pantheism* holds that God is immanent in, but not transcendant to, nature; He and the universe are one and the same.

During the 1960s, spearheaded by the Second Vatican Council, Pope John XXIII set a course of church reform aimed to push the Roman Catholic Church more into the midstream of twentieth-century social living. While church institutions retained their primary position, the people of the Church and the larger society were given greater importance than in the past. For example, the liturgy was changed in an attempt to convert worshipping Catholics from spectators of priestly activities to active participants, and priests began to face worshippers and recite the mass in the language of the people. Thus, Catholicism has attempted to meet modern human needs, without modifying its basic creed or structure.

Dualistic Theism: The Nature of Reality

For dualistic theists, first of all, an all powerful, all knowing, and all benevolent supernatural God exists. This divine being, God, is the ultimate author and ruler of everything. Absolute reality is the existence and presence of God, Christ, and their created Church. Jesus Christ is God and man in one person, and God is both one and three: God and Father, Son, and Holy Spirit. Whereas change characterizes the natural order of things, God is changeless. Furthermore, what people can know about man and his destiny from theology, science, philosophy, aesthetic experience, and common sense, are interpreted to form a single harmonious mosaic.

Dualistic theism adheres to a *realistic ontology*, it holds that the world exists independently of human knowledge of it, and for the most part, it can be known as it is. Both mind and matter are genuinely real, and both are the creations of God. So, this philosophy is a mind-matter dualism, but one that emphasizes the orderly coordination and synthesis of physical and mental aspects of reality.

Dualistic theists recognize the existence of a number of seeming discontinuities or antinomies in their thinking such as eternity and measured time, church and state, spiritual religion and social morals, Divine Grace and nature, faith and works, freedom and responsibility, and contemplation and action. But, they overcome the apparent contrasts and oppositions by forming *syntheses* of them. Their syntheses, however, consist of *combinations of opposites*, not of *emergent concepts*.

> Since grace transforms and elevates nature but neither destroys nor negates it, it is not surprising to find a similar tension running throughout the natural order and requiring the resolution of a number of apparent antinomies. Time and eternity, the sacred and the profane, the person and the community, the civic commonwealth and the Church, action and contemplation, freedom and responsibility—in each case it is necessary to affirm both elements and to unify them in life itself, so that they coexist in a harmony that overcomes contrasts and oppositions without destroying either of two complementary values or dissolving them both into a lifeless mix.[2]

So, while there are essential differences between God and creation, Supernature and nature, spirit and matter, universals and particulars, and substance and accidents, these dualities are welded into accordant wholes.

For Aristotle, from whom St. Thomas got many of his ideas, a thing came into being through the union of its *form*, which is *actuality*, and *matter*, which is *potentiality*. In its production, a thing assumed a character of its own, an *essence* so the *essence* of anything was its basic *whatness*.

St. Thomas, in synthesizing of Aristotle and Christianity, was more interested in the fact that things *exist* than in what they are, *their whatness*. So, for him, the problem of *essence* was made secondary to the problem of *existence;* the root ingredient of all things was *existence*. Hence, whereas *actuality* for Aristotle was *form*, for St. Thomas it was *existence*. *God* and *Being* are one and the same. But, God also is the ultimate union of whatness (essence) and isness (existence). When essence and existence come together, there results Being. The world consists of both mind and things; their unifying force is Being or God. So, St. Thomas demoted essence to the principle of potentiality, and promoted existence to the principle of actuality.

Dualistic Theism: The Nature of Human Motivation

Dualistic theism, like classical realism, assumes that people are rational animals, but in addition it ascribes to them immortal souls. Their purpose on earth is basically theological in nature. A human being is an animal endowed with reason, a sinful wounded creature called to divine life and the freedom of grace, and a free individual in intimate relation with God; a human being holds himself or herself in check by the exercise of personal intelligence and will. A person is a fusion of material, mental, and spiritual reality. So, people are *bad-active* rational animals in which soul, mind, and body are united as one.

The *bad-active* assumption harmonizes with various *dualistic theisms*. There are, however, two quite distinctly different positions in regard to the nature of the badness. The most extreme position is *total depravity* as developed by John Calvin and the Puritans. For example, Jonathan Edwards, an eighteenth century Connecticut Calvinist minister, argued that people are wholly under the power of sin and utterly unable, without the interposition of sovereign grace, to do anything that is good. A less extreme position is represented by Roman Catholicism and many Protestant groups. They think that, with the fall of Adam, people lost their Godlike supernature, but they still have a human nature to begin life with, and this human nature is blessed with a goodness of intent that vies with original sin for the control of the moral life of each person.

A child, from the moment of conception, is a person who has a physical body and lives in a material world, but who also has a spiritual soul. For this reason a person is fundamentally different from the material universe and anything in it. Whereas one's body is natural, one's soul is spiritual and immortal. But, one's body is a real material, not merely a thought in the mind of God, as is the position of idealism. Every individual has not only an animal dimension, but also is a self-contained center of intelligence and freedom that is destined never to be destroyed. Each individual represents a combination of eternity and time, religion and morals, grace and nature, faith and works, freedom and responsibility, contemplation and action, spirit and flesh, human essence and personal history. Human processes are not mechanically determined and are not potentially explainable by laws of physics and chemistry; they are not merely some sort of concentration of force or energy within a larger physical field.

People, as rational creatures and body-soul units, have the powers of *understanding* and *free will*. Their final end is happiness to be achieved fully only by union with God. It is the dual capacity of thought and freedom that makes people human. All persons are capable of free choice, but the actual fullness of their freedom is a mark of maturity that is developed only by time and effort. So, in addition to having a *kind* of *intelligence* that does not exist below them in the animal kingdom, people have *free wills*. Having spiritual souls fundamentally different from any aspects of the physical universe gives them a value beyond anything else in the world.

As free agents, persons are personally responsible for their own salvation. Through Christ, they are able once more to find grace and with it the means of achieving their supernatural destiny (See page 72 for a definition of *grace*). Newborn babies, having the inborn weaknesses of human nature, have been temporarily deprived of supernatural life. However, they are not *depraved*. So through faith and works they may achieve a supernatural life for themselves. Yet, from birth, their fallen bad-active substantive minds continue active until they are curbed.

Dualistic Theism: The Nature and Source of Truth and Knowledge

Truth, for theistic supernaturalists, is the apprehension of a reality that is permanent, universal, and absolute. Since theology is made central to philosophy, truth is considered to be conformity of thoughts to things as they eternally are, their essence or reality. Reality is what exists independent of the mind, and knowledge is a value in itself and an end in itself. Truths are eternal only insofar as they exist in the mind of God.

There are many truths in human intellects, but in the divine intellect there is one primary overarching truth, which each existent thing reflects in its own way. All truth is anchored in God in such a way that one true proposition cannot contradict another. Hence, all truth forms a unity. However, whereas God's existence can be shown by reason, we cannot, in any way, completely grasp God's essence. "Truth resides in the human intellect, but also in things insofar as they are designed and sustained by the divine intellect. . . . Truth has eternity in God's intellect, not in man's."[3]

Sources of Truth

The three recognized sources of truth are revelation, self-evident intuition, and science. Revelation is the highest source of truth known to man. It is based on faith and the conviction that revealed truth comes from God and that God has entered human history and is actively engaged in shaping events. Since God reveals himself through human intellects, if there is conflict between revealed and either intuitive or scientific truth, revelation carries the day.

Self-evident truth is immediately apprehended by intellects; it is intuited by minds. Since minds reach out and grasp truth in and by itself, self-evident truths need not be tested in action. Any first principles not gained by inspired revelation must be gained through intuition. Such principles are truth grasped for the sake of truth.

Scientific truth is synthetic, it requires checkable evidence to support it, and it is not a source of ultimate truth. The eternal verities (truth, goodness, and beauty) are available through revelation, intuition, and logical reasoning, but they are not necessarily either available or validated through scientific investigation.

Means of Achieving Truth

There are two distinct orders of gaining supernatural knowledge (faith and reason) and two types of natural knowledge (bodily sensory experience and intelligence). "Faith is believing all that God has revealed because he has revealed it."[4] Revealed truth is a basic disclosure from God in His nature and His place for human beings.

Through reason, a human mind can work its way to absolute truth or a priori knowledge. So, Being or God is accessible through both faith and reason. Reason can show that the mysteries of Christian doctrine are plausible; that is, they are free from internal contradictions and harmonious with established knowledge. It also can suggest metaphors and analogies that, while not explaining revealed mysteries, do cast some light upon them. Christian thought finds perfect, absolute unity in the Source of the universe, but not in the universe itself. Through deductive reasoning from the knowledge supplied by faith, people can achieve indirect or a posteriori knowledge.

There is a difference in nature between the senses and the intellect, but both are a means of achieving truth. Whereas senses are biologically centered, the intellect, in essence, is spiritual. Through our senses we know particulars; through our intellects we grasp universals and compare particulars by relating them to one another. "Through his senses, which are indeed bodily powers, a man knows individual, singular objects of a material nature—the color and scent of this rose. But through his mind, which is itself human but immaterial, he grasps 'universal' aspects."[5]

Intelligence comes from God and is a power of the soul. Since it is what makes us human, we should exercise it. It has both passive and active roles. Intellect, then, is a nonmaterial power that grasps the nonmaterial essence of things. Since knowledge transcends the sensory order, it "is an unfortunate mistake to define human thought as an organ of response to the stimuli and situations of the environment."[6]

Maritain recognizes two basically different states of intelligence, *natural intelligence* and *intellectual virtues*. Natural intelligence operates at the level of *universal* knowledge; this level is neither scientific nor speculative. Natural intelligence consists of the right opinions about the nature and meaning of knowledge. Intellectual virtues consist of intelligence that is scientifically formed and equipped: the arts, the sciences, and "wisdom."

Tests for Truth

The test for revealed truth is divine inspiration. The Church through the Pope or the Bible tells people what is true, and the people have little or no desire to check it. "The essence of Catholicism is that the Pope, when speaking *ex cathedra*, states a theological position because it is true, it is not true because he proclaims it."[7] Hence, the test for such absolute, universal truth is its metaphysical roots.

The test for scientific truth is a statement's correspondence to preexisting natural laws. Such truth consists of correspondence between intellects and objects, and it is possible for people, as scientists, to know things as they really are.

Dualistic Theism: The Nature and Source of Human Values

The value system of theists is based on the conviction that a universal moral "natural" law has been established by God and that we can understand much of it through reason. For theists, a value system based on naturalistic, humanistic ethics is inadequate. Certain absolute values have been revealed to people by God. Thus, their essence is in no way contingent on the variations of culture, custom, or local practice. These values are interpreted by the priesthood; God's earthly intermediates. So, the primary aim of education, in its broadest sense, is formation of a moral life and its accompanying virtues and values in such way as to develop a faithful relationship with God.

"If the existence of the One who is the Absolute Being and the Absolute Good is not recognized and believed in, no certitude in the unconditional and obligatory value of moral law and ethical standards can be validly established and efficaciously adhered to."[8] It is, therefore, an obligation for schools and colleges, not only to enlighten students on moral matters, but also to allow them to receive full religious education. Christians are summoned both to life in time, on the earth made by God, and life in the age-to-come, union with God. "Although the mind cannot reach God immediately, the heart can. . . ."[9]

The Doctrine of Original Sin

Dualistic theists make much of the original sin doctrine. For them, humankind has had a common beginning and a common nature, hence a universal history. The first generation of people broke their loving relationship with God, and thereby lost their *supernature*. However, the Roman Catholic Church and many protestant churches differ from the Calvinists, who thought that people are born totally *depraved* of anything good. Roman Catholics and others do not accept the concept of human depravity; they think that, even after the fall, people still retained a unique *human* nature that contained much goodness, but through the sins of Adam and Eve they had lost their benign *supernature*.

Since humanity, through primordial sin, lost the original bond of divine friendship and the gifts that went with it, all people begin life in a sinful condition. This original sin is a moral disorder because it alienates people from God and embodies a willful preference to pursue their own purposes. So, earthly people have a divided nature involving both sin and goodness. The Apostle Paul wrote in Romans 7:15, ". . . I really want to do what is right, but I can't. I do what I don't want to—what I hate."

Christian theists believe that Christ, through His death and resurrection, overcame original sin, so people, with Christ's help, can vanquish their personal sin. Christ died for all people so that, through their faith in Him, they all might share in His resurrection. All persons are born without the gift of redemption, but they have the means of reestablishing friendship with God through an encounter with Him.

Through baptism, people are inserted into the Christian community, and through the other sacraments, they maintain and strengthen their Christian commitment. In the sacrament of penance or confession, they examine their consciences, confess their sins, and perform the assigned penances.

Hierarchy of Values

Maritain describes a hierarchy of Christian values as follows:[10]

1. Knowledge and love of what is above time. This is superior to, and embraces and quickens, knowledge and love of what is within time.

2. Charity, within which one loves God and embraces all people in this love, is the highest form of love.

3. In the intellectual realm, wisdom, which knows things eternal and creates order and unity in the mind, is superior to science or knowledge gained through particular cases.

4. The speculative intellect, which knows for the sake of knowing, comes before the practical intellect, which knows for the sake of action.

5. The practical intellect involves appreciation of secular or earthly values—arts, sciences, technology, and enterprises involved in building civilization as both the support and expression of human life.

Levels of Contemplation

Theists emphasize the importance of contemplation in Christian lives. Contemplation consists of mental concentration on spiritual matters as a form of private devotion. It is the intellectual grasping of reality and enjoyment of knowledge for its own sake. For theists, contemplation has three interrelated levels of meaning: (1) a natural inward activity of mind that creates a disposition of creativity for contemplation in the other two senses; (2) prayerful study of divine matters as manifested by Christ and proclaimed in the scriptures, such study presumes the presence of grace; (3) prayer in the purest sense—a reverential, loving awareness of the presence of God; an upward-mounting of the mind and heart to God, "The heart of Christian life is knowing and loving God, particularly in Christ, the Divine Word."[11] This level of contemplation requires the divine assistance called grace; it is superior to the other two levels.

Grace consists of unmerited divine assistance given to people by God for their regeneration or sanctification. God enhances the natural powers of intelligence and will with grace. Each person is either actually or potentially a synthesis of nature and grace. Christian education, as one of its most important aims, fosters this synthesis by helping people become more aware of its existence and importance.

Dualistic Theism: The Purpose of Education

Dualistic theists deduce the ultimate aim of education from what they consider to be the true nature and destiny of human beings. This aim is to "cooperate with Divine grace in forming the true and perfect Christian."[12] It entails people reclaiming the life of grace, which was lost through the fall of Adam. Hence, education should develop supernatural persons who judge, think and act rightly, in accordance with reason illuminated by supernatural guidance, so as to achieve grace free from mortal sin.

The purpose of education, then, is the propagation of faith and salvation of souls. It encompasses physical, spiritual, intellectual, moral, individual, and social aspects of life with the purpose of elevating, regulating, and perfecting it in keeping with eternal, Divine principles. So, people should be educated in such way as to educe the highest possible fulfillment of their powers of intelligence and will. An educated person is a mature thinker, who works with others and travels toward God.

"A true [theistic] education aims at the formation of the human person with respect to his ultimate goal, and simultaneously with respect to the good of those societies of which, as a man, he is a member, and in whose responsibilities, as an adult, he will share."[13] So, education should help every person achieve eternal salvation by striving for the glory of God both on earth and hereafter in heaven, and make his way on earth by loving both God and his neighbor. The dual nature of human beings as immortal souls and members of society, requires both supernatural and natural education. To summarize, the twofold purpose of theistic education is "(1) the development of a true interior life whose most important element will be a prayerful familiarity with God, and (2) the development of the capacity for contributing to the welfare of others, particularly through one's work."[14]

Dualistic Theism: The Nature of the Learning Process

Dualistic theists, in actual practice, often employ various psychologies of learning. But the various theories are frequently made subservient to *mental discipline* and *faculty psychology*. Learning is primarily intellectual and moral; it involves people's minds and hearts. Theists, like classical realists, assume that learning is accomplished by active minds. But, they differ from classical realists in that, whereas classical realists assume the minds of babies to be morally neutral, theists assume them to be inclined toward moral badness; they, however, are not totally depraved of any goodness.

The central idea in mental discipline is that the mind, envisioned as a substance, or its various faculties lie dormant until they are exercised through the active efforts of the person whose mind is involved. Faculties such as memory, will, reason, and perseverance are the "muscles of the mind." Like physiological muscles, they are strengthened through exercise and subsequently operate automatically. Hence, learning is a matter of strengthening, or disciplining, the faculties of the mind, which combine to produce intelligent behavior. Just as exercising an arm develops the biceps, exercising the mental faculties makes them more powerful.

According to *mental discipline learning theory*, rudiments of the various faculties are in each individual from birth, and learning is a process of developing these germinal, underdeveloped faculties into powers or capabilities. When teachers are questioned concerning the value of students' studying their particular subject and they reply, "it sharpens the mind and improves the memory," or "it cultivates the reasoning faculty," they are thinking of learning as the product of mental discipline that is transferred to other learning situations by a generally exercised mental capacity. Consequently, they think that they are building in their students great reservoirs of intellectual power that will automatically go into operation in any subsequent mental activity.

The various faculties can be developed through training and can become capable of effective performance in all areas in which they are involved. The training of the faculty of memory through memorizing even nonsense syllables presumably improves one's memory for names, for meaningful material, and for anything that calls for memory. Likewise, it is assumed that after training in reasoning through a study of geometry, a person can reason effectively in realms of philosophy, mathematics, social issues, and housekeeping.

Learning, then, for dualistic theists is a process of corrective disciplining of wills, intellects, and bodies. From Aristotle comes the dictum that, "All teaching and all learning are constituted out of pre-existing knowledge."[15] Hence, there are no innate ideas. While self-evident truths or principles are not innate, they can be known immediately and with certainty through intuition, as soon as the terms in which they are formulated are known. For example, a person or a thing cannot, at the same time, both *be* and *not be*.

Through employment of the uniquely human abstracting function, knowledge or learning has a sensory beginning, but an intellectual end. Intelligence is the power that does the abstracting. Existent reality provides the intelligible, and learners provide the intelligence. Human thinking begins, not with difficulties, but with already gained insights. It ends with new insights whose truth has been established either by rational deduction or experimental verification. The intellect forms concepts by abstracting universals from particulars. People then use these concepts in future judgments. The judging function combines the particular and the universal, sense and intellect, and concrete and abstract. Through this process, "A whole person knows a whole thing."[16] So, "this is a horse" means this particular object that I can see and touch has the nature of horseness, a universal found wherever there are horses.

Concepts, then, are abstracted universals; we can utilize them in both judgments and deductions. A *universal* is any trait or relationship that is able to characterize more than one particular instance. To abstract is to apprehend mentally the nature and value of something apart from all of its material and individual conditions.

Theists emphasize that new gains and discoveries should be used, not to shatter and reject what has been acquired from the past, but to augment the perennial truths that are carried over from the past. They strive to maintain a careful course between denying the possibility of objective knowledge and asserting that such knowledge comes easily, without stringent intellectual discipline.

Dualistic Theism: The Nature of the Teaching Process

The primary aim of theistic teachers, as such, is to move children and youth from their deprived natural state toward a divine, supernatural one, to develop their religious maturity along with other aspects of their personal-social growth, and to harmonize the two. So, a theistic teacher combines harmoniously the contributions of religious faith and educational philosophy so as to communicate wisdom and integrate cultural knowledge.

For theistic teachers, the basic principles of education are everywhere, and at all times, the same. However, different mechanisms may be used in implementing these principles. Teachers use the various techniques of modern education, but they constantly direct the entire process toward awakening students' intellectual powers and development of their sense of truth through a mental disciplining process.

Educational practices centered on mental discipline are largely a matter of training or disciplining minds with vigorous mental exercises in religion, the classics, grammar, logic, mathematics, and pure science on the assumption that such training makes a person equally effective in all areas where a given faculty is to be employed. To a mental disciplinarian, the direct utility of a subject is of only secondary importance; exercise of the mental faculties is what counts most. Hence, the primary value of science or any other disciplinary subject is the training effect it has on the minds of students. Certain mental powers or faculties such as tenacity and logicality, exercised and developed in the study of a disciplinary subject, are expected to carry over automatically to all aspects of life wherein the same mental powers are required.

Since people are assumed to be psychologically active, the principal, but not the *dominant*, agent in the educational process is not the teacher but the student. Teachers center upon students' acquisition of knowledge and the solid disciplined formation of their minds so as to free the students' intuitive powers. In teaching, adults lead students from what they know to what they do not know by conveying to them new sets of relations among the things that they know. They get students to use their minds to understand matters that they did not understand before. *Catechetical drill* in the form of questions and their correct answers is often used for training of intrinsic mental powers and to promote an awareness of God's presence.

Knowledge, fundamentally, is contemplative in nature. To contemplate means to see and to enjoy seeing. Education, in its finest and highest achievements, tends to develop the contemplative capacities of human minds. "Christian contemplation, being rooted in love, superabounds in action."[17] Genuine contemplative or truth-grasping learning fails in its very nature if it does not develop in youth both critical activity and a kind of thirst and anguish whose reward will be the very joy of perceiving truth.

Since God provides man's spiritual intelligence, He is the principal teacher. Just as nature is the principal healer, God is the principal teacher. Teachers, however, can present selected sense data to help learners' minds abstract the correct ideas. But, more important, teachers can lead learners from the known to the unknown by rational discourse. In teaching, art imitates nature by developing and extending, but not copying it. "A teacher is a physician of the mind, dependent upon its natural operations."[18]

In theistic perspective, "what matters most is to develop in the child the 'intuitivity' of the mind and its spiritual discriminatory and creative energies. The educational venture is a ceaseless appeal to intelligence and free will in the young person."[19] In the educational task, the service of adults to youth requires from them first love and then authority. This authority should be genuine, not arbitrary power. Genuine authority of teachers is intellectual authority to teach and moral authority to be respected and listened to. "For the child is entitled to expect from them what he needs: to be positively guided and to learn what he is ignorant of."[20]

The Subject Matter Emphasis of Dualistic Theism

Dualistic theists believe that religious values should permeate all parts of the curriculum. So, educational subject matter should consist of intellectually disciplinary subjects that elevate and regulate the moral, mental, and physical aspects of life. Christian doctrine must pervade everything that is taught. There is a Christian way to teach everything, even the alphabet. Teachers constantly promote an awareness of God's presence. School programs, in addition to conventional subject matter, include religious materials in the form of holy scriptures, catechisms, and explanations of Christian doctrine and dogma.

Whereas higher learning or graduate studies deal with a world of knowledge appropriate to *intellectual virtues,* basic *Christian liberal education* deals with knowledge that is appropriate to *natural* intelligence, it is "education for freedom." It is directed toward wisdom and centered on the humanities. Its aim is to develop in people the capacity to *think correctly* and to enjoy truth and beauty. It should extend through both high school and college.

We grasp the meaning of a science or an art when we understand its object, nature, and scope, and the particular species of truth or beauty it *discloses* to us. The objective of basic liberal education is to see to it that young persons grasp this truth or beauty through the natural powers and gifts of their minds and the natural intuitive energy of their reason backed up by their whole sensuous, imaginative, and emotional dynamisms.

Whatever type of curriculum is offered, first place must be reserved for religion. The primary purpose of education is not merely to teach given subjects or disciplines, but to help students understand the reality around them and see that all reality is related to God. The most crucial features of education are not the procedural aspects, but the aim that is espoused. Hence, there is a distrust of those novelties in education that originate in non-Christian circles. "Reality is what it is, while the various disciplines, as such, even theology, are abstractions."[21] So, abstraction takes students toward the intelligibility of reality.

The function of science is to organize its observations methodically and systematically so that the properties of things can lead us to an understanding of their inner Aristotelian essences. Science is a new method of understanding the inner whatness of our universe. "Physics and the natural sciences, if they are taught not only for the sake of practical applications but essentially for the sake of knowledge, provide man with a vision of the universe and a sense of the sacred, exacting, unbending objectivity of the humblest truth, which plays an essential part in the liberation of the mind and in liberal education."[22]

Footnotes

[1]Merrimon Cuninggim, "A Protestant View of Education," in *Philosophies of Education*, ed. Philip H. Phenix (New York: Wiley, 1961), pp. 67–68.

[2]John W. Donohue, *Catholicism and Education* (New York: Harper & Row, 1973), p. 124.

[3]Adrian M. Dupuis and Robert M. Nordberg, *Philosophy and Education: A Total View*, 3rd ed. (Beverly Hills, Calif.: Benzinger, Bruce, and Glencoe, 1973), p. 31.

[4]Ibid., p. 11.

[5]John W. Donohue, *Catholicism and Education*, p. 52.

[6]Jacques Maritain, "Thomist Views on Education," in *Modern Philosophies and Education*, ed. Nelson B. Henry, (Chicago: The University of Chicago Press, 1955), p. 59.

[7]William Oliver Martin, *Realism in Education* (New York: Harper & Row, 1969), p. 115.

[8]Maritain, "Thomist Views on Education," p. 83.

[9]Donohue, *Catholicism and Education*, p. 91.

[10]Maritain, "Thomist Views on Education," pp. 65–66.

[11]Donohue, *Catholicism and Education*, p. 108.

[12]Robert J. Henle, "A Roman Catholic View of Education," in *Philosophies of Education*, ed. Philip H. Phenix (New York: Wiley, 1961), p. 76.

[13]Dupuis and Nordberg, *Philosophy and Education: A Total View*, p. 288.

[14]Donohue, *Catholicism and Education*, pp. 81–82.

[15]Dupuis and Nordberg, *Philosophy and Education: A Total View*, p. 38.

[16]Ibid., p. 33.

[17]Maritain, "Thomist Views on Education," p. 65.

[18]Dupuis and Nordberg, *Philosophy and Education: A Total View*, p. 35.

[19]Maritain, "Thomist Views on Education," p. 71.

[20]Ibid., p. 69.

[21]Dupuis and Nordberg, *Philosophy and Education: A Total View*, p. 9.

[22]Maritain, "Thomist Views on Education," p. 78.

BIBLIOGRAPHY

Butler, J. Donald. *Four Philosophies and Their Practice in Education and Religion* 3rd ed. New York: Harper & Row, 1968, Chapters 12, 15, and 16.

Cuninggim, Merrimon. "A Protestant View of Education." In *Philosophies of Education*, edited by Philip H. Phenix. New York: Wiley, 1961.

Donohue, John W. *Catholicism and Education.* New York: Harper & Row, 1973.

Dupuis, Adrian M., and Nordberg, Robert B. *Philosophy and Education: A Total View*, 3rd ed. Beverly Hills, Calif.: Benzinger, Bruce, and Glencoe, 1973.

Maritain, Jacques. "Thomist Views on Education." In *Modern Philosophies and Education*, edited by Nelson B. Henry. Chicago: The University of Chicago Press, 1955.

Martin, William Oliver. *Realism in Education.* New York: Harper & Row, 1969.

Morris, Van Cleve, and Pai, Young. *Philosophy and the American School* 2nd ed. Boston: Houghton Mifflin, 1976.

Neff, Frederick. *Philosophy and American Education.* New York: Center for Applied Research on Education, 1966, Chapter 3.

Shermis, S. Samuel. *Philosophic Foundations of Education.* New York: American Book Company, 1967.

Wynne, John P. *Theories of Education.* New York: Harper & Row, 1963, Chapters 1 and 9.

Chapter 5
Logical Empiricism, a Tough-Minded Determinism

Logical empiricism, through its emphasis upon the use of scientific procedures as the only source of truth has "presented itself as a philosophy to end all philosophies."[1] Its adherents make much of Auguste Comte's thesis that the intellectual development of humankind begins with a theological phase, passes through a metaphysical phase, and finally culminates in a positive, scientific phase. For them, the only kinds of statements that involve truthful meaning are statements of empirical facts that can be confirmed by sensory observation and statements of logic and mathematics that can be checked by deduction or calculation.

This philosophy has made its major contributions in the realms of the language and logic within the natural sciences. Its basic premise is that all meaningful statements are either analytic ones or ones verifiable by observation and experimentation. Hence, it set the stage for development of *analytic philosophy*, which will be treated in Chapter 6. Whereas logical empiricism focuses upon the scientific method as the source of all truth, analytical philosophy gives much greater emphasis to the logical, rational aspects of logical empiricism and has developed methods for carrying out these aspects. Hence, although there is much in common between the two positions, there is also enough difference for them to be treated as separate philosophic positions.

The thinking of the leading logical empiricists shows great divergence, but they do have one basic area in common; they all adhere to a nonmetaphysical, nonspeculative philosophy. Their philosophical purpose is to eliminate metaphysical-speculative statements, which are meaningless, and to develop a more precise and complete definition of scientifically tenable statements.[2] For them, the future task of philosophy is not to build grand metaphysical systems, but to study the consequences of linguistic usage. They think that metaphysical statements about preexisting absolutes really say nothing. They only express some emotional attitude and the means for expression of emotions are art, lyric poetry, and music. So, their philosophy has been an attempt "to make philosophy scientifically tenable through critical analysis of details rather than to make it universal by vague generalizations and dogmatic construction of systems. . . ."[3]

The empiricism of logical empiricism means that all knowledge originates through sensory experience in the form of observation and experimentation as practiced in the natural sciences. The logical of logical empiricism means using reason in a formal, orderly, and cogent fashion. So, logical empiricists emphasize the use of formal logic and language analysis in philosophy.

Historical Background of Logical Empiricism

Logical empiricism grew out of *logical positivism*, which was developed in the Vienna Circle. The *Vienna Circle* consisted of a revolutionary group of philosophers who assembled at Vienna in 1924. This group was lead by Gustav Bergmann (1906–   ), Rudolf Carnap (1891–1970), Herbert Feigl (1902–   ), Philipp Frank (1884–1966), and Moritz Schlick (1882–1936).

The philosophical view of logical positivism emerged from the work of Bertrand Russell (1872–1970) and his student, Ludwig Wittgenstein (1889–1951). It was considered to be the logical outcome of the earlier positivistic empiricisms developed by people such as Auguste Comte (1798–1857), David Hume (1711–1776), Ernst Mach (1839–1916), and J. S. Mill (1806–1873). A. J. Ayer (1910–   ) and Herbert Feigl have become leading contemporary advocates of logical empiricism. Hence, we draw heavily from the works of these two scholars in the development of this chapter.

Russell's hard data consisted of the particular facts of sense data and the general truths of logic. As a mathematician, he thought that pure mathematics could be reduced to formal logic. Hence, he attempted to develop a generalized symbolic logic to be used in all sciences.

Wittgenstein was greatly influenced by Russell. His *Tractatus Logico-philosophicus*[4] was an exposition of logical atomism and an account of the conditions under which language has meaning and can make a claim for truth. He thought that most propositions that had been written about philosophical matters were not false but being metaphysical and mystical statements they were senseless. For him a true proposition was a picture of reality, and in any such picture, there must be a one-to-one correspondence between the picture and the state of affairs it purports to represent.

Wittgenstein's logical atomism entailed that (1) the world consists of facts independent of each other, (2) atomic facts are combinations of simpler parts, (3) the totality of true thought is an accurate picture of the world, (4) the real sense of a proposition is its agreement and disagreement with the possibility that its atomic facts exist or don't exist and (5) the specification of all of the true elementary propositions describes the world completely. In his later *Philosophical Investigations,*[5] Wittgenstein rejected some aspects of his logical atomism. This position, however, continued to be implicit in logical empiricism.

After his graduation from Oxford, Ayer studied logical positivism at the University of Vienna. He published his *Language, Truth and Logic*[6] in 1936 when he was only twenty-six. As a professor of logic at the University of Oxford, he has continued to write books and treatises that expand and clarify his position. Ayer's second important work, the *Foundations of Empirical Knowledge* (1940), dealt mostly with problems of philosophical psychology; that is, with the philosophy of perception. This book deviated considerably from the hard line of earlier positivism. The second edition of *Language, Truth and Logic* (1946) showed a similar softening trend, which continued in *Philosophical Essays* (1954), *The Problem of Knowledge* (1956), *The Concept of a Person* (1963), and *The Central Questions of Philosophy* (1973).

Herbert Feigl was professor of philosophy at the University of Minnesota and director of the Minnesota Center for Philosophy of Science, where he spearheaded the *Minnesota Studies in the Philosophy of Science.* Volumes 1 and 2 of these studies involved the meanings of basic psychological concepts.

The Task of Logical Empiricism

Logical empiricists think that philosophers of the future should not attempt to formulate speculative truths, to look for first principles, or to make nonscientific judgments about the validity of empirical beliefs. Instead, they should confine their operation to verbal clarification and analysis. For them, language analysis and language analysis alone is the fundamental, defensible future role of philosophers. Language analysis includes the analysis of everyday common language as well as the technical language of the natural sciences, logic, and mathematics. They think that through this procedure, philosophers can move people in the direction of "maturer ways of thinking, thinking which possesses the virtues characteristic of science: clarity and consistency, testability and adequacy, precision and objectivity."[7]

The task of philosophy contrasts sharply with the task of the sciences, which is to add to the volume of our reliable knowledge. Philosophical propositions are not factual, but linguistic in nature. They express either definitions or the formal consequences of definitions. Hence, philosophy is actually a part of logic. "The way to the solution of a philosophical problem leads . . . through the explication of the philosophical use of some key words."[8] Accordingly, this philosophy is concerned more with the meanings that are carried by propositions or sentences than with the pursuit of truth as such.

Critics of logical empiricism, however, continue to think that a nonsystematic, analytic, piecemeal philosophical method, centered upon analyses of isolated concepts allows philosophers to gloss over the challenging task of integrating the composite meaning among a group of related concepts (such as reality, truth, meaning, and causality) in order to develop a synthetic reconstruction of the whole. Thus, they think that the more defensible role of philosophy, and especially educational philosophy, is to develop an integrated, systematic outlook in regard to human life and its problems.[9]

Logical Empiricism: The Nature of Reality

Within logical empiricism, "there is an empirical, cognitively meaningful concept of reality, [that is] used in common life and merely refined in science."[10] This reality consists of the perceptible properties of physical objects, and a physical object can be known to people only through its various appearances. The role of science is to develop the relation of the appearances of physical objects to the reality of the objects themselves. However, Ayer has written "there is an intelligible sense in which our ordinary judgments of perception may truly be said to go beyond the evidence on which they are based."[11]

An Antimetaphysical Philosophy

Since knowledge is limited to statements based on *observable* facts, metaphysical theses concerning a world of reality that transcends the world of science and common sense are brushed aside as meaningless or nonsensical. All metaphysical statements are either meaningless combinations of words or they are concealed scientific statements whose truth can be ascertained by scientific methods of observation and experimentation. Religious and mystical hypotheses are assessed in terms of scientific theory and evidence. So, for logical empiricists, there are no meaningful metaphysical statements. Many logical empiricists recognize that, "The search for an ultimate reason [for things] is emotionally understandable but it is not intellectually coherent."[12]

Since the ontology of logical empiricists is a physicalistic one, nothing should be asserted to be real or meaningful unless, through observation, it can be objectively studied, using only publicly verifiable data. If anything exists, it exists in some amount; if it exists in some amount, it can be measured. So, logical empiricists think that we should abandon "dogmatic, other worldly, supernaturalistic, tender-minded, rationalistic, parochial preconceptions and . . . replace them by critical, worldly, naturalistic, fact-minded, empirical, experimental, and universally applicable ways of thinking."[13]

A Realistic Ontology

Logical empiricists are convinced that the physical world that is experienced by human beings is real and essentially what it appears to be when observed through the senses. Furthermore, even if there were no human beings around to observe it, the world would exist in the same state. Therefore reality or objective existence is independent of a thing's being known. "The great majority of philosophers nowadays do, indeed, believe in the capacity of material objects to exist unperceived. . . ."[14] Reality refers to physical objects and processes, which are out there in their own right. So, "it is possible to start with sensory qualities and construct on this basis a realistic theory of the physical world."[15] The chair on which the reader is sitting may be said to exist and, to logical empiricists, the chair is a good example of reality (not someone's impression of the chair, but the chair itself). The chair exists in its own right; the way one perceives it is not relevant to its reality.

Logical empiricists tend to assume that the physical world is governed by natural laws, which operate inexorably and without change. They further assume that a basic principle of the universe is sequential cause and effect; every event is determined by events that have gone before. Thus, the universe is a vast mechanism governed by natural laws.

Logical Empiricism: The Nature of Human Motivation

The naturalistic view of logical empiricists carries with it the concept of the *causal determination* of human behavior. Logical empiricists consider "human beings with their drives and interests, reflections and deliberations, purposes and ideals, preferences, choices and actions, as links in the causal chains of the processes of the universe."[16] They interpret the causal necessity of these processes essentially in terms of lawfulness and predictability. Thus, their understanding of an individual centers upon that person's past pointed toward the present.

In terms of their conception of humankind, logical empiricists are psychophysiological monists as opposed to mind-body dualists. They "look with great suspicion upon the hypotheses of vitalism in biology, of mind-body dualism, of psychical research, and of so-called 'empirical theologies' which base their arguments on the observable facts of the world."[17] For them, human activity is better explained in terms of physical, biological, and psychological behavioristic principles. Immaterial mentalistic substances are absolutely incapable of being tested, therefore factually meaningless.

Human beings are not *rational animals* in the sense of being biological organisms with ethereal spiritual minds. Instead, they are talking, tool-using, symbolic-reasoning animals; "the most profound difference between human and subhuman organisms consists in the exclusively human possession of language."[18] *Homo Sapiens* is the biologically determined *talking animal*. So, we no longer need the hypothesis of an immaterial soul or spirit that controls one's brain activities.

The causal determination outlook of psychophysiological monism expresses itself as a behavioristic psychology such as that developed by B. F. Skinner within which a person is taken to be a neutral-passive biological organism whose behavior is determined by its original genetic pattern and the physical environment that has impinged upon it. Any organism will respond according to its genetic inheritance and prior conditioning. All talk about mind is replaced by talk about behavior. Even in the case of emotions, behavioral dispositions are what really count.

The causal determinism of logical empiricism is not a fatalistic concept. All behavior is determined by *prior* causes, not by future ones. Hence, there is no fatalistic predetermination of human behavior; no destiny that guides our actions. Logical empiricists think of *free will* as being exercised within *causal determinism*. It simply means freedom from the future, though not from the past. And prior causes are interpreted in keeping with natural lawfulness and predictability.

Logical empiricists tend to consider the concept that people are goal-directed or purposive human beings as teleological (supernaturally purposively) designed. To them teleological means deriving present behavior from the future, and consequently it sounds mystical and superstitious. So, in an effort to escape any commitment to the view that the future has a bearing on causation, they emphasize that past events are the cause of present behavior. Accordingly, logical empiricism treats human beings within a behavioristic frame of reference; people are basically extremely well-designed, clever machines who learn through their accumulating memories in an additive process. Human responses are chance affairs without intentional purpose, and a human being is a biological organism with a history of conditioned behavior.

So, for a logical empiricist, words such as foresight, purpose, and desire are literary terms, not scientific ones.

Logical empiricists and their counterparts in behaviorist psychology continue to think in terms of stimuli as causes and responses as effects, and of a time lapse occurring between physical stimuli and organic responses. "Temporarily integrated behavior, extended over a period of time, is treated as a series of reactions to a series of stimulation. . . . Stimulus followed directly by response is the archetype of behavior. . . ."[19] Explanation for what organisms, including people, do is sought in the environmental circumstances that surround them, the stimuli that impinge upon them, and the actions, including verbalizations, that they emit. These actions or behaviors are either respondents or operants. A respondent is behavior that is elicited by a stimulus. An operant is behavior that is controlled by its consequences, that is, by the stimulus that follows it.

Logical Empiricism: The Nature and Source of Truth and Knowledge

The goal of knowledge, for logical empiricists, consists of adequate descriptions, explanations, and predictions of the facts of experience. A basic assumption is that all knowledge is carried in language. The three functions of language are representation, expression, and appeal. The function that is unique to humankind, however, is *representation* of objects and relations. Lower animals, in contrast, communicate almost exclusively by expression and appeal.

Reliable knowledge is based in science. It consists of a body of testable, precise, coherent, and comprehensive facts. These facts basically fall into two categories: knowing that so and so is true, and knowing how to do so and so. The meanings of statements made in empirical science can be determined through the process of logical analysis and can be reduced to simple sentences about empirically given data. In contrast, animistic, theological, and metaphysical assertions are often completely immune to objective tests and thus become a matter of pure faith. In that case they must be considered as nonscientific ". . . even if they operate with . . . sharply defined concepts, display a rigorous logical structure and . . . offer comprehensive explanations of all there is."[20]

A Hierarchy of Unified Sciences
Logical empiricists think that there is a kind of hierarchy of the sciences, some being much more objective and reliable than others. At the top of the hierarchy are physics and chemistry, aided by mathematics. These sciences are regarded as models that other sciences should emulate. "There is good reason to believe that the laws of chemistry

can be derived from those of physics, and that biological laws are derivable from chemical laws. If it could then be shown that the laws of psychology and sociology were derivable from biological laws, the programme would be complete."[21] This is the basis for their commitment to the *unity of science*. A goal of their language analysis is to develop a universal mathematical and symbolic scientific language that can be used in all the sciences.

Principle of Verifiability

The keystone principle of logical empiricism is that meaningful knowledge is verifiable. Succinctly stated, a statement is meaningful if, and only if, it is either an analytic one or is empirically verifiable. Ayer has written "the necessary and sufficient conditions for knowing that something is the case are first that what one is said to know be true, secondly that one be sure of it and thirdly that one should have the right to be sure."[22] So, knowing something is distinguished from believing it. A person who claims to *know* something that is not true, only *believes* it. For one to know something one's knowledge must be conclusively verified and one must deserve the right to be sure about it.

The test for the meaningful truth of a sentence or proposition, then, is its *verifiability*. "A sentence is factually significant to any given person if, and only if, he knows how to verify the proposition which it purports to express—that is, if he knows what observations would lead him, under certain conditions, to accept it as being true or reject it as being false."[23] Accordingly, "the meaning of a sentence is equated with the truth-conditions of the proposition which it serves to express."[24] Likewise, a concept is meaningful if and only if there are possible sense-perceptions that will verify the presence or absence of what is designated by that concept.

It is within the verifiability principle that the *logic* of logical empiricism comes to the forefront. This logic centers on categorization and classification of concepts in much the same way that Aristotle had arranged concepts into hierarchical cubbyholes. Its purpose is to analyze the language that we use in the expression of our concepts and ideas in the form of propositions.

A *proposition* is a declarative sentence that consists of a *subject*, a *predicate*, and a *middle term*, such as "is" that connects the subject and predicate. The subject represents a thing, process, event, or concept. The predicate states something about the subject in terms of either what it is part of, what it is like, what it does, or how it behaves. Predicates give basic data about the world.

Based upon the nature of their content, there are two basic kinds of propositions: empirical and logical ones. *Empirical propositions* contain statements about matter of fact reality. *Logical propositions* indicate the ways in which the terms (subject and predicate) relate to each other and how a proposition relates to other propositions. Propositions are either true or false, as tested by empirical science, or valid or invalid, as tested by logic.

Then, based upon their subject-predicate relationships, there are both synthetic and analytic propositions. *Synthetic* propositions are statements about the physical world. A synthetic proposition attaches a related predicate to a subject on the basis of empirical (scientific) evidence. Synthetic propositions are the only kind that are capable of producing knowledge. For example, "a wolf is a carnivore" or "the pen is on the desk."

Analytic propositions consist of the propositions of logic and pure mathematics. They are consistent with other statements or definitions, but they do not say anything about the world as such. An analytic proposition is one in which the predicate merely repeats what already is contained in the meaning of the subject. Such a proposition is absolutely true because it is a tautology.

A *tautology* is a statement that, because of its logical form, is true by definition. Some examples of analytic tautologies are "Hereford cattle are white-faced," "a quadruped has four legs," or "two plus two equals four." A tautology has a useful meaning but it cannot produce knowledge. Statements of mathematics are necessarily true, however, only insofar as they are analytic and dependent upon the meaning of mathematical terms. When they have empirical referents, they no longer are necessarily true but depend upon observation for their verification.

Then, finally, based upon their derivation, propositions may be either a priori or a posteriori ones. An *a priori* proposition is derived from a set of self-evident first principles. An *a posteriori* proposition is derived from observed facts; it involves an inductive process. Meaningful propositions involving empirical evidence are all synthetic *a posteriori* ones.

Synthetic *a priori* statements are statements of self-evident first principles arrived at through intuition or inspiration and not based on empirical evidence. They are pseudopropositions that grammatically resemble synthetic statements such as those made by scientists, but that have no method of verification. There is no way to apply empirical evidence to them so as to test their truth. Some examples of synthetic a priori statements are "God is love," "people have substantive, nonphysical minds," or "reality basically is mental or spiritual in nature." For logical empiricists, since synthetic a priori statements are based on metaphysical speculation, they are meaningless or nonsensical.

The meaning of any proposition then is to be established through its method of verification. If it has no valid method of verification, it has no meaning. In order for a proposition to have meaning it either must be true by definition (an analytic tautology) or its truth must be testable by relevant sense experience. If a statement about reality fails to satisfy this principle, "it is metaphysical, and . . . being metaphysical, it is neither true nor false but literally senseless."[25] So, all statements or propositions are either synthetic a posteriori, analytic, or meaningless ones.

Logical Empiricism: The Nature and Source of Human Values

For logical empiricists, whereas facts are descriptive of an independently existing reality, values are only normative; that is, either they are subjective, emotional matters of desire or they are absolute, nonempirical pronouncements. In neither case are they amenable to empirical study. They, therefore, are removed from any sort of scientific inquiry. To logical empiricists there is no way of bridging the gap, no argument capable of advancing logically from an "is" premise in regard to reality to an "ought" conclusion, which is normative.

A moral code cannot be founded on either metaphysics, authority, or science. However, since it is legitimate to analyze and clarify concepts in these areas, scientific and factual considerations are indeed relevant to morals.[26] Once basic principles are intuitively set, we may use a scientific approach to learn how to achieve them. But, what has to be admitted is that there is no way of proving that the principles are either correct or mistaken.[27] What we can do through scientific procedures is to know what the moral situation in which we are placed is like and what the consequences of different actions are likely to be. Furthermore, using logical processes, we may show that certain moral principles either are inconsistent with one another, are based on false factual assumptions, are the product of bad reasoning, or lead to consequences that the persons involved do not desire.

"Logically empiricists are generally agreed to draw a sharp distinction between the *study* of evaluation and the *making* of evaluations."[28] Since their philosophy centers on *is's*, not *oughts*, they study the evaluations that occur in social, cultural, and psychological contexts, using the criteria of scientific inquiry to decide upon the presence or absence of certain properties or relations. They, however, think that all values are humanmade, and that they are dependent upon human needs and interests. Hence, there are no absolute values. In the current age of scientific enlightenment, "human knowledge and human love and sympathy are the only firm foundations on which moral conduct can be built."[29]

Since ethical judgments have no objective status, it is impossible to find any criterion for determining their validity. Since they are pure expressions of unverifiable feelings, there is no sense in asking whether they are true or false. "For in saying that a certain type of action is right or wrong, I am not making any factual statement, not even a statement about my own state of mind. I am merely expressing certain sentiments."[30] Expressions of feelings or sentiments, however, are not uncaused events. They, like other behaviors, are determined by prior circumstances.

"The scientific outlook in philosophy proposed by the logical empiricists has no room for 'absolute values'—if this phrase is understood to mean values that could be demonstrated or otherwise justified independently of any reference to human needs, interests, and ideals as they naturally arise in the bio-psycho-socioeconomic-historical matrix of civilization."[31] So people need to learn to live with their knowledge about themselves through combining scientific insights with serious social, moral commitments. Their fuller insight into factors that determine their outlook on life will help to eliminate infantile fixations and their regression to less mature levels of development.

Feigl states that, "Only the deterministic view provides an adequate basis for an interpretation of moral responsibility."[32] The deterministic view is that all human behavior is *determined* by prior causes. Freedom for people to choose does not mean their freedom from prior causes. In fact, it is only if we, with our character and personality as it is constituted at a given moment of our life, are deemed the doers of our deeds that we can be held responsible for our deeds.

Logical Empiricism: The Purpose of Education

As a philosophy of science and theory of knowledge, logical empiricism has had a great effect on the purposes and procedures of today's education and especially upon the kinds of psychological approaches within education. But, since this philosophy essentially is one that develops a philosophical methodology, its goals for education can be arrived at only indirectly, in one of two ways. Either the basic evaluations that underlie the outlook of the philosophy may be made explicit and discussed critically, thus certain aims and ideals of education may be formulated; or the ways and means of education may be appraised in the light of criteria for their validity.

Logical empiricists think that education should dislodge the confusions with which tender minded, wishful, prescientific thinking abound and replace them with a tough-minded, scientific approach to all areas that lend themselves to descriptive study combined with training in the analysis of the function of language. Since education, like medicine, is essentially an applied science, the major part of education should be devoted to inculcating the scientific attitude in all areas of inquiry and to giving students an understanding of the problems and results of applying both natural and social science in the modern world.

Training students in analysis of the functions of language enables them to recognize the necessary sharp distinctions between descriptive cognitions consisting of "is's" or "whats" and prescriptive valuations consisting of "oughts" or "whys." It also helps them recognize propaganda and see the necessity for careful, sound definitions. Achievement of educational goals is a matter of behavioral engineering. Leaders should plan the nature of future society and its various members then change the observable behaviors of students in the planned direction.

In addition to the enhancement of scientific and linguistic procedures and the promotion of rational thought and conduct, some logical empiricists think that, "education should foster the development of constructive and benevolent attitudes."[33] Thus, it should help students maintain sufficient high levels of aspiration for self-perfection, but it should guard against overdoing this function to the point of endangering the mental health of students.

Logical Empiricism: The Nature of the Learning Process

In regard to the learning process, Feigl states,

> No matter how the present controversies in the psychological theories of learning may ultimately be settled, there are some conclusions which are fairly firmly established: Patterns of expectation and of action develop through the responses of the organism to repeated stimuli (or stimuli-configurations), and through trial and error (fumble and success), i.e., under conditions of positive or negative reinforcement. These reinforcements consist in the satisfaction (or frustration) either of basic biological needs (like hunger or sex) or of the varieties of secondary and tertiary needs (interests) as they are typical of the human cultural level (needs for security, recognition, love, equity, new experience, pure knowledge, or aesthetic gratification).[34]

Thus, logical empiricists generally are committed to a *neobehavioristic* outlook on learning within which people are assumed to be neutral-passive biological organisms.

In the eyes of neobehaviorists, learning is a more or less permanent change of behavior that results from practice. Accordingly, the learning process consists of impressions of new reaction patterns on pliable organisms. Since learning arises, in some way, from an interplay between organisms and their environments, the key concept of neobehaviorists are *stimuli* (excitement provided by an environment) and *responses* (reactions made by an organism). Consequently, the problem of the nature of the learning process is the study of relationships among processions of stimuli and responses and what occurs between them.

Within neobehaviorism or stimulus-response conditioning theory, one thinks of all learning as S-R conditioning and divides conditioning into two basic categories: *classical conditioning* (that without reinforcement) and *instrumental conditioning* (that which occurs through reinforcement). *Conditioning* is formation of some sort of stimulus-response sequential relation that results in an enduring change either in the pattern of behavior or in the likelihood of an organic response. *Reinforcement* is a special type of conditioning in which the reduction of an organic need or the satisfaction of a drive stimulus increases the probability of the organism emitting a given response or behavior on subsequent occasions. Reinforcement occurs through satisfaction of either basic biological needs, like hunger or sex, or secondary needs such as security, recognition, or aesthetic gratification. There are both positive and negative reinforcers. A *positive reinforcer* is a stimulus whose *presence* strengthens a behavior; a negative reinforcer is a stimulus whose *withdrawal* strengthens a behavior.

A *need* as used here is an objective, biological requirement of an organism that must be met if the organism is to survive and grow. Examples of needs are an organism's requirement for food or escape from pain. A *drive stimulus* is an aroused state in an organism. It is closely related to the need that sets the organism into action and may be defined as a strong, persistent stimulus that demands an adjustive response. Whenever an organism is deprived of satisfaction of a need, drive stimuli occur.

Classical conditioning, that is, conditioning with no reinforcement, is stimulus substitution; it is based on the adhesive principle. The *adhesive principle* means that a stimulus is attached to a response through occurring just prior to the response so that the revival of the stimulus evokes that response. Reinforcement, also called instrumental or operant conditioning, is response change or modification; it is based on the feedback principle. The *feedback principle* means that the reduction or satisfaction of an organic need or drive stimulus increases the probability of future responses of the kind that the organism emitted immediately prior to being fed, watered, satisfied sexually, or otherwise satiated. There is feedback from the satisfaction of some deprivation to the type of behavior that preceded it.

Primary Reinforcement

Reinforcement may be either *primary* or *secondary*. Primary reinforcement strengthens a certain behavior through the satisfaction of a basic biological need or drive.

The drive-reduction sequence of primary reinforcement proceeds as follows.

1. Deprivation of satisfaction of a basic requirement, such as that for food, produces a state of need in an organism.

2. The need expresses itself as a tension state or drive stimulus, which energizes the organism into action (a food-deprived animal shows the restless activity whose manifestation is called the hunger drive).

3. The activity achieves satisfaction of the need and relieves the tension state.

4. The form of the activity that immediately preceded the satisfaction of the need or reduction of the drive is reinforced.

Secondary Reinforcement

Secondary reinforcement sometimes is called high-order reinforcement. The reinforcers in secondary or high-order reinforcement have acquired their power of reinforcement indirectly through learning; poker chips for which a chimpanzee will work and money for which a person will do almost anything are secondary reinforcers. Secondary reinforcement is brought about by an originally neutral stimulus occurring along with a reinforcing stimulus. When a neutral stimulus such as a sound or light is repeatedly paired with food in the presence of a food-deprived (hungry) animal, the formerly neutral stimulus becomes a secondary, conditioned reinforcer. Thus, secondary reinforcement results when originally neutral stimuli become closely associated with primary reinforcing stimuli and thereby become effective in reducing needs. In this way, neutral stimuli acquire the power of acting as reinforcing agents; a chimpanzee learns to accept the poker chips that accompany food as a "reward" just as readily as he accepts food. Consequently, future actions of the chimpanzee are reinforced by his receiving poker chips immediately after he performs them; this is secondary reinforcement.

In addition to the two kinds of positive conditioning (*classical* and *instrumental*) there also is a negative conditioning process (*extinction*). Through classical and instrumental conditioning, an organism *gains* responses or habits; through extinction it *loses* them. Extinction is the process whereby an organism gradually loses a response or habit through repeating the response a number of times while no reinforcing stimulus accompanies it. Any habits gained through either classical or instrumental conditioning may be lost through extinction.

For logical empiricists, one's knowing and the learning process of achieving knowledge are defined in terms of gaining empirically testable truths. Thus, perception is prominent in the learning process, and what we perceive is equated with physical states or processes within our behavioral dispositions. Since metaphysics is equated with non-sense and science is equated with sense, "It is vain to attempt to dissociate the world as it is in itself from the world as we conceive it."[35] Even though some things we perceive are real and some are not, the things we perceive are all nonmental. However, "the positing of physical objects leads us to our drawing a distinction between the objects as they are in themselves and the experiences through which we come to know them."[36]

The Meaning of Memory
In keeping with their denial that substantive minds exist, logical empiricists have their unique characterization of processes such as memory and thinking that are involved in learning. To remember a fact is to have the disposition or ability to state that fact. Such a disposition, to be actualized, must become a thing remembered. Actualization consists of being able to talk about the fact or event that is being remembered. So memory is a called-for performance, description, or statement of something learned or experienced in the past.

The Meaning of Thinking
The activity, thinking, is not sharply distinguishable from other acts of a person; there is nothing called mind that underlies mental events. So mental events are simply thinking; that is, organisms behaving symbolically. In cases "where thought *is* given expression, the expressing and the thinking merge into a single process."[37] When a person talks intelligently to another, talking is evidence that the person is thinking; the person is making certain utterances and understands them. Thinking and using words intelligently are one and the same process, whether done vocally or subvocally. The process of thought and the medium of thought are one and the same. Since what people know consists of symbols, when they think of something they think in symbols.

For most logical-empiricistic behaviorists, an idea or thought consists of a symbolic movement that constitutes an intermediate step between overt stimuli and responses. Symbols are events that represent something beyond themselves. They may be either substitute stimuli or substitute responses. Whenever an organism is responding in a certain way, and the stimulus that was originally adequate to evoke the response is absent, the organism is responding to a symbolic stimulus. A symbolic response is an incipient (partial) movement that takes the place of a completely expressed pattern of behavior. It may be a shrug of the shoulders, a facial expression, a nod of the head, or a change in posture. In thinking, symbolic movements may be so slight that the individual may only be aware of a thought divorced from any movement. Nevertheless, behaviorists believe that when one thinks, at least some slight muscular, glandular, or organic action does occur.

Thinking, then, is a person behaving symbolically or incipiently in a random, trial-and-error fashion. Thought is not some mentalistic process that is the cause of behavior, but the behavior itself. Thus, thinking is symbolic or incipient trial-and-error behavior that culminates in learning. Like all other instances of an organism's behavior, it is a function or result of a set of antecedent conditions.

In thinking, an organism makes symbolic miniature responses that sample the feedbacks that would occur if the actions represented symbolically or incipiently were really carried out. Thus, to behaviorists, thought consists of very small preparatory responses. So construed, thinking can be observed in the incipient or miniature trial-and-error movements of a rat at a "choice point" in a maze. Here small movements, this way and that, often precede the rat's actual movement down a pathway. In human beings this process is subtle and more elaborate, but is no different in kind from that of rats and other lower animals.

In its broadest sense, thinking behavior is both verbal and nonverbal, both overt and covert. However, any nonverbal or covert aspects of behavior are considered to function much like the observable ones; they too are segments of stimulus-response sequences. Accordingly, behaviorists assume that, once natural laws governing the relationship of observable stimuli and responses are identified and established, internal processes likewise can be described in terms of stimulus-response sequences, which conform to the same laws. Thus, ideational thought, a variable that intervenes between observable stimuli and responses, likewise consists of stimuli and responses, albeit covert ones.

Although B. F. Skinner and some other behaviorists consider the study of any private, internal events irrelevant to a functional analysis of behavior, many contemporary behaviorists follow John B. Watson's earlier leadership in regarding thinking as basically a matter of implicit speech, talking to oneself. Thus, they associate thought very closely with language, which is a rich collection of symbols. So considered, thought is basically a laryngeal activity mediated by a nervous system. However, it is closely aligned with gestures, frowns, shrugs, and grimaces that symbolize, that is, take the place of, more overt actions or behaviors.

In the thinking process, words, other symbols, and incipient movements become cues for behavior. Cues are stimuli of faint intensity that evoke or guide an organism's movements. Any uniqueness humankind may have involves his "better" use of cues. Three principal factors make humankind's thinking processes higher than those of other animals. First, a human being has greater capacity to respond selectively to more subtle aspects of the environment as cues. Secondly, a person is able to make a greater variety of distinctive responses that constitutes cues for actions. Finally, he or she can emit a greater number of cue-responses simultaneously. Thus, he or she can elicit many more future responses based on patterns of cues that represent, or result from, several different earlier patterns of stimulation.

Logical Empiricism: The Nature of the Teaching Process

For logical empiricists, a child or youth is basically an extremely well-designed, clever machine who learns through accumulating memories in an additive process. Human responses are chance affairs without intentional purpose, and a human being is a biological organism with a history of conditioned behavior that is to be molded in the proper fashion. Learning primarily is a process within which both verbal and nonverbal behaviors are changed. Such behaviors are inculcated by adults telling, showing, directing, guiding, arranging, manipulating, rewarding, punishing, and at times, coercing the activities of children and youth. Accordingly, teaching is a matter of adults setting behavioristic environmental conditions (stimuli) to make sure that the students accomplish those goals. Teachers strive to change the behaviors of their students in the desired direction by providing the right stimuli at the proper time.

Probably the most efficient mechanistic method of changing the behavior of either students or rats involves the use of programmed instruction, or in other words operant conditioning. Programmed instruction is a system of teaching and learning within which pre-established subject matter is broken down into small, discrete steps and carefully organized into a logical sequence which can be learned readily by the students. Each step builds deliberately upon the preceding one. Progress through the sequence of steps is at the learner's own rate and the learner is reinforced immediately after each step. In a rat or a very young child, reinforcement consists in receiving bits of food or other organically satisfying substances. In an older child, or an adult, it consists of being given the correct answer or by being permitted to proceed to the next step immediately following the correct response.

Teaching, then, is a process of conditioning passive biological organisms. Conditioning is any sort of stimulus-and-response manipulation that results in either an enduring change in the organism being taught or an increase in the likelihood of certain behavior occurring. Conditioning takes the form either of stimulus substitution or response modification. Stimulus substitution is called classical conditioning; it is based on an adhesive or associative principle. (This is what Pavlov used on his dog.) Response modification is called instrumental or operant conditioning; it is based on a feedback or reinforcement principle, see pages 93–94.

Since logical empiricists interpret all learning in terms of caused changes in observable behavior, they consider teaching to be the process of causing the desired behavioral changes in students. Accordingly, teachers or other authorities decide which specific responses they want students to display. They then stimulate the student in such a way as to evoke and then reinforce the desired behavioral responses. The success of the process is judged by how dependably the behavior is manifested in the future.

Logical empiricists tend to think of democracy as a political system within which each mature and competent person, through voting, contributes his instructed judgment to a common good. They believe that people should make little or no attempt to arrive at consensus on decisional matters. Rather, each person should vote according to his own conscience and majority rule should prevail. Since they emphasize the teaching of scientifically ascertained facts and reprove the indoctrination of values, logical-empiricistic teachers, in instructing their students, strive to maintain complete neutrality on social issues. They therefore promote *axiological autonomy;* the freedom of students to arrive at their respective valuational positions all on their own. Consequently, within logical empiricism, democracy entails a compromise between factual indoctrination and valuational autonomy.

"The elements of a philosophy of language can furnish important suggestions for the teaching and learning procedures on all levels."[38] Thought depends almost entirely on modes of linguistic representation and symbolization. Its confusion and perplexity can be avoided only by teachers' giving greater attention to the rules of meaningful discourse. Techniques of definition can be used quite implicitly and informally with children and then applied with increasing explicit awarenesses with those in higher stages of maturity.

> Training in the analysis of the functions of language is, educationally, extremely valuable in that it provides the tools for recognizing propaganda, for persuasive definitions, and, more fundamentally, for an understanding of the distinction between cognition and valuation. It helps in spotting disguised tautologies and disclosing their factual emptiness. And last, but not least, it makes possible the distinction between information on the one hand and exhortation, edification, etc., on the other, which scientific enlightenment must insist upon if it is to dislodge the confusions with which tender-minded, wishful, and prescientific thinking abound.[39]

The Subject Matter Emphasis of Logical Empiricism

The primary purpose of education, for logical empiricists, is to transmit the great body of scientifically well-ascertained knowledge in the various fields. Children, adolescents, and adults need information both for the immediate practical purposes of their existence and for that broadening of their experience that is the essence of intelligent, cultural living.

Within the *unity of science* traditional departmental divisions are regarded as only practical conveniences, not fundamental lines of cleavage. There is an essential unity of both the method and the subject matter of science. "The natural and social sciences differ in their special techniques, but the methods of validation are essentially the same."[40]

In their giving physical science a priority among subject matters, logical empiricists place at the top of their hierarchy of science physics and chemistry, aided by mathematics. These are regarded the models for all other sciences to emulate; they are more objective and reliable than the others.

Training in the sciences and the scientific attitude should be combined with studies in history, literature, and the arts. Science and the humanities are not incompatible with one another. "Only those who insist that the higher values of life are sustained by supernatural powers will find the scientific outlook severely sobering or disappointing. But once the other-worldly and obscurantist conceit is abandoned, our lives will be enriched by a better understanding of ourselves."[41]

Footnotes

[1]Herbert Feigl, "Aims of Education For Our Age of Science: Reflections of a Logical Empiricist," in *Modern Philosophies and Education*, ed. Nelson B. Henry (Chicago: The University of Chicago Press, 1955), p. 304.

[2]See Joergen Joergensen, *The Development of Logical Empiricism* (Chicago: The University of Chicago Press, 1951), p. 4.

[3]See ibid., p. 4.

[4]See Ludwig Wittgenstein, *Tractatus Logico-Philosophicus* (New York: Harcourt Brace, 1922).

[5]See Ludwig Wittgenstein, *Philosophical Investigations*, 3rd ed., trans. by G. E. M. Anscombe. (New York: Macmillan, 1973).

[6]See A. J. Ayer, *Language, Truth, and Logic* (New York: Dover Publications, 1946).

[7]"Logical Empiricism," in *Twentieth Century Philosophy*, ed. Dagobert D. Runes (New York: Philosophical Library, 1943), p. 376.

[8]Gustav Bergmann, *Logic and Reality* (Madison, Wisc.: University of Wisconsin Press, 1964), p. 302.

[9]See M. Markoic, "Is Systematic Philosophy Possible Today?" *Contemporary Aspects of Philosophy*, ed. Gilbert Ryle (Stockfield, England: Oriel Press, 1976).

[10]Feigl, "Aims of Education for Our Age of Science: Reflections of a Logical Empiricist," p. 318.

[11]A. J. Ayer, *The Central Questions of Philosophy* (London: Weidenfeld and Nicolson, 1973), p. 89.

[12]Ibid., p. 216.

[13]Feigl, "Aims of Education for Our Age of Science: Reflections of a Logical Empiricist," p. 306.

[14]Ayer, *The Central Question of Philosophy*, p. 41.

[15]Ibid., p. vii.

[16]Feigl, "Aims of Education for Our Age of Science: Reflections of a Logical Empiricist," p. 322.

[17]Ibid., p. 311.

[18]Ibid., p. 307.

[19]Donald O. Hebb, *A Textbook of Psychology* (Philadelphia: Saunders, 1958), p. 46.

[20]Feigl, "Aims of Education for Our Age of Science: Reflections of a Logical Empiricist," p. 312.

[21]Ayer, *The Central Questions of Philosophy*, p. 3.

[22]A. J. Ayer, *The Problem of Knowledge* (Baltimore: Penguin Books, 1956), p. 34.

[23]Ayer, *The Central Questions of Philosophy*, p. 24.

[24]Ibid., pp. 25–26.

[25]Ayer, *Language, Truth, and Logic*, p. 31.

[26]Ayer, *The Central Questions of Philosophy*, p. 226.

[27]See ibid., p. 227.

[28]Feigl, "Aims of Education for Our Age of Science: Reflections of a Logical Empiricist," p. 325.

[29]Ibid., p. 332.

[30]Ayer, *Language, Truth, and Logic*, p. 107.

[31]Feigl, "Aims of Education for Our Age of Science: Reflections of a Logical Empiricist," p. 331.

[32]Ibid., p. 322.

[33]Ibid., p. 336.

[34]Ibid., p. 309

[35]Ayer, *The Central Questions of Philosophy*, p. 12.

[36]Ibid., p. 112.

[37]Ibid., p. 7.

[38]Fiegl, "Aims of Education for Our Age of Science: Reflections of a Logical Empiricist," p. 340.

[39]Ibid., p. 340.

[40]Ibid., p. 339.

[41]Ibid., p. 338.

BIBLIOGRAPHY

Ayer, A. J., *Language, Truth, and Logic*. New York: Dover Publications, 1946.

Ayer, A. J., *The Problem of Knowledge*. Baltimore: Penguin Books, 1956.

Ayer, A. J., "An Honest Ghost?" in Oscar P. Wood and George Pitcher, eds., *A Collection of Critical Essays*. Garden City, N.Y.: Doubleday, 1970.

Ayer, A. J., *The Central Questions of Philosophy*. London: Weidenfeld and Nicolson, 1973.

Ayer, A. J., *Thinking and Meaning*. London: H. K. Lewis, 1947.

Bergmann, Gustav, *Logic and Reality*. Madison, Wisc.: University of Wisconsin Press, 1964.

Feigl, Herbert, "Aims of Education for Our Age of Science: Reflections of a Logical Empiricist," in Nelson B. Henry, ed., *Modern Philosophies and Education*. Chicago: The University of Chicago Press, 1955.

Joergensen, Joergen, *The Development of Logical Empiricism*. Chicago: The University of Chicago Press, 1951.

Nelson, Thomas W., *A. J. Ayer and John Dewey: Two Theories of Knowledge from the Perspective of Education*, Fresno, Calif.: California State University, 1966 (unpublished master thesis).

Ryle, Gilbert, *Contemporary Aspects of Philosophy*. Stockfield, England: Oriel Press, 1976.

Skinner, B. F. *Walden Two*. New York: Macmillan, 1948.

Skinner, B. F. *Beyond Freedom and Dignity*. New York: Knopf, 1971.

Titus, Harold H., *Living Issues In Philosophy*, 5th ed. New York: Van Nostrand Reinhold, 1970, pp. 286–291.

Chapter 6
Analytic Philosophy
and Education

Analytic philosophy focuses on the rational, logical analysis of words, concepts, and propositions. It has two principal historical roots: twentieth century logical empiricism and perennial rationalism extending back into antiquity. For analysts the proper role of philosophy is simply to analyze the meanings of both ordinary language and meaningful technical concepts. For them, the range of data for philosophy is very wide: "the specificity of the data of philosophy together with the breadth of human concerns makes it necessary to draw upon all the available means whereby human beings give symbolic expression to their experiences, whether it be in the language of science, politics, art, religion, or even mythology."[1]

Analytic philosophy is a direct challenge to traditional philosophies. Traditional philosophers have sought a general perspective to life on a rational basis. Hence, they have speculated in regard to the nature of reality, man, truth, and values. Analysts, in contrast, conceive of philosophical activity as consisting of rational reflection, critical analysis or arguments and assumptions, and systematic clarification of fundamental ideas. The essence of analytic philosophy is critical precision.

Analysts note that philosophers back through antiquity have used analytic procedures. But simultaneously, they are extremely critical of the various philosophies that have preceded theirs. Specifically, they contrast their approach with that of speculative philosophies, pragmatic philosophy, irrational existentialism, and skepticism. They think that adherents of the speculative philosophies, both medieval scholastics and modern metaphysicians, have overplayed their hands, whereas pragmatists, irrational existentialists, and skeptics have underplayed theirs.

Analysts relegate the tradition of metaphysics, ethics, and supernatural religion to a realm of purely emotional utterances. An analytic philsopher "wants to achieve comprehensive analytical understanding not for some ulterior practical motive, but for its own sake, although he does not . . . deny that understanding may affect practice."[2] In fact, he may think that "Theoretical inquiry, independently pursued, has the most powerful potential for the analysis and transformation of practice."[3] But, theory is effective only insofar as it provides insight into fundamental processes.

Philosophical Analysis—A Rationalistic Process

Analytic philosophy basically is a rationalistic process that is anchored to a perceived physical world. It represents a union between scientific spirit and logical method. This philosophy is asserted to be a genuine, but nonmetaphysical, branch of knowledge. Although modern analysts differ from Aristotle in some respect, their process of reasoning is fundamentally Aristotelian. Hence, for them, linguistic analysis has been a method of philosophy for centuries. Since philosophizing consists of conceptual analysis, philosophy is an activity and not a subject, something to do rather than something to study. So, analytic philosophers *do* philosophy; they engage in *philosophical analysis*.

Philosophical analysis is a method, not a doctrine. Its purpose is to provide understanding instead of advice, clarity instead of guidance. Rather than being a set of recommended substantive conclusions, it is a set of procedural principles that is being applied.

Analytic philosophers see three main parts to their works. They act in a purely critical capacity in either correcting or refuting the theories of other philosophers. They trace the logical and historical interconnections of certain crucial concepts that experience has shown to be centers of philosophical disputes and puzzles. They construct philosophical theories to systematize and elucidate human experience, but in doing so, they do not indulge in any "transcendental, metaphysical extravagances."

Analysts sometimes reformulate existing theories by interpretation of experience in terms of experience, but never in terms of entities that go beyond human experience. "By reformulating and reinterpreting the common content of human experience it [analytic philosophy] tries to provide the same sort of unifying overall views of experience as traditional metaphysical systems purported to supply."[4]

Philosophical Analysis—An Art

Philosophical analysis is an *art* and, like any other art, its practice requires discrimination, judgment, and good taste. Israel Scheffler states that, in applying philosophical methods of analysis, we are "concerned directly with solving intellectual rather than practical difficulties—with removing the perplexities that arise in our attempt to say systematically and clearly what we are doing in education and why."[5] "Philosophers have thus naturally tended . . . to seek general perspective not by gathering the fruits of knowledge, but by analysis of the roots,—the basic concepts, assumptions, arguments, and inferences characteristic of different domains."[6]

Philosophical analysis doesn't start with the definition of pertinent terms. Instead it starts by examining some concrete, specific examples of very common experiences and it terminates with some sort of refinement of definition. An educational philosopher who is an adherent of a systematic philosophy might well need to read analytical books and articles backwards in order to understand the nature of their procedures.

In an analysis of *teaching*, Paul H. Hirst maps the features that distinguish teaching activities from all others. To do this, he summarizes the activities of teaching in great detail. He next describes in detail how teaching activities can be distinguished from nonteaching activities. He then characterizes specific teaching activities. Throughout the discourse he uses several examples in each step. Well along in the chapter he arrives at the formula "teaching is the label for those activities of a person A, the intention of which is to bring about in another person, B, the intentional learning of X."[7] He, then, analyzes in detail the aspects of this formula.

The analysis of any concept always proceeds from the study of examples that are specific, concrete, rooted in quite familiar human experiences, and elaborated with much detail. To analyze the meaning of a term, analysts start with one or more exemplifying cases of its most literal, ordinary, and conventional usage. They study the term's use, examples of its use, and examples of situations in which it cannot be used. Examples may consist of either model or paradigmatic, contrary, borderline, or invented cases. Invented cases often are the most interesting and fruitful sources of philosophical data. For example, what would be the meaning of death if we were not to die at all?

In the world of a philosophical analyst, thought and reason really count for something. The analytic task is *reflexive*. That is, it is thinking turned back on itself or thinking about thinking. Analysts not only make distinctions, they also think about the distinctions themselves. They also *reflect* upon the full range of human experience. For philosophical analysts, to analyze means to take apart, dismember, and scrutinize; to distinguish. Analysts select questions that are deemed worth clarifying and proceed to clarify them. In this way, they provide students with something to emulate as they develop skill in making distinctions. "Let us distinguish the conditions of knowledge, the modes of teaching, the different senses of 'learn,' a priori and contingent claims, the different types of explanation. But making distinctions with skill, with clarity, and above all, with tenacity, letting our distinctions carry us where they may."[8] (A priori statements are derived from self-evident metaphysical principles. Hence, they purport to be true in all imaginable worlds. They stand in contrast to empirical statements that are true only for the existing world.)

Analysts distinguish three different kinds of language: empirical, analytical, and emotive. *Empirical* language is the language of science; it is about the world and thus verifiable. *Analytical* language is purely conceptual; it is not about the world. Instead it follows clear logical prescriptions. *Emotive* language, by its very nature, is nonverifiable in any way. Language serves three general purposes: In its *descriptive* use, informative facts are stated. Its *expressive* function is to show our feelings and attitudes. Its *persuasive* use is to influence the feelings and attitudes of others.

Analytic philosophers of education apply the concepts and methods of general analytic philosophy to an analysis of both the *ordinary language* and the *special concepts* of education. They analyze educational concepts such as knowing and teaching with emphasis on how they are put in verbal form. They aim "explicitly at improving our *understanding* of education by clarification of our conceptual apparatus—the ways in which we formulate our beliefs, arguments, assumptions, and judgments concerning such topics as learning and teaching, character and intellect, subject-matter and skill, desirable ends and appropriate means of schooling."[9]

Analytic philosophers think that they may contribute to the quality of educational practices through (1) an analytical description of the forms of thought that are represented in different school subjects, (2) an evaluation and criticism of such forms of thought, (3) an analysis of specific teaching materials so as to systematize and exhibit them as exemplification of forms of thought, and (4) an interpretation of particular exemplifications in terms that are accessible to novices.

Analytic philosophers of education have striven to examine educational concepts in verbal forms. For them, a concept is a rule for the use of a certain term. When learning a concept, someone learns either a rule of language, or more generally, a rule of behavior. The way people view the world is shaped, in a large part, by what their language permits them to say about it.

Since, *"The analysis of a concept is the description of its use,"*[10] the analysis of any concept cannot even begin unless there is a rough idea of its meaning. The objective of analysis is to study, clarify, and more thoroughly understand the meaning of a concept. Conceptual analysis, then, is talk about talk. Insofar as a philosophy is analytic, it is concerned primarily with the clarification of concepts and their relations. Matters for philosophical study that are related to teaching and learning are: the nature of knowledge and belief, the requirements of explanation, the criteria for definitions, and the foundations of wonder and imagination. In treating these matters, analysts study the verb forms that are related to the activity of thinking, namely: knowing, believing, learning, explaining, judging, wondering.

The principal goal of conceptual analysis in education is to make a conscious effort to remove ambiguity and vagueness by carefully distinguishing between the different senses in which educational concepts are used. The first step in analysis is to remove a term's ambiguity, then attack its vagueness. A term is *ambiguous* if it can receive more than one meaning. Ambuguity may be either *conceptual* or *contextual*. The term *trunk* has conceptual ambiguity, but its context usually tells us whether it means a piece of baggage, a part of a tree, or the nose of an elephant. "Real difficulty in thinking arises primarily when conceptually ambiguous terms remain ambiguous even when placed in context."[11] The word teaching, as commonly used, is often ambiguous in both senses.

Ambiguous terms do not have *no meaning,* they have *too many meanings. Equivocation* is a form of ambiguity; it involves an outright mistake in reasoning. There are two kinds of equivocation: the mistaking of a process for a product and vice versa, and the fallacies of composition and division. The fallacy of composition is reasoning from what is true of a single individual to what is true of a group, attributing a member's personality traits to the entire group that is represented. In the fallacy of division a single term may be used to apply both to members of a group and to the group itself, for example, members of a talented family. A concept is vague when it is not clearly and precisely expressed or when it is stated in such indefinite terms that it does not have a clear and precise meaning. Its boundary lines are hard to set and one cannot tell what is or is not included in the concept.

Analytic Philosophy: The Nature of Reality

It is in their dealing with the nature of reality that philosophical analysts show their roots in logical empiricism. In a logical empiricist tradition, they assume that scientists have the only means whereby *truth* may be *found.* Truth must correspond with natural reality. Reality is the reality of common sense. The role of scientists is to find and report this reality. Whatever is knowable (the facts and regularities of nature) are confirmable only by sensory experience. Knowledge so gained takes the form of empirically verified propositions. Truth is knowledge about reality, and to be true, it must be absolutely so.

As stated on page 106, language may be either empirical, emotive, or analytical. But only empirical language concerns the real world and is verifiable through the use of scientific procedures. So, truths about the universe, reality, and man are empirical, not philosophical, matters. Analytic philosophy is both naturalistic and empiricistic in its orientation. But, analysts concern themselves with words and concepts rather than sensory experiences. For them, science alone is equipped to handle empirical matters, and philosophy is an art.

Any metaphysical concepts are meaningless because they are neither empirical nor logical, only emotive. "We have the same reason for rejecting metaphysics as we have for rejecting witchcraft, astrology, or phrenology; it cannot do what it claims to do."[12] Thus for analysts, there are positive grounds for rejecting the grandiose claims of metaphysicians. Analysts seek factual naturalistic answers, not metaphysical ones.

Analytic Philosophy: The Nature of Human Motivation

For analytic philosophers people are *rational animals,* but there is no place in this philosophy for any kind of body-mind dualism. As rational animals, people have both an *animal nature,* which is susceptible to scientific observation and measurement, and a *rationality,* which is the capacity to reason, solve problems, and answer questions. But, mind is not "the ghost in the machine."

Reason does not refer to some general faculty of a mind. Instead, it is always used in the plural and refers to the mutual sharing of reasons. It means the general capacity of people to solve problems and to answer questions appropriately. People may justly be called rational animals, but this does not mean that they have any nonphysical mind to do their reasoning. Rationality is a matter of degree, not a clear-cut all or nothing affair.

Analytic Philosophy: The Nature and Source of
Truth and Knowledge

For analytic philosophers, a truth is absolutely so. It is impossible to know something that is not the case. When the truth condition is unsatisfied, then what one took to be *knowledge* turns out to have been only *belief.* Knowing, then, is a special kind of believing; it is *believing that* something is true, arrived at on the basis of adequate evidence. But, "a due regard for truth must be accompanied always with the sense of doubt that the whole truth, or even the important truth, is yet within grasp."[13]

Whereas beliefs have a tentative nature, knowledge does not. Whereas *believing that* something is so aims at the truth, *knowing that* something is so succeeds in this aim. There can be no false knowledge. "When a person believes something, he believes it to be a reasonable approximation to *the* truth."[14] But knowing is incompatible with mistakes; knowing requires not only the proper state of the subject's mind but also the proper state of the world. Knowing is not a task, activity, or performance, but an achievement state relative to belief.

An explanation of a belief that is constructed without logical fault is a good explanation. Whether reasons are good or adequate to support a certain belief depends upon the logical properties of the relation between the belief and its reasons, not upon the psychological fact that someone happens to accept those reasons.

For analysis, we need not doubt that the world is, that we are, that robins produce robins, and that growing grass is green. We are absolutely certain of these simple truths, but we are equally certain that they need not be truths. Things could be quite different. "The existence of the world and everything within it is contingent. It could be very different."[15] Only logical, not empirical necessities may be taken for granted. Though the order of the world is dependable, it is nonetheless contingent; it could be other than it is.

"Some questions, characteristically those of the natural and social sciences, can be settled by empirical methods, by hypotheses arising out of observation and observation confirming hypotheses. Other questions, characteristic of logical and mathematical subject matters, can be settled by calculation in accordance with settled rules of deduction."[16] Then, any other meaningful questions are the province of philosophy; they lie completely outside the realm of scientific procedure. For analysts, logical truths, as contrasted with scientific ones, neither require support from empirical evidence nor can they be supported by such means.[17]

Statements may be either *scientific* or *nonscientific* ones. Science consists of a body of statements purporting to be true, on the best available evidence. It is because of its abstraction from the practical world that scientific inquiry is able to provide compact, comprehensive principles or statements explaining what goes on in the world. Scientific definitions are to be judged, roughly, by their contribution to the adequacy of their respective scientific networks in accounting for the facts. They are continuous with the theories and evidence in their respective domains. The various disciplines are dependent upon the availability of germane established scientific principles: theories and laws. The terms of a discipline are those terms by means of which such principles are formulated.

Statements in nonscientific discourse may be either statements of general definitions, statements containing metaphorical descriptions, or statements embodying educational slogans. Statements of general definitions may be either stipulative, descriptive, or programmatic. *Stipulative definitions,* such as the abbreviations grade A, B, C, are used to facilitate discourse or communication, but they do not purport to accord with their prior usage. They in no way express truth. *Descriptive definitions* are explanatory accounts of meaning; they purport to explain terms by providing an account of their prior usage in such way as to clarify the normal application and meaning of the terms. *Programmatic definitions* are moral ones. They are intended to embody programs of action. Hence, they act as expressions of practical programs.

Metaphors point to what are conceived to be significant parallels, analogies, and similarities within the subject-matter of the discourse itself. Unlike stipulations, which express no truth at all, and unlike descriptive definitions, which normally fail to surprise, metaphors often express significant and surprising truths. Like programmatic definitions, they frequently convey programs of action. But, metaphors always do so by suggesting some objective analogy that purports to state truths discovered in the phenomena before us. However, "The line, even in science, between serious theory and metaphor, is a thin one if it can be drawn at all."[18]

Analytic Philosophy: The Nature and Source of Human Values

A major reason for philosophical criticism of an educational theory is to distinguish and make plain its guiding values. In the process of teaching others, a teacher is called upon to reveal, and risk, personal judgments and loyalties. Far from denying responsibility, the increase of scientific knowledge, by rendering our choices more effective, makes us more responsible morally for our behavior. "To sum up, the scientist's goal of exhibiting the causal background of human behavior is not at all incompatible with freedom in the only morally relevant sense."[19] Within the analytic position *free* means voluntary, not uncaused. So, the meaningfulness of moral notions and the deterministic goals of a science of human affairs are not incompatible. But, "as long as we assume that moral judgments lie somewhere on a scale of objectivity . . . between hard concrete statements of public facts at one end and private expressions of taste or emotion at the other, we shall never arrive at a proper conception of them."[20] Further, "the moral point of view is attained, if at all, by acquiring a tradition of practice, embodied in rules and habits of conduct."[21]

For analytic philosophers, their *rational morality* is a *form* of moral experience that has emerged, in part, as a response to the conflict between traditionally held moral codes. However, the *contents* of moral experience deriving from different traditions may be fitted under the analytical, rational form of experience. But, rational morality stands over against all traditional or authoritarian-based forms of conduct. For example, adherents of rational morality think that, just as stoics need to make some room in their reasoning-centered system for compassion, Christians must make some room in their compassion-centered system for reason.

Richard S. Peters, a leading analytic moral philosopher, links his thoughts in regard to the source of human values or morality to the "genetic epistemology" of Jean Piaget as refined and applied to moral stages by Lawrence Kohlberg's *social values theory.* Peters, however, develops only three stages of morality, whereas Kohlberg has six.

For Piaget, the mental development of children consists of a succession of three stages, namely, sensori-motor, symbolic, and concrete operations. Each stage "extends the preceding period, reconstructs it on a new level, and later surpasses it to an even greater degree."[22]

During the sensori-motor stage (birth to eighteen months or two years) an infant lacks any symbolic function, so it displays only direct action on reality. During the symbolic, preconcrete operational stage (eighteen months to age seven or eight) a child uses differentiated signifiers, but does not think about things. Then, during the stage of concrete operations (ages seven or eight to eleven or twelve) a child internalizes actions as related to objects; that is, thinks about things but does not yet use verbally stated hypotheses. Such hypotheses appear only in either preadolescence or adolescence.

Kohlberg has claimed, on the basis of investigations performed in many countries, that, although cultures differ in regard to the *content* of moral beliefs, the *form* of moral beliefs is a "cultural invariant." He is convinced that there are sequential stages of patterns of moral thought that are cross-cultural and invariant. But, such morality is revealed not in the *content,* but in the *form* of decisions. Morality lies in reasonings, not acts. There are cultural variations with regard to thrift, punctuality, sexual relationships, and so on (content), but there are unlearned cross-cultural uniformities in how such rules are conceived (form). Will, for Kohlberg, is a complex of all the factors and motives that determine the doing of an act; whoever knows the good does the good.

Whereas Kohlberg emphasizes the development of the form of moral experience rather than the content, Peters gives a significant place to both. Peters sees the content of rules being learned by instruction and imitation aided by reward and punishment or praise and blame. However, his *rational morality* emphasizes the emergence of a *rational form* of morality. Accordingly, he states that "the type of 'reinforcement' used by Skinnerians can be shown to be peculiarly appropriate to learning specific types of *content* at certain stages of development. . . . But learning the *form* of experience may be a very different matter."[23] So, for Peters, the distinction between the development of the form of morality and the learning of its content is crucial to his conception of rational morality.

The Form of Morality

When applied to the realm of the forms of morals, which are the roots of values and motivation, Piaget's sensori-motor stage becomes Peters' egocentric stage; his preconcrete operational stage becomes Peters' stage of code-encased morality, and his stage of concrete operations becomes Peters' autonomy stage, Kohlberg's sixth stage.

The Egocentric Stage.   In this stage a child is acquiring the general apparatus for reasoning and the beginnings of concern for others. He becomes a *chooser*. Although his specific teachings are influenced by social conditions, his attitude toward rules is basically egocentric; it consists of conformity as a way of avoiding punishment and obtaining rewards.

The Stage of Code-Encased Morality.   This is the good-boy stage of peer group conformity and authority-based morality. It involves a child's realization of what it is to follow a rule; to accept a rule as binding on one's conduct. A rule comes to be seen as a rule and to depend for its existence on the approval and disapproval of both peer groups and authority figures. In this crucial stage children come to enjoy following rules and to revel in the sense of mastery that this gives them. But, they, as yet, have no notion in regard to the *validity* of given rules. During this stage, imitation and identification are extremely important factors in children's learning.

Achievement of the Autonomy Stage.   The autonomy stage is a self-exploratory one. It is marked by the notion of authenticity or genuineness. In this stage, one resolves moral dilemmas by appealing to principles within which the values of justice and human dignity are incorporated. People develop rules and principles through ethical reasoning. A person accepts or rejects rules for himself and follows certain rules because of the valid reasons for them. Hence, an individual, through questioning the validity of moral or political beliefs, performs a leading role in determining his destiny. In this stage rules, activities, and emotional responses are criticized in regard to their validity and appropriateness through a process of critical reflection. Autonomy suggests integrity and strength of will, the ability of hold to a judgment or course of conduct in face of any counter-inclinations.

"In the development of autonomy, first-hand experience is essential. But it must be informed and sensitized by initiation into those imaginative explorations which are part of our cultural heritage as civilized men."[24] Children need to pass from their seeing rules as connected with punishment and reward to seeing them as ways of maintaining either a gang-given or an authoritatively-ordained governing structure before they can adopt a more autonomous attitude toward them. But, when a system that is maintained purely by naked force and the dispensation of rewards gives way to a system that is dependent on belief in the sanctity of rules enshrined in tradition or laid down by authority, force and rewards are not abandoned; they still are in the background as support for the authoritative structure. Likewise, "when traditional systems are challenged, authority becomes rationalized, not superseded. Its structure is adapted to the reasons for having it. But the insistence that a rule is a rule . . . persists."[25] So, autonomous man has a rational attitude toward both tradition and authority.

Learning the Content of Morality

Peters sees the crucial problem of methods in early moral education as involving how a basic content for morality can be provided that gives individuals a firm basis for moral behavior without impeding the development of a rational form of it. He is concerned with which nonrational methods aid, or at least do not impede, students' development of rationality. For both social security and self-preservation, small children must be taught a moral code that, when internalized, will, to some degree, regulate their behavior when they are unsupervised. Also, since a great number of people never reach a rational or autonomous level of morality, teaching the content of morality is crucially important. Before being able to follow rules autonomously, a person first must learn what it is to follow a rule for other reasons.

Analytic Philosophy: The Purpose of Education

Within analytic philosophy, education is a practical art with a scientific basis; it refines students' beliefs in the direction of absolutely true knowledge and enhances their capacity to think rationally. Teachers should teach both science and morals, and the fundamental trait that is to be cultivated in both is *reasonableness*.

"The heart of education is the effort to enhance the human capacity to think."[26] Hence, in a basic sense, "the schools *ought* to stand apart from life. . . ."[27] In doing this, however, they should not cultivate pedantry or myth. Instead, they should illuminate a wider world and they should sustain those habits of mind that fit minds for breadth, penetration, and objectivity of vision. So, a teacher should be a person committed to the values of truth, reason, and the enlargement of human powers.

"The function of education in a democracy is . . . to liberate the mind, strengthen its critical powers, inform it with knowledge and the capacity for independent inquiry, engage its human sympathies, and illuminate its moral and practical choices."[28] So, the responsibility of education is not only to serve society but also to provide techniques for critical, informed, and humane persons.

> Education that attempts only to inculcate good behavior without developing good thinking about behavior cannot be good education. It follows that good education must run the risk of bad behavior. Schools that in their institutional structure and process do not encourage such thinking cannot be good schools, no matter how successfully they teach mathematics, science, and history. And a society whose basic institutions do not encourage that kind of thinking cannot be a good society, no matter how successful and how affluent it may be in other ways.[29]

Analytic Philosophy: The Nature of the Learning Process

For analytic philosophers, knowledge, by definition, is always *true*, never false. When we learn, we either come to believe or to know that something is true or we come to know how to do something. One's believing something is one's thinking that that thing is a reasonable approximation to *the truth*. So, both believing and knowing are cognitive terms, their meanings differ only in degree.

Analysts make a point of the fact that, whereas there is a propositional use of both *know* and *believe*, there is only a procedural use of know, not of believe. *Propositional* use is either to *know that* or to *believe that* such and such is the case. Procedural use is to *know how to* do such and such.[30] We may either believe or know that a whale is a mammal, but we can only know, not believe, how to catch a whale.

There are three necessary conditions for knowing that such and such *is* the case: the *belief* condition, the *evidence* condition, and the *truth* condition. One knows such and such if and only if one believes such and such, one has adequate evidence that such and such is true, and such and such is true.[31]

Learning involves matters of truth or falsity, and understanding of truth is complete or not at all. In students' efforts to understand, they question, explore, doubt, and evaluate. Practice, in the form of repeated performances, may be employed to learn skills and know-hows, but it is not relevant to deliberation and inquiry. People can learn to do certain things through being trained. But, they do not achieve understanding through practice. Learning at its best, then, is thinking. Through thinking people not only change their minds in regard to what they believe is true but they also change their minds about what they decide to do.

"Words and concepts are the tools with which we think."[32] Analytical thinking centers upon the way words are used, not upon their psychological results. Hence, analysts consider both the *designation* view and the *semantic* view of learning as obstacles to philosophical analysis. The *designation view* is that the meaning of a word is that to which it points, its referent. The *semantic view* is that the meaning of a word is what it calls forth in the mind of the hearer or reader, its connotations. Both of these views of learning direct attention away from the way the word is used (the analytic view) and instead, fix it upon its psychological results.

A genuine analysis of learning and thinking cannot go far without the employment of metaphors. Also, whereas we cannot think without the use of metaphors, we cannot think well without thinking about the metaphors that we use. A *metaphor* is an implicit comparison. It is much like a simile except that a simile is an explicit comparison. A metaphor, then, is a way of establishing thoughtful relations between things.

A metaphor may be either a "dead" one or a constructive one. A dead metaphor is one that we use in our thought as if it were literal, for example, the sun rises and sets. A *constructive* metaphor is used in the process of invention through which we create statements for examination. A constructive metaphor is employed not only to formulate new ideas for study, but also to revive old, unnoticed assumptions as though they were fresh, new formulas.

Beliefs always occur in sets or groups; nobody holds a belief in total independence of all other beliefs. Furthermore, beliefs are always gathered as part of a belief system. A *belief system* is a metaphor. The actual logical order of beliefs is based upon their content and structure. However, a quasi-logical order and structure of beliefs lends itself more to analytical study, the quasi-logical order is the order that beliefs receive in somebody's belief system. The quasi-logical relation between beliefs makes some of them derivative and some primary. However, there is no reason a priori to suppose that primary beliefs might not become derivative ones and vice versa.

Analytic Philosophy: The Nature of the Teaching Process

Within analytic philosophy, whereas believing and knowing are cognitive terms, teaching and learning are educational ones. Whereas teaching is an active process, learning is a passive one. "Teaching . . . involves trying to bring about learning . . . within the limitations imposed by the framework of rational discussion."[33] A teacher, as an example of logical thinker, sets precise rules for class discussions, demands clear definitions, and insists on objective proof for every statement presented as true. When teaching, a teacher risks his or her own particular truth judgments to the free critical judgment of his students' minds. Teaching generally involves an effort to achieve learning, but the converse is not true; efforts to achieve learning cannot generally be said to involve teaching. Teaching is directed toward some goal whose attainment normally involves attention and effort and provides a relevant definition of success.

"Teaching is a practical activity like laying a dry wall or baking a loaf of bread."[34] It consists of either transmitting knowledge or shaping behavior. Teaching someone that so and so is true is focused on the transmission of knowledge. Teaching someone to do so and so is focused on formation of behavior.

Learning Is Not Gaining Patterns of Movements
Although learning may involve shaping behavior, it is a mistake for us to suppose that learning geometry is a matter of mastering some distinctive patterns of movements, or that teaching geometry consists of prescribing the pattern of movements to be made. So, to think of problem solving as a complex sequence of movements governed by rules is a myth. Furthermore, teaching cannot be construed as some distinctive pattern of movements executed by the teacher. "Attempts to think of teaching in extreme behavioristic terms are, at best, ambiguous and, at worst, totally misguided."[35]

"Schools and methodological programs are the lifeblood of thought; they provide direction and organization to the efforts of individual thinkers."[36] So, "For the teacher to conceive his role after the analogy of industrial production is . . . a distorting fallacy of far reaching consequence."[37] Students enter into communication with their teacher, and through the teacher, they communicate with the cultural heritage that is common to both students and teacher. Such communication broadens and refines students' outlooks, and thereby increases their understanding.

Three Categories of Teaching
The activities of teaching fall into three different categories—logical acts, strategic acts, and institutional acts. Logical and strategic acts are indispensable to the conduct of teaching, but institutional acts are not.

The *logical acts* of teaching include those activities relating primarily to the elements of thinking or reasoning in the conduct of teaching. The performance of logical acts can be evaluated independently of their practical consequences. However, logical acts occur only in the context of some teaching strategy. Insofar as the activity of teaching involves giving reasons, evidence, explanations, and conclusions, it can be evaluated quite independently of its results in getting someone to learn. *"The performance of the logical act of teaching is appraised on logical grounds."*[38]

The *strategic acts* of teaching concern primarily the teacher's plan for teaching, the way that instructional material is organized or that students are directed in the course of teaching. "Performance of the strategic acts of teaching are appraised by their consequences for learning."[39] Whereas *logical* acts require a knowledge of the methods of knowing, knowledge of the laws of thought, strategic acts require knowledge of human behavior and motivation, that is, knowledge of the laws of learning and human growth.

The teacher's reasons related to the logical acts of teaching will have much to do with the subject to be taught and the ways of knowing within that field. But, the teacher's strategic reasons will more often be related to the nature of the students to be taught. Strategic reasons involve how well students "understand what was done before; whether they are tired, anxious, motivated, prepared to advance, and so forth."[40] Teaching can be improved by improving either kind of activity, but it cannot be excellent without giving attention to both.

Within the strategic acts of teaching, "What is reasonable to believe must be rendered reasonable for the student to believe."[41] *"Teaching is an activity aimed at developing belief systems of a particular kind."*[42] In these belief systems evidential beliefs are maximized and core unsubstantiated beliefs are minimized.

The institutional acts of teaching include those activities that arise primarily because of the way the teacher's work is organized by the teaching institution. They are not necessary to the activity of teaching. Teaching may proceed even when institutional acts of teaching are not going on; for example, a father may teach his own child.

Forms of Teaching

Teaching, for analytical philosophers, may take the form of *training, conditioning, indoctrinating,* or *instructing.* But in its best sense it consists of instructing. *Training* is aimed primarily at acquiring habits or modes of behavior. It is teaching someone *to do* so and so; it is shaping behavior. Hence, it is only a part of teaching. As training is aimed less and less at the display of intelligence we have *conditioning.* An individual who *obeys* a command is displaying training; when one *responds* to a command one is showing conditioning. Whereas we train a dog to fetch or heel, we *condition* him to salivate at the sound of a bell. "In short, *as the manifestation of intelligence aimed at in training declines, the concept of teaching seems to be less and less clearly exemplified and the concept of conditioning more and more clearly exemplified.*"[43]

Indoctrinating is that mode of teaching most closely concerned with *what* people believe; it is aimed at developing a nonevidential way of holding beliefs. Indoctrinating aims at inculcating the *right answers* though not necessarily for the *right reasons,* or even for good reasons.

Instructing is that mode of teaching that is most closely associated with a concern for *how* people believe. It always involves matters of truth and falsity. Teaching in terms of instructing requires teachers to reveal their reasons to students and, by so doing, to submit them to student evaluation and criticism. Instructing, then, is primarily concerned with matters of belief and knowledge, not behaviors. "It makes sense to tell a student to practice [repeat] playing a certain piece of music, it makes no sense to tell him to practice appreciating what he plays."[44] Practice seems clearly relevant to skills and know-how, typically built up through repeated trials or performances, but it is not relevant to the activities of deliberation and inquiry. Teachers can train people to do certain things without bringing them to an understanding of what they do, but this is not the mode of instruction.

Through instruction, teachers try to get students to believe that such and such is the case. They also try to get them to believe it for reasons that, within the limits of the students' capacity to grasp, are the teachers' reasons. Such teaching requires teachers to reveal their reasons to students and, by so doing, to submit them to the students' evaluation and criticism. To instruct, then, is to acknowledge students' demand for and judgment of reasons, but such demands are not uniformly appropriate at every phase of a teaching interval.

"Instruction is an activity which has to do not with what people believe but with how they believe it."[45] It involves arriving at answers on the right kind of grounds. Since it is essentially the pursuit of truth, it involves giving reasons, evidence, argument, and justifications. The manners of instruction are the manners of civility expressed in the institutions of free speech, due process, and freedom of dissent. These are essential for the preservation of any civilization of free men.

Manners of Argument

"The manners of teaching are the manners of argument."[46] They involve two kinds of questions: What is it reasonable for students to believe? What should students do? Hence, the competencies that are required of a successful teacher in instruction *"are simply those that . . . are required for a teacher to change the truth value of the premises of the practical argument in the mind of the child,"*[47] to complete those premises, or to add to the range of premises accessible to the child in the formation of practical arguments. Whereas the purpose of theoretical reason or thought is to arrive at truth, that is, to establish what we are to believe or what we can justifiably claim to know, the purpose of practical reason or argument is to decide what to do. The conclusion of a practical argument, however, is not an act, but a statement about what should be done.

Since students should spend much of their time refining their beliefs in the direction of true knowledge, analysts think we "can identify the competencies needed by a successful teacher in instruction without any *immediate* and *direct* reference to concepts of learning. Instead, we require concepts of truth, and reasoning, and their connection with doing."[48]

The Subject Matter Emphasis of Analytic Philosophy

For analysts, the activities of teaching can be fully displayed only under certain conditions: (1) There must be access to information. (2) The information must be brought to bear on two questions. These are what is it reasonable for students to believe, and what is it their duty to do. (3) There must be a way to introduce new ideas of what is relevant in order to gain new perspectives on old beliefs, and to direct attention to what has gone unnoticed. The existence of the activities and the conditions that are conducive to them rely on three factors for their realization: There must be freedom of access to information. The capacity must exist to bring information to bear upon problems of knowledge, beliefs, and conduct. There must be freedom to review old ideas and decisions in light of newly gained perspectives.[49]

The subject matter of education should consist of knowledge of what is known, what to believe, and what to do along with understanding of the nature and source of reliable knowledge. All such knowledge and understanding centers upon the meanings and uses of *words*. Since acceptable subject matter is limited to verifiable synthetic propositions, its scope is much reduced from that of traditional education.

Footnotes

[1]Thomas F. Green, *The Activities of Teaching* (New York: McGraw-Hill, 1971), p. 206.

[2]Israel Scheffler, *Reason and Teaching* (Indianapolis: Bobbs-Merrill, 1973), p. 37.

[3]Ibid., p. 133.

[4]D. J. O'Connor, *An Introduction to the Philosophy of Education* (London: Routledge and Kegan Paul, 1957), p. 112.

[5]Israel Scheffler, ed., "Introduction to the First Edition," *Philosophy and Education*, 2nd ed. (Boston: Allyn and Bacon, 1966), p. 4.

[6]Israel Scheffler, *The Language of Education* (Springfield, Ill.: Charles C Thomas, 1960), p. 6.

[7]Paul H. Hirst, "What Is Teaching," in *The Philosophy of Education,* ed. R. S. Peters (London: Oxford University Press, 1973), p. 172.

[8]Green, *The Activities of Teaching,* p. 203.

[9]Scheffler, Introduction to the First Edition," p. 4.

[10]Green, *The Activities of Teaching,* p. 11.

[11]Ibid., p. 34.

[12]O'Connor, *An Introduction to the Philosophy of Education,* p. 114.

[13]Green, *The Activities of Teaching,* p. 226.

[14]Ibid., p. 43.

[15]Ibid., p. 195.

[16]O'Connor, *An Introduction to the Philosophy of Education,* p. 22.

[17]See D. C. Phillips, "Post-Kuhnian Reflections on Educational Research," in *Philosophy and Education: Eighteenth Yearbook of the National Society for the Study of Education,* ed. Jonas F. Soltis. (Chicago: The University of Chicago Press, 1981), p. 259.

[18]John B. Magee, *Philosophical Analysis in Education* (New York: Harper & Row, 1971), p. 47.

[19]Scheffler, *Reason and Teaching,* p. 110.

[20]O'Connor, *An Introduction to the Philosophy of Education,* p. 61.

[21]Scheffler, *Reason and Teaching,* p. 142.

[22]Jean Piaget and Barbel Inhelder, *The Psychology of the Child* (New York: Basic Books, 1969), p. 152.

[23]Richard S. Peters, *Reason and Compassion* (London: Routledge and Kegan Paul, 1973), p. 35.

[24]Ibid., p. 54.

[25]Ibid., p. 57.

[26]Green, *The Activities of Teaching,* p. 218.

[27]Scheffler, *Reason and Teaching,* p. 155.

[28]Ibid., p. 139

[29]Green, *The Activities of Teaching,* p. 218.

[30]Israel Scheffler, "Knowledge and Teaching," in Van Cleve Morris, *Modern Movements in Educational Philosophy* (New York: Houghton Mifflin, 1969), p. 224.

[31]Ibid., p. 231.

[32]Green, *The Activities of Teaching,* p. 13.

[33]Ibid., p. 431.

[34]Ibid., p. 2.

[35]Magee, *Philosophical Analysis in Education,* p. 67.

[36]Scheffler, *Reason and Teaching,* p. 19.

[37]Ibid., p. 87.

[38]Green, *The Activities of Teaching,* p. 8.

[39]Ibid, p. 8.

[40]Ibid, pp. 8, 9.

[41]Ibid., p. 221.

[42]Ibid., p. 52.

[43]Ibid., p. 26.

[44]Scheffler in Morris, *Modern Movements in Educational Philosophy*, p. 229.

[45]Green in Morris, *Modern Movements in Educational Philosophy*, p. 247.

[46]Green, *The Activities of Teaching*, p. 218.

[47]Thomas F. Green, "Teacher Competence as Practical Rationality," in *Philosophy of Education 1976* (Urbana, Ill.: Philosophy of Education Society, 1976), p. 8.

[48]Ibid., p. 9.

[49]See Green, *The Activities of Teaching*, pp. 219–228.

BIBLIOGRAPHY

Christensen, James E. and Fisher, James E. *Analytic Philosophy of Education as a Sub-Discipline of Educology: An Introduction to Its Technique and Application*. Washington, D. C.: University Press of America, 1979.

Dearden, R. F., Hirst, P. H., and Peters, R. S., eds. *Education and the Development of Reason*. London: Routledge and Kegan Paul, 1972.

Dixon, Keith, ed. *Philosophy of Education and the Curriculum*. Oxford: Pergamon Press, 1972.

Gage, N. L. *The Scientific Basis of the Art of Teaching*. New York: Teachers College Press, 1977.

Green, Thomas F. *The Activities of Teaching*. New York: McGraw-Hill, 1971.

Green, Thomas F. "Teacher Competence as Practical Rationality." *Philosophy of Education 1976*. Urbana, Ill.: Philosophy of Education Society, 1976.

Hirst, Paul H. *Knowledge and the Curriculum*. London: Routledge and Kegan Paul, 1974.

Langford, Glenn, and O'Connor, D. J., eds. *New Essays in the Philosophy of Education*. London: Routledge and Kegan Paul, 1973.

Magee, John B. *Philosophical Analysis in Education*. New York: Harper & Row, 1971.

Martin, Jane R. *Explaining, Understanding, and Teaching*. New York: McGraw-Hill, 1970.

Morris, Van Cleve. *Modern Movements in Educational Philosophy*. New York: Houghton Mifflin, 1969. Part 4, "Analytic Philosophy in Educational Thought," pp. 173–281.

O'Connor, D. J. *The Correspondence Theory of Truth*. London: Hutchinson & Co., 1975.

O'Connor, D. J. *An Introduction to the Philosophy of Education*. London: Routledge and Kegan Paul, 1957.

Peters, Richard S. *Authority, Responsibility, and Education*. London: Allen & Unwin, 1973.

Peters, Richard S. *Ethics and Education*. London: Allen & Unwin, 1970.

Peters, Richard S. *Education and the Education of Teachers*. London: Routledge and Kegan Paul, 1977.

Peters, Richard S., ed. *Nature and Conduct*. New York: St. Martin's Press, 1975.

Peters, Richard S. *Reason and Compassion*. London: Routledge and Kegan Paul, 1973.

Scheffler, Israel. *Conditions of Knowledge*. Glenview, Ill.: Scott Foresman, 1965.

Scheffler, Israel. *The Language of Education*. Springfield, Ill.: Charles C Thomas, 1960.

Scheffler, Israel, ed. *Philosophy and Education*, 2nd ed. Boston: Allyn and Bacon, 1966.

Scheffler, Israel. *Reason and Teaching*. Indianapolis: Bobbs-Merrill, 1973.

Soltis, Jonas F., ed. *Philosophy and Education, Eightieth Yearbook of the National Society for the Study of Education*. Chicago: The University of Chicago Press, 1981.

Steinberg, Ira S. *Behaviorism and Schooling*. New York: St. Martin's Press, 1980.

Chapter 7
Existentialism,
an Irrational
Educational Philosophy

Existentialism is a nineteenth and twentieth century philosophy that centers upon the unique way individuals find themselves existing in the world. This philosophy begins and ends not in reason, but in wonder. However, it is a philosophy of personal life that emphasizes passioned reason, which is a state of heightened feeling throughout the whole person. So existentialism is an educational philosophy of personal autonomy that rejects all rationalistic, speculative philosophies. It emphasizes the importance of human feelings and places individual persons in charge of their own destinies. It centers upon self-actualized existences expressed in terms of feelings.

Existentialists dare to dwell upon such unpleasant subject matter as nothingness, anxiety, dread, anguish, death, and absurdity. "If the lack of an essence signified a nothingness at the heart of my being, it is precisely this awareness of the void that can summon me to live out a more meaningful life."[1]

The Existentialist Tradition

Existentialism can claim some ancient roots extending back to fourth- and fifth-century B.C. Greek philosophers. However, its first modern developer was the Danish religious philosopher, Sören Kierkegaard (1813–1855). Some other leaders in the development were Martin Buber (1878–1965), Martin Heidegger (1889–1976), Karl Jaspers (1883–1969), Gabriel Marcel (1889–1973), Friederick Nietzsche (1844–1900), and Jean-Paul Sartre (1905–1980). Some leading contemporary American existentialist writers are William Barrett, Maxine Greene, Ralph Harper, and Van Cleve Morris.

Morris, and a nonexistentialist writer, George F. Kneller, have probably done the most to apply the existentialist outlook to the problems of teaching. This chapter draws heavily from the works of these authors especially those of Professor Morris, who appears to draw more from Sartre than any other existentialist philosopher.

Existentialist thinkers characterize existence in nonscientific terms that stress the freedom and responsibility of each person. They are primarily concerned with presenting personal responses to their own consciousness of their conscious existence and with authenticating themselves as persons. The positive common core of existentialism consists of its adherents' commitment to humanity's active consciousness and the complete, absolute freedom of will and choice. Implicit in existentialist thinking, is the idea that the exercise of one's active, conscious, and absolute freedom is *good,* or at least better than any alternatives.

In addition to its *positive* aspects, existentialism has some negative features. Existentialists reject both philosophical and scientific *systems* that have been used to explain human existence. Since people are not considered to be *objects* of impersonal, analytic study, all traditional systems of thought have no existential significance. In existential situations, reason is neither adequate nor inadequate, it is totally irrelevant; all that is vital is irrational. Since people are not considered to be rational animals, existentialists place their faith in neither metaphysics nor logic.

Blackham has stated,

> Classical philosophy comes to an end in Hegel, because it has become folly to construct intellectual totalitarian systems in which everything is taken up, harmonized, rationalized, and justified. Such palaces are still marvelous, but nobody can live in them. The savour and reality of human existence, its perils and triumphs, its bitterness and sweetness, are outside in the street.[2]

In studying existentialism, readers should constantly keep in mind that, the more systematic we become in describing both an existential philosophy and philosophy of education, the farther we get from the central message of existentialism, which is centered in a concern for the individual's personal beliefs and commitments.

Existentialists oppose all positions that stress the physical, mechanical natures or aspects of human functioning. They berate studying first metaphysics, then the natural sciences including anthropology, and placing human beings in the context of such study. They also attack a social science that has involved the discovery of humankind as an objective fact in the world—a behaving organism whose behavior is, at least in principle, open to public inspection in somewhat the same manner as the behavior of molecules, stars, and frogs.

Existentialists grant that man is a social animal, but they do not view his sociality as an unmixed blessing. For example, they note that modern industrial organization turns people into replaceable *things*. Morris states, "It is when I weaken and yield to the gaze of 'the other' and simply follow the conventional path tramped down in front of me that my freedom as a man is put in jeopardy."[3]

These are some of the basic themes of existentialism.

1. The absolute, incurable isolation of each individual.

2. The absurd mechanisms of society that destroy individuals.

3. The courage of each person to face death while affirming the reality of life.

4. Humanity has no genetic essence of human nature, only a history.

5. A person's being evolves through a history that the individual creates.

6. Each person living in such a way as to deserve something better than nothingness.

7. A life without pretense, though difficult and hazardous, is to be preferred over a life of illusionary false security.

Radical Existentialism

Like other philosophies, *existentialism* represents diverse strains of thought, all with a common core. Its interpretation extends from an individual-centered radical, atheistic existentialism, such as that developed by Jean-Paul Sartre, to a group-centered psychedelic-humanistic position, such as that of Carl Rogers.

Since it would be nearly impossible to develop one existentialist position that would truly represent the various strains and space does not permit examining each strain, this chapter centers upon radical existentialism within which each individual is completely the sole judge both of right and wrong and of the criteria for judging rightness and wrongness. There is a radical necessity for personal responsibility in making moral decisions. Furthermore, humankind is what each person conceives and wills himself to be, and each person *creates* his or her own private world of meaning and destiny in which other people and objects merely play supporting roles. Morris summarizes this existentialist position:

> Thus we behold man, aboriginal man that is, as pure existent devoid of any essence whatsoever. He is not bound by any antecedent or a priori human nature but is completely free to determine

his own nature. This freedom is total; man can choose what he shall be. It is this process of choosing and of becoming which describes, as accurately as one can, what the Existentialists believe is fundamental to human existence. If man has essence, it is literally his freedom from essence and the consequent freedom to choose and become what he will.[4]

For radical existentialists, life is a tour from, and back to an *ocean of nothingness,* and it consists of encounters with this nothingness. Within life, one is either self-created or one is formed by one's own organism and its physical-social milieu. So existentialists place each human being in an existential stance where one must choose one's own destiny beyond the limits of rational knowledge and scientific proof, guided only by a consciousness of one's own conscious subjectivity.

Each human being is confronted with the reality of three dreadful alternative choices: To adjust to the social situation and become a slave to it while hoping to gain some momentary relief at the whim of the gods and nature who have been appeased by the person's submission. To choose neither to adjust nor to revolt but to escape facing the brutal dilemma through suicide. To assert one's absolute freedom and ask no quarter from any god or human institution, thereby assuming the endless burden of tension and struggle that a life of revolt against organized society demands. Here, one finds in such rebellion a *value* that is one's own and that gives meaning and purpose to one's life. This value is the exercise of unlimited, absolute freedom and choice. "*Either,* man chooses existentialism with its commitment to self, character, choice, and will; *or* man embraces modern humanism with its faith in the absolute wisdom of organismic and cosmic consciousness."[5]

Sartre: A Radical Existentialist Philosopher

Jean-Paul Sartre served in the French Army from 1939 to 1941. He spent nine months as a German prisoner of war, and was released from prison in 1941. He then became active in the French resistance movement. It was during his participation in the underground movement that his atheistic existentialist philosophy crystallized. *Existentialism and Humanism* was published in 1950. He also has published other books, novels, and plays, that delineate his philosophical position. His ideas were the principal driving force behind the existentialism that emerged in the United States during the 1950s and 1960s.

Sartre was greatly influenced by both Kierkegaard and Heidegger. However his atheism contrasts with Kierkegaard's religious orientation, and he reversed Heidegger's position that people's essence, or being in general, is prior to their existence. Whereas Heidegger studied the psychological existence of concrete individuals only as a means to understand the philosophical basis of *being* in general, Sartre was concerned almost entirely with the existence of concrete individuals. So, whereas Heidegger, in a sense, thought that essence precedes existence, Sartre has emphasized that *existence* precedes *essence*.

Sartre used atheism as an argument for rejecting not only God, but any genetic nature or innate essence of human nature as well. "If man as the existentialist sees him is not definable, it is because to begin with he is nothing. He will not be anything until later, and then he will be what he makes of himself. Thus, there is no [innate] human nature, because there is no God to have a conception of it. . . . Man is nothing else but that which he makes of himself. That is the first principle of existentialism."[6]

For Sartre, a human being is forever in a state of becoming, is totally free to make a self, and is totally responsible for the self that is so made; the individual has unlimited freedom and unlimited self-responsibility. One is not a *determined* object, but a conscious subject who can freely choose and will the relationship to oneself and to one's world; choice is the main aspect of human life.

Sartre considered his writings to be psychological in nature. In them he has discussed despair, dread, decision, and self-deception. Through using fictional writing to develop his theory, he emphasized the tragic human condition and the absurdity of human life. Tragedy lies in the fact that a person is required to make commitments and decisions without having proper knowledge of their consequences, both personal and for others.

Existentialism: The Nature of Reality

For existentialists, reality is existence as lived in terms of expressed feelings, and ultimate and final reality resides within the self of each individual. "Reality in Existentialist language is 'self-operating-in-cosmos-of-choice' or simply 'self-choosing'."[7] The only reality, then, that existentialists recognize consists of lived *existences*. "The only reality that exists for an existing individual is his own ethical reality."[8]

What Is Existence?

A person is a mortal being, on earth for a brief time, born by chance at a chance place, and affected by some circumstances beyond its control throughout this short, uncertain life. But the person does have a subjective awareness of his or her own being; this is the person's existence. So, all philosophizing begins with an existing being's being aware of its own existing. "The first thing to exist is me."[9] Then, every act that I perform derives its existence from my prior existence.

A key idea of existentialism, held by many though not all existentialists is that existence precedes essence; first of all "I am." As a human being, I have been thrown into existence; my awareness of this is the absolutely raw datum of the world. But, since humankind arrives on the scene devoid of any whatness, my existence does not make me, I must make myself. So, existence is one's brute being in the world. Essence, in contrast is the identity that one defines for oneself as one lives one's life.

That one reality that we all can discover from within is a concrete, living, experiencing, struggling, and suffering existent self. But, our existence does not make us, instead, we must make ourselves. Humankind is its own designer and essence giver. I must create my essence by *choosing* the kind of person I am to be moment by moment and year by year.

The Metaphysics of Existentialism
For existentialists the physical universe, in the sense of a world apart from humankind, has neither meaning nor purpose. Reality is not a state of being, but a process of becoming; it is human made. Whereas traditional speculative philosophies have centered their inquiry on the metaphysical question of the fixed essence of reality, God, the universe, and humankind, existentialists relegate this question to a largely meaningless position. For example, their study centers on the fact that human beings exist individually: humankind is. They are little concerned with the nature of any metaphysical essence of humankind. Consequently, "Ultimately, when all the sham of Reason, and Nature and Science have been stuffed away, there stand you and I, our choosing selves naked before a cosmos of alternatives."[10]

Existentialists have little sympathy with the metaphysical views that either the physical world of things, the Platonic world of Ideas, or a combination of the two represents ultimate reality. They do, however, have their own unique meaning of metaphysics; it is the fundamental happening within human existence: *Dasein.*

Dasein is present only in humanity. It is a consciousness of conscious Being; the *is* of what is. Humankind first is (it exists) then it defines itself by thinking, what does it mean to say that I am? The *Dasein* of each individual includes potential for both authenticity and inauthenticity. But these are not determined by genetic and environmental causes; instead they transcend them.

Existential Nothingness
For all of us human beings, nothingness is coiled, like a worm, in the heart of our being. It is at the heart of our being because it is brought in by humankind—the very agent who has established being. Humanity is the very being by which the nothingness-idea comes into the world. No awareness of existence (being) may be had without one's also having an awareness of nonexistence (nothingness); the two awarenesses must always occur together.

Nothingness, then, is a wound in our being, but because of this wound, our being becomes intensified within the process of our awareness. Figuratively speaking, nothingness is the hole in the doughnut. "Of course, without the doughnut, no hole. But keep in mind that without the hole, no doughnut."[11] Without original nothingness there is no selfhood and no freedom.

Atheistic Existentialism
For adherents of the atheistic wing of existentialism, the concept *God* is completely irrelevant. They note that within the various theistic and deistic positions essence has preceded existence; the Creator had the pattern for humankind before creating any human beings, just as a carpenter has the idea of a table before creating a specific table. However, since human beings truly are thrown into existence, one's existence occurs without any prepatterned essence. Atheistic existentialists note that if, as evangelists often say, "God's will is working through me," then God uses and manipulates people as instruments. This completely contradicts any consideration of people as free, choosing beings.

Reality Is Humankind Made
What is ultimately real in this world is the selfhood of a single human being: the existential I. This does not mean that nothing exists except people, but it does mean that everything else exists in the light of human consciousness. As one lives one's life, carrying on various activities and making various choices, one is engaging in defining oneself, of giving oneself an essence. A person is only what that person does.

One's subjective awarenesses constitute one's self as a subject in a world, which appears to be made up of objects. To other people, one is both a subject and an object. But, everything that is subjective is grounded upon something that extends beyond the dichotomy or split of subjective and objective matters.

Existentialism: The Nature of Human Motivation

Whereas traditional philosophies have assumed that the *essence* of human beings occurs prior to their *existence;* for existentialists, *existence precedes essence.* People, at birth, are absolutely free awarenesses thrown into an existence, but they must find their essence. "Man is the measure of all things" becomes an absolute moral imperative. One's birth and death consists of one's coming from and returning to an ocean of nothingness. People are free, but their freedom is no longer considered the gift of God.

Existence Precedes Essence

Existentialists are convinced that there is no innate human nature that is, in any way, foreordained. Instead, human nature is whatever people actively choose to become as they assume responsibility for the choices they make. So, existentialists begin with conscious human experience.

People, however, not only are conscious; they also are self-conscious. In a sense, one always stands outside oneself. One not only thinks, contemplates, and feels; one also can think about one's thinking, one can contemplate one's facility for contemplation, and one can have feeling about one's feeling. A human being, then, unlike other beings, can question the nature of its own being. The dawn of consciousness is consciousness becoming aware of itself as existing; it is consciousness of consciousness. So, "we mean by 'man' a being aware of being."[12] The emergence of the awareness of existence has been simultaneous with the emergence of humanity. Humankind became aware of its own existence and gave it a name.

An existentialist may not be able rationally to know that he exists through using a definition of his existence, but he can *feel* his existence. "Our existence is given; we wake up to it. Our essence is what is in question; it becomes our project."[13]

Being or existence is the supreme genus; it is impossible to find a higher genus within which it would be included. Hence, any definition of being is logically impossible. However, being or existence is something given here and now that emphasizes one's inner life and introspective awareness. Humankind first is, then it defines itself. So, since humankind is not born with an essence, it is useless for us to search for humanity's essence before we understand its existence.

Within existential thought, there is an absolute uniqueness about my own selfhood; I am genuinely different from all other things or persons. Furthermore, my singular existence will never be repeated. Nevertheless, my existence is a big joke or a huge delusion. Actually, I count for absolutely nothing. Since there has been no essence of humanity prior to my existence, there is nothing about the cosmos that requires my presence. All this means that I am aware of my existential nothingness. Although, human beings have attempted to structure their sciences, arts, and religions into some kind of rational order, design, and purpose; existence itself is devoid of any such qualities.

Humankind's Absolute Freedom

Humankind is condemned to be free with all of the potentiality and tragedy that this entails. Since humankind's essence is not predetermined, one can choose one's own nature. Hence, one wills one's own essential nature out of the depths of one's own inward anxiety. One is free and one's freedom is essentially an inner matter. The human predicament is that people have the awesome responsibility of choice whether or not they choose to accept it. A human being chooses its lot in life even by refusing to make a choice. The only thing that we are not free to do is not to choose. It is this power of choice, operating within the necessary medium of responsibility that sets us off as human beings. Awareness, choosing, and freedom are interlocking notions; they all come together in the awareness of one's freedom in the acts of choosing.

Existential freedom is the freedom to set goals, but not necessarily to achieve them. Freedom is absolute because there are no limits on the freedom to set goals for oneself; there are no goals that one cannot choose. The setting of goals comes first. Only later is this or that feature of the phenomenological environment recognized as a limit to accomplishing this or that aim in life.

Man Is the Measure of All Things
Existentialism sponsors the absolute, final fulfillment of the dictum, arising in ancient Greece, "man is the measure of all things." The human power and necessity of choice sets us off as human beings, sets the criteria for determining truth, decides what is true, determines the standards to be used in choosing between criteria, and sets the judgments to be used in deciding on the standards. "Human choice is the ultimate court of judgment both in morals and in practical judgment."[14] What one becomes is one's own responsibility (to oneself). An individual either chooses a personal essence—what that person will be—or the individual allows this to be chosen by others. We all are proactive (forwardly active) beings who, in choosing, are free and responsible agents who actively use our environment through exercising absolute autonomy.

A person's basic motivation is neither biological satisfaction nor psychological adjustment; it is creation and discovery of one's own self. A person's existence, then, is a choice among the possibilities that are open to one. It is a self in its inseparable relations with the world of other persons and things into which the self always finds itself inserted.

Being-For-Itself
Humankind is the only being that exists before it can be defined by any concept. It is constantly in a state of becoming. Furthermore, it is always more than science can disclose about it. Also, it is ultimately opaque to rational understanding.

Whereas a physical object or a lower animal constitutes being-in-itself, humankind constitutes being-for-itself. Physical objects and lower animals cannot master their thrown conditions. Instead, they have a *determined* existence. Humankind, in contrast, moves toward a future that is self-chosen and self-created. Thus, being-for-itself makes itself.

Sartre has written, "When we say man chooses himself, we do mean that every one of us must choose himself, but by that we also mean that in choosing for himself he chooses for all men. . . . What we choose is always the better; and nothing can be better for us unless it is better for all. . . . Our responsibility is thus much greater than we had supposed, for it concerns mankind as a whole."[15]

The Authentic Life

Life's task, for an existentialist, is to assert one's selfhood in such a way as to make any nothingness that awaits one an injustice. One does not rest one's case with the symptoms of anxiety. Instead, one summons oneself onward beyond initial psychic states to a higher level of awareness that achieves an *authenticity* that leads one to take charge of one's own symptoms.

"Childhood is a pre-Existential phase of human life."[16] It is followed in the life of each person by *The Existential Moment*. This is the moment when an individual first discovers himself as existing, when one recognizes one's own presence in the world as a person. Quite without any say in the matter, a person is confronted with existence and the absolute necessity of making choices.

People are equally susceptible to the human condition, but they differ in the degree to which they respond to it authentically; the degree to which they are aware of their freedom, baselessness, and responsibility for the way they are living their lives. However, an existentialist need not be a radical iconoclast. "Even the man who consents to convention can be the existential man *if* he is *aware* of the act of consenting, and hence of the necessity that he take *personal* responsibility for living his life in a conventional way. . . . The people who say, 'I couldn't help it; I had no choice,' are the nonauthentics; they do not know they are human."[17]

Human Transcendence

Humankind, unlike any other phenomenon in the universe, is always oriented toward its possibilities. *Transcendence* is the existentialist name for this unique mode of existence. It is a dynamic self confidence within which an individual is constantly struggling for a new, higher definition of himself. The concept *transcendence* implies that humankind is constantly reordering human nature. Human nature is not a *given*, but a *question*. Growth, in the sense of self-transcendence, entails one's activity of choosing without having any external guides or criteria for choice.

Existentialism: The Nature and Source of Truth and Knowledge

The two modes of being imply two modes of knowing: scientific and existential. Scientific regularities are there all right, but they have no direct human significance. A perceived object is just what it appears to be and no more. This is its *facticity*, which means that objects in existing simply exist as they are in themselves; this is being-in-itself. Both objects and other persons have facticity; they can be studied scientifically. But persons, so studied, exist just as objects do. So, whereas Mode 1 centers upon consciousness of an external world and objective research in regard to it, Mode 2 is scientifically out of reach. The prime epistemological task of existentialists is to apply Mode 2 knowing to facticity situations. But, this mode of knowing almost defies description and definition. It is a kind of total feeling-tone that simply is *had* by the individual. In the knowing, an awareness of my awareness process, I feel myself as an existential center of knowing.

Knowledge is not something purely objective that is laid out to be learned. Neither is it something merely functional and useful in the management of experience. "At bottom, knowledge *becomes* knowledge only when a subjectivity takes hold of it and puts it into his own life."[18] In this sense, the individual is responsible for his or her own knowledge. A person is responsible for attaching meaning to cold brute facts. For example, each student must become a baseless chooser of the meaning of the American Revolution.

Science gathers factual evidence on a problem; it gathers data. But it does not prescribe answers. It is the individual who selects the answers, and he or she does so without outside help. One, by nature, may select any answer and one alone is responsible for one's selection. One may, but also may not, select the answer of the majority. So a person lives in constant anguish and doubt as to whether the choice was the right one.

There is no way to truth except through individual judgment. Knowledge is acquired through appropriation, personally taking and adopting something that is available to all. What is *taken* in the form of ideas, attitudes, and points of view is common property. "What is uncommon and really unique is how each of us uses and appropriates these 'data' in interpreting the world."[19] This calls for a whole new understanding of the word truth within which the learner's *feeling toward* truth comes to play as significant a role as does the mere cognitive understanding of truth. "Knowledge is always in part subjective. That is, for anything to be true, it must first pass into and be taken hold of by some subjective consciousness. It must be chosen, i.e., appropriated, before it can be true for that consciousness."[20]

It is the individual self that must make the ultimate decision as to what is true. Truths are not forced upon one by either an external, objective reality, a necessary logic, or an absolute Being. "Each person is his or her own supreme court of epistemological judgment and is, therefore, in an ultimate sense, absolutely on his or her own when it comes to deciding between candidates for truth."[21]

Truths, then, are personal not social. They do not happen to people but are chosen by them, and one's subjective feelings are the final authority for truth. Truths are revealed in the subjective experience of living. No truth by itself has reality. A flower is a flower all right, but its meaning to anyone who views it depends upon that person's relationship to it. An object is there but each of us sees it in a unique way.

Existentialism: The Nature and Source of Human Values

Except for human existence itself, "the entirety of philosophical content in Existentialism may be described as axiological."[22] So, existentialism is obsessed with value theory. In fact, "To *be* means to be engaged in choosing."[23] However, there are no values external to humankind. All persons merely turn up and through being discover themselves. No one chooses whether to exist; human existence is the result of chance or accident.

Humankind, then, has to make itself and choose the conditions under which its members are to live. People arrive on the scene devoid of any *whatness*; they have only *isness*. They are committed to something that they did not ask for, and they are locked in a condition from which there is no escape. Their life consists of the totality of their acts, and their living is an affair of risks and uncertainties. Since no one way of life can be defended as being more rational than another, creative movement is possible for each individual only by a "leap of faith" grounded in the passion of subjective truth and personal commitment.

Opposition to Metaphysical and Social Values

Existentialists revolt against either metaphysical or social standards of value. Since, for them, the idea of mankind is not yet finished, the highest form of human existence entails the repudiation of all paradigmatic (perfect) ideas of humankind. Classical Realist philosophy, religion, and social ethics are all constructed on a faulty basis of value. They all have an erroneous notion of where the values by which one intends to live are found. They all begin looking for *human values* in the world instead of in humankind.

Classical realism looks for values in sets of independent categories that would go on existing even if there were no human beings. Religion looks for them in a superhuman being who personally underwrites certain values regardless of people's attitude toward them. Social ethics looks for human values in institutional arrangements and social conventions that are necessary for effective group effort; the values according to which people are expected to live are those of the social system. In all three cases, values are considered to be entities already present in situations prior to the entry of individual persons. So, the crowd is the untruth "by reason of the fact that it renders the individual completely impenitent and irresponsible, or at least weakens his sense of responsibility by reducing it to a fraction."[24] Sartre thought that "Hell is other people" by this he meant that other persons are capable of making a given person a mere thing in their experience. However, he recognized that other people could encounter one as a subject like themselves. In an I and Thou encounter, one may be so desperately trying to exercise one's own subjectivity that one attributes to others an objectivity that is externally defined rather than a true subjectivity like oneself. Nevertheless, according to Morris, "If man is to regain that which makes him human, he must be willing once again to stand alone, willing to withstand the pressures of history and culture, and to chart the course of his own life, not only for himself but on behalf of Man."[25]

Absolute Freedom

To be human is to be absolutely free. Humankind is the determiner of its own nature and the definer of its own values. People cannot attribute their faulty values, their barbaric politics, or even their personal neuroses to membership in a given social group—family, community, or nation—because each one could have had it otherwise. Humankind's freedom to choose which way it will go distinguishes it from all other phenomena in the universe. "In choosing we make our values *out of nothing.*"[26]

Each person, then, is a personal supreme court of values; each is a benign anarchist. "The value-making agent in the world is the free subjectivity of man."[27] Each of one's words, deeds, and choices becomes a building block in one's existential edifice of value. In the valuing process, a human being creates, not discovers, personal values and projects them onto the world.

Baselessness of Human Values

Since an existentialist repudiates all moral absolutes, the business of choosing is really baseless. There is no structure of either essences or values that has any being prior to humankind's individual and collective existence. Hence, an individual is a baseless source of values. Each person is the originator, inventor, and creator of values. Humankind, as existential chooser, is the being by which values enter the world. In the act of choosing, a person creates values out of nothing. Individuals frequently are in anguish over the baselessness of their values; freedom simply is too much for them. Hence they try to escape this condition by submitting to determinants of conduct that are external to their own wills. However, one cannot escape being the creator of values, for one cannot escape choosing. To repeat, even to choose not to choose is a choice.

One discovers values through the way one lives one's life. One discovers them in the choices one makes, the things one does, the attitudes one holds, and the goals one sets for oneself; so, one is the ultimate author of all of one's choices. In the sense that there is no certifying agency for one's choices, they are really baseless in nature.

Existential Anxiety

There is a paradox with which every person must live; one is of absolute value in the world and simultaneously one is absolutely of no value in the world. Since each person must create his or her own ends or goals, each person is conscious of anxiety in terms of anguished freedom; this is the human predicament. Existential anxiety is not mere psychological tension. Rather, it is dread of the necessary irrational choice between absolutely irreconcilable alternatives.

Anxiety is the numbing feeling of being aware of one's possible continuance in the nothingness in which one was born. It involves the question, "what am I doing here in the world?" It is possible for me merely to exist without any quality, value, or meaning in my existing selfhood; I can continue in nothingness. So, my self is ill-at-ease in the world. I fear the inauthenticity of my own selfhood.

Humankind's anxiety is partly rooted in the fact that human beings are fastened to dying animals. Both persons and beasts die, but a human being is more than a beast in that a human being knows, and can live with the knowledge, that the final destiny is death. Death, and the dread attending it, is the means by which the true exaltation of being human can be realized. It is not the nothingness, but our encounter with it, that provides the vehicle for our humanness. Within this encounter, each person must personalize death, embrace it as a central element in one's being.

Our lack of an essence, our lack of a basic definition of whatness is at once our agony and our glory. We suffer the agony in exchange for our *absolute freedom*. If we ever did *find* the essence of humanity, "Man—the chooser, the value maker—would dissolve and disappear and become merely an odd, hairless anthropoid, balanced on his hind legs, living out a prescribed existence."[28]

One's existentialism must begin with agony, but it is capable of developing exhilarating sensations of human power. Within the privacy of one's own subjectivity, one can have certain feelings and awarenesses that are authentic and laden with personal meaning. The way to an authentic—good—life is for each individual to realize himself or herself by assertion of individuality and by making personal choices instead of being stampeded into the choices of collective groups.

Individual Choice and Human Society

"If the authentic man is our aim, then the authentic society is also our aim."[29] A society is authentic to the degree that it fails to provoke in individual citizens urgings to escape from their freedom and one that refuses to specify what is good to its citizens. The only adequate sociopolitical order is that which recognizes and values the absolute freedom of human persons. In such an order, each person takes personal responsibility for the laws that are obeyed, the conventions that are followed, and the values that are appropriated for each one's own life.

When choosing, a person chooses for humanity, and one's life and conduct become that person's definition of humanity. In macrocosmic terms, humanity had begun to awaken to its moral predicament. In microcosmic terms, each individual must awaken to it in his or her own life. At about puberty, there is an abrupt awakening to the fact of one's own existence in the form of the first agonizing recognition of being responsible for what one does and how one behaves.

What a person should like can be answered only in terms of what each individual chooses subjectively. An existential oriented student or teacher may rightly say, "I have a subjective knowledge of beauty and goodness, one that is completely baseless in the sense that it is absolutely nonreferable to any final criteria, but it is one that just the same is authentic."

Existentialism: The Purpose of Education

Since the end product of existentialist education is a completely autonomous person, existentialist educators have little interest in imparting abstract, objective knowledge about reality, truth, and goodness. Instead, they are concerned with what a given piece of knowledge or belief means to the individual existences of persons. They grant that objective knowledge is possible, but they see little point in promulgating it as such. Hence, they consider both metaphysics and science to be existentially impotent. Knowledge, in its best sense, exists only as it rises from human consciousness and feelings.

Education, then, is the process of developing free, self-actualized persons, centered on their feelings. It is a student-centered process within which students generally are considered to be good and active. Hence, in the education process, no coercion, presciption, or imposition of either ideas or actions is advised or necessary. Learners choose and make their natures and themselves.

"If education is to be truly human, it must somehow awaken [and intensify] *awareness* in the learner—existential awareness of himself as a single subjectivity present in the world. . . . To be human is first to exist, and to exist is to be aware of being, to be aware of existing."[30] Existential awareness is manifested most vividly in one's awareness of one's choosing. So, education should enhance a person's choosing process.

Existentialist educators, then, are committed to development of the choice making powers of individuals. Thus, their emphasis moves away from the physical and social sciences and turns more to the humanities and the arts, where man's aesthetic, emotional, and moral proclivities are more exercised. Schools, however, definitely are not to be places where specified values, skills, attitudes, and modes of response are selected and inculcated as appropriate cultural conditions to be propagated.

Existentialism: The Nature of the Learning Process

It is in the treatment of learning that the irrational nature of existentialist philosophy comes to the front. Existentialists fairly well agree in their opposition to both behavioristic and Freudian psychologies and align themselves with a *third force* psychology. But, there is a lack of agreement among adherents of this position in regard to what third force psychology really means. It may be that existential philosophy, by its very nature, precludes a rational description of the learning process.

Existentialists adhere to the "metaphor of an inner space, with its intentions, thoughts, feelings, crises, rhythms, order, surprises, events and situations."[31] But there is no existential learning *system*. Instead, existentialists have an ever-shifting vision of what transpires in conscious minds; human mentalities are always in process. As long as one lives, one's unfinished experience is always shifting and changing. The five major themes of existentialism (existence, insecurity, the void, self-isolation, and presence) are bound together by a state of experience always being unfinished and by one's absolute freedom. This freedom is not so much a freedom to choose this or that, but a freedom to choose oneself.

To be consciously aware is for one to experience a sometimes painful and sometimes exhilarating awareness of oneself as a baseless base of knowledge and values. So, to be aware is to be conscious of the fact that one is the author of one's own dispositions. One's awareness is of being a choosing, free, and responsible agent who actively uses the environment through exercise of one's autonomy. "Man is nothing else but what he makes of himself."[32] Humankind "is better defined not as a rational animal but as a *choosing*, and therefore valuing, animal who *can* think and *does* think if he chooses."[33] So, one's cognitive development is subordinate to one's affective or emotional growth. In final analysis the test for truth is each person's feelings about the matters at hand in terms of intuitive awareness.

"An existentialist is one who should know one thing well, himself, as one who measures his experience against the categories of his own and other people's insights."[34] A human being is first a seeker, then only secondly an analyst.

Existentialists reject the idea that psychology is a physical science. They emphasize willed responses in people as opposed to the conditioned responses of behaviorists and the organismic responses of humanists. They place the concrete existence of individuals above the logical manipulation of abstractions. General laws and abstract systems cannot solve the specific problems that confront a concrete individual.

We terminate this section with an attempted formal definition of learning that draws its substance fron Professor Ralph Harper. Learning, for an existentialist, is the process of using one's mind to organize experiences and ideas into some kind of coherent structure that can help one unify one's relationship to reality and at the same time make that relationship one's very own; it is a search for personal truth.[35]

Existentialism: The Nature of the Teaching Process

Existential education is a process of self-actualization within which one makes oneself and in the process develops a self-directed intuitive awareness. Such education starts, not with the nature of the world and man, but with the human *self*. Furthermore it starts, not with knowledge, but with the moral self. Though education is an activity usually conducted with children and youth in groups, this does not preclude our psychologically seeing active personalities existing alone as individuals, and considering groups to be only physical phenomena.

Children have been thrown into the world. Yet, they are not passive things to be worked over in a fashion that brings them into alignment with some prior notion of what they should be. Instead, they are active conscious selves who have absolute freedom. A teacher's job is to awaken in students an awareness of their subjective freedom. Education, then, becomes a matter of awakening each student to the full intensity and potentiality of selfhood. *Self*, as used here, is a subjective awareness that one's being is an unanalyzable, indefinable point of origin for all subsequent awareness.

To become an authentic person, one must penetrate one's own inwardness so as to make genuine choices and to take responsibility for those choices. "The school's job pre-eminently is to awaken each child to the ultimate responsibility he or she must bear for the selections made between alternative sets of consequences."[36]

Teaching Freedom and Responsibility

A teacher's imperative is to arrange learning situations so as to bring home to every student the truth of three basic propositions: I am a *choosing* agent, who is unable to avoid choosing my way through life; I am a *free* agent, who is absolutely free to set the goals of my own life; and I am a *responsible* agent, who is personally accountable for my free choices as they are revealed in how I live my life.[37]

The discovery of people's subjective freedom can occur only in the freest possible atmosphere. Accordingly, in an educational institution there should be no hierarchy of authority, no domination by teachers over students, and no external standards of achievement of success. So, any need for tests, grades, and report cards would disappear. In place of external standards, each student would be free to establish personal standards in terms of what the student chooses to learn. It would "Let learning be the sharp and vivid awakening of the learner to the sense of being personally answerable for his own life."[38] Complete freedom is the only medium in which genuine communication can be effected between teacher and learner.

Existentialism brings the learner's self-determination to the very center of the learning process. Teachers promote an intensity of awareness of each student's own precarious role as a baseless chooser who cannot escape choosing and therefore creating a personal answer to all normative and moral questions that arise. "The environment of the child should be one of complete and absolute freedom, a freedom where selfhood can operate without hindrance. We should not impose upon a youngster any environments whatever—neither Mind, nor things, nor God, nor Truth, nor Experience lived with and among other human beings."[39]

A human being cannot acquire moral and ethical principles from either other persons or social institutions except by choosing them from the baseless platform of a personal awareness of what is transpiring in contemporary life. Hence, students should be encouraged to react to the world and other persons, but in a subjective individualistic way, not a social one.

The Individual vs Society

Existentialist teachers combat all social forces that tend to dehumanize people by denying their inherent autonomy. They think that the reduction and destruction of human freedom has been the reduction and destruction of humanity and has tended to bring creative processes to an end. Because of their preoccupation with order, discipline, and punishment for failure, many of today's schools are repressive and inhumane. Thus, they destroy student's spontaneity, inquisitiveness, and creativity. Since every human being has an innate curiosity, any punitive or repressive environment that threatens the self is not conducive to its development.

A good existential teacher recognizes that he or she is one resource for students' use in achieving self-directed growth. Hence, the teacher provides a setting for permitting each student to decide consciously upon his or her freedom and becoming. In development of his freedom, the student may be enabled to distinguish among the various perspectives available and to adjust them to one another. Learning occurs whenever a person feels responsibility for achieving and enhancing oneself. What is learned must make a difference in the learner's life. That is, a student must go beyond mere intellectual acceptance of knowledge and values and *live* them.

The Teaching Dialog

An existentialist teacher is not an instructor. Instead, the teacher is a participant in dialogs with students. In each dialog each participant, teacher and student, is a subject for the other. Thus, there is an I-Thou relationship going both ways. Since the business of knowing is essentially one of coming into some kind of human touch with reality, learning occurs more effectively if the learner is permitted to explore freely in an enriched environment where appropriate materials, including a teacher, are provided and made readily accessible. The teacher provides no answer and makes no suggested solutions. Instead, each student is asked to create a unique solution. The teacher, as a resource for student use in achieving self-directed growth, offers but does not transmit knowledge. The teacher constantly urges students to assume responsibility for, and deal with, the results of their actions. Also, the teacher helps each student become what it is that student wants to become.

Existentialist education may help provide students with a knowledge of the various ideological choices people, to date, have made. "But, finally, it returns the children to themselves; it awakens children to the final knowledge that each one of them is alone, completely and beautifully alone, in the value enterprise."[40] Individuals not only must awaken to their own existential condition and the responsibility that it entails but also to the alternatives before them from which their choices should be made. Students must be given every conceivable latitude to find for themselves all of the possibilities open to them. Any and all subject matters are appropriate. But students must be perfectly free to follow their own inclinations in learning.

Teaching—A Gadfly Function

An existentialist teacher emphasizes human experiences such as suffering, conflict, guilt, and death. The teacher helps students see that life is compounded of growth and decay, joy and tragedy, pain and happiness, suffering and ecstacy, and life and death; thus taking existential anxiety fully into account (see page 138 for the meaning of anxiety). Like a gadfly, a teacher seeks to sting fellow human beings into pursuing the only life that is worth living and thereby becoming *authentic selves*.

An existentialist teacher is searching for personal truth; a truth that is always new to the teacher- or student-searcher. "In the most literal and profound of ways, he will learn along with his students."[41]

A good teacher aims to produce, not replicas of the teacher or anyone else, but people who stand apart as individuals even more distinctly than they did when the teacher first met them. "When that individual stands apart and alone, awake to his existing, aware of his freedom, responsible and in charge of his life, he will see for himself why he may, for the first time, be called authentic."[42] Then the person, completely independent, is sufficient for every situation. The student arrives at decisions on all issues in accordance with the way he or she feels and is completely confident that the decision is right. Leaders in promulgating this subjective emphasis promote each individual's intuitive self-awareness and the artistic expression of the individual's self-actualization.

The Subject Matter Emphasis of Existentialism

Subject matter, for existentialists, is a means of self-development and self-fulfillment that is subjected to students; students are not subjected to it. Students appropriate to themselves the knowledge that they make their own in the process of their self-fulfillment. Hence, relevancy of the subject matter to the student is all-important. School subjects are only tools for the realization of subjectivity.

The curriculum of a school, in its various forms, represents the extant knowledge of the world; it consists of the lines spoken by others in their interpretation of the world and humanity. Subject matter is there for the taking, but each learner must do his own taking. Subject matter is there neither to be mastered nor to be experienced, but to be either chosen or rejected. "The subject matter and experiences in a curriculum shall be merely *available*; to be learned, they must first be opted for, sought out, and appropriated by the student,"[43]

Schools should promote the idea that whatever a student produces in either the classroom or at home is largely original. Thus, the student will see himself in the role of a creative innovator. Morris states that "Experience in music, the dance, drama, creative writing, painting, and the plastic arts seem to me the chief contenders for this kind of education."[44] However, even here, no artistic standards are to be followed.

Artistic experiences should be in keeping with the way the student, not the teacher or the master, sees it. What a student creates is less important than that something is created that the student can interpret to be a private artistic statement about personal experience.

Since existentialists are more concerned with matters relating to feelings and commitment, they are relatively disinterested in matters such as physics, mathematics, and sociology. They, however, are moderately interested in history and literature, but only as they conceive of it. For them, the meanings to be attached to the past are created by each of us in terms of our particular personal life projects. In a sense, each person creates a personal history. "History can be understood only forward, not backward."[45] One finds meaning in history only in terms of present circumstances. For example, the meanings of the Constitution of the United States are authored in the here and now. History and literature, the normative segments of the curriculum, must include not only subject matter but also experiences in which sharp pro- and con-ethical dimensions are intensified. "Past events may be said to exist in a brute, documentary, 'archive' sense. But what they *mean* is always for us to say."[46] We create the value contents of our heritage by examining that heritage in a particular light.

Footnotes

[1]Van Cleve Morris, *Existentialism in Education* (New York: Harper & Row, 1966), p. 28.

[2]H. J. Blackham, *Six Existentialist Thinkers* (London: Routledge and Kegan Paul, 1952), p. 44.

[3]Morris, *Existentialism in Education,* p. 66.

[4]Van Cleve Morris, "Existentialism and Education," in *Educational Theory,* IV, no. 4 (October 1954): 250.

[5]Richard E. Johnson, *In Quest of A New Psychology: Toward a Redefinition of Humanism* (New York: Human Sciences Press, 1975), p. 322.

[6]Jean-Paul Sartre, *Existentialism and Humanism,* trans. by Philip Mairet (London: Methuen 1963), p. 28.

[7]Van Cleve Morris and Young Pai, *Philosophy and the American School,* 2nd ed. (Boston: Houghton Mifflin, 1976), p. 71.

[8]Soren Kierkegaard, *Concluding Unscientific Postscript,* trans. by David F. Swenson and Walter Lowrie (Princeton, N.J.: Princeton University Press, 1944), p. 267.

[9]Morris, *Existentialism in Education,* p. 12.

[10]Morris and Pai, *Philosophy and the American School,* p. 71.

[11]Morris, *Existentialism in Education,* p. 22.

[12]Ibid., p. 19.

[13]Morris and Pai, *Philosophy and the American School,* p. 71.

[14]Ibid., p. 71.

[15]Sartre, *Existentialism and Humanism,* p. 29.

[16]Morris, *Existentialism in Education,* p. 112.

[17]Ibid., p. 48.

[18]Ibid., p. 121.

[19]Ibid., p. 120.

[20]Ibid., p. 121

[21]Morris and Pai, *Philosophy and the American School,* p. 154.

[22]Morris, Existentialism and Education, p. 255.

[23]Ibid., p. 255.

[24]Soren Kierkegaard, *The Point of View For My Work As An Author: A Report to History,* trans. by Walter Lowrie (New York: Harper Torchbooks, 1962), p. 112.

[25]Morris, "Existentialism and Education," p. 256.

[26]Morris and Pai, *Philosophy and the American School,* p. 257.

[27]Morris, *Existentialism in Education,* p. 45.

[28]Ibid., p. 45.

[29]Ibid., p. 103.

[30]Ibid., p. 110.

[31]Ralph Harper, *The Existential Experience* (Baltimore: Johns Hopkins Press, 1972), p. 10.

[32]Jean-Paul Sartre, *Existentialism* (New York: Philosophical Library, 1947), p. 18.

[33]Morris, *Existentialism in Education,* p. 90.

[34]Harper, *The Existential Experience,* p. 136.

[35]Ibid., p. 142.

[36]Morris and Pai, *Philosophy and the American School,* p. 284.

[37]See Joshua Weinstein, *Buber and Humanistic Education* (New York: Philosophical Library, 1975), pp. 51–53.

[38]Morris, *Existentialism in Education,* p. 117.

[39]Morris and Pia, *Philosophy and the American School,* pp. 80–81.

[40]Ibid., p. 267.

[41]Morris, *Existentialism in Education,* p. 137.

[42]Ibid., p. 154.

[43]Ibid., p. 124.

[44]Ibid., p. 125.

[45]Ibid., p. 126.

[46]Ibid., p. 142.

BIBLIOGRAPHY

Abbs, Peter. *Reclamations: Essays on Culture Mass-Culture and Curriculum.* London: Heinemann Educational Books, 1979.

Barrett, William. *What is Existentialism.* New York: Grove Press, 1964.

Barrow, Robin. *Radical Education: A Critique of Freeschooling and Deschooling.* New York: John Wiley & Sons, 1978.

Bedford, Mitchell. *Existentialism and Creativity.* New York: Philosophical Library, 1972.

Blackham, H. J. *Six Existentialist Thinkers.* London: Routledge and Kegan Paul, 1952.

Buber, Martin. *I and Thou.* New York: Scribner's, 1970.

Greene, Maxine, ed. *Existential Encounters for Teachers.* New York: Random House, 1967.

Harper, Ralph. "Significance of Existence and Recognition for Education," in Nelson B. Henry, ed., *Modern Philosophies and Education.* Chicago: National Society for the Study of Education, 1955.

Harper, Ralph. *The Existential Experience.* Baltimore: Johns Hopkins Press, 1972.

Heidegger, Martin. *Being and Time,* trans. by J. MacQuarrie and E. Robinson. New York: Harper & Row, 1962.

Johnson, Richard E. *In Quest of a New Psychology: Toward a Redefinition of Humanism.* New York: Human Science Press, 1975.

Jouard, Sidney M. *Disclosing Man to Himself.* Princeton, N.J.: D. Van Nostrand, 1968.

Kierkegaard, Sören. *The Point of View for My Work as an Author: A Report to History,* trans. by Walter Lowrie. New York: Harper Torchbooks, 1962.

Kierkegaard, Sören. *Concluding Unscientific Postscript,* trans. by David Swenson and Walter Lowrie. Princeton, N.J.: Princeton University Press, 1944.

Kneller, George F. *Existentialism and Education,* New York: Philosophical Library, 1958.

Kneller, George F. *Introduction To the Philosophy of Education,* 2nd ed., New York: John Wiley & Sons, 1971.

Misiak, Henryk and Virginia S. Sexton. *Phenomenological, Existential, and Humanistic Psychologies: A Historical Survey,* New York: Grune & Stratton, 1973.

Morris, Van Cleve. *Existentialism in Education,* New York: Harper & Row, 1966.

Morris, Van Cleve, and Pai, Young. *Philosophy and the American School,* 2nd ed. Boston: Houghton Mifflin, 1976.

Neff, Frederick C. *Philosophy and American Education*. New York: Center For Applied Research in Education, 1966, pp. 96–104.

Pratte, Richard. *Contemporary Theories of Education*. Scranton, Pa.: Intext Educational Publishers, 1971.

Rogers, Carl R. *Carl Rogers on Personal Power*. New York: Delacorte, 1977.

Sartre, Jean-Paul. *Existentialism and Humanism*, trans. by Philip Mairet. London: Methuen, 1963.

Sartre, Jean-Paul. *Existentialism*. New York: Philosophical Library, 1947.

Weinstein, Joshua. *Buber and Humanistic Education*. New York: Philosophical Library, 1975.

Chapter 8
Behavioral Experimentalism in Education

Behavioral experimentalism is a twentieth century science-oriented educational philosophy implemented by a social behavioristic psychology. It emerged from a more generalized *pragmatism*, which was founded by C. S. Peirce and William James and refined by John Dewey. The terms *behavioral experimentalism* and *pragmatism* may be used interchangeably. However, in this book we use *behavioral experimentalism* to distinguish this position from that of *cognitive-field experimentalism*, the subject of Chapter 9, which may also be called *pragmatism*.

In the early 1900s Edward L. Thorndike's *connectionism* and John B. Watson's physicalistic *behaviorism* were rising to challenge the prevailing mentalistic psychologies of *mental discipline* and *mind structuralism*. Although Thorndike spoke of both physical units and mental units, in their broadest meanings, both of these newer psychologies were naturalistic, mechanistic, behavioristic, and nonmetaphysical. Both of these psychologies greatly influenced the developing behavioral experimentalist educational philosophy.

The two pivotal concepts of behavioral experimentalism have been *naturalism* and *empiricism*. Adherents of this philosophy have tended to debunk all traditional dualistic metaphysical views and replace them with a comprehensive naturalistic, though not materialistic, theory of reality and truth. Rejection of both mentalism and materialism is one of the distinctive features of this philosophy.

Behavioral experimentalists have placed humankind in, not apart from, nature. Since, for them humankind is both an integral part of and continuous with nature, they have rejected the dualistic view that a person is composed of a material body and a nonmaterial mind. For them, people are highly developed biological organisms. Taking the theory of evolution very seriously, they have assumed that human beings, too, have evolved from natural sources. So, people are no different, in kind, from other material beings. They are more complex than other beings, but they have evolved in the same way as trees, flowers, amoebas, rats, and cats. Humankind is a part of the natural world.

Behavioral experimentalism is one of the three leading empiricist educational philosophies. To review, empiricists emphasize that human learnings are centered in perceptual experience, not in mentalistic reason, intuition, or speculation. Readers should bear in mind that the other two empiricisms (logical empiricism and cognitive-field experimentalism) also emphasize a scientific approach to learning, but each of their positions differs significantly from that of a behavioral experimentalist educational philosophy.

In the development of behavioral experimentalism, Dewey's educational philosophy has been interpreted and expanded by William H. Kilpatrick, John L. Childs, Sidney Hook, Ernest Nagel, and many others.

A logical, but radical extension of behavioral experimentalism has been *social reconstructionism*. Whereas experimentalists, in general, have promoted a gradual evolutionary improvement of society, social reconstructionists have thought that educational institutions should take the lead in reconstructing the social order. George S. Counts' *Dare the Schools Build a New Social Order*[1] epitomized this movement. Other leading social reconstructionists have been Theodore Brameld and Harold Rugg.[2] They have urged educators to turn the schools into the central headquarters for deliberate social planning, directed social change, and reconstruction of society. Since they have deemed society to be in a crisis state, there constantly has been a sense of urgency in their writing.

Social reconstructionism developed as a scientific rebellion against the excessive formalism of traditional education. It recognized the rapid cultural changes of modern society and proposed that, through education, these changes be responsibly directed. It is an internationally minded educational philosophy; its goal is a worldwide democratic government within which people think, plan, and reach decisions from the bottom up instead of from the top down. Teachers, students, and parents should be involved in community making and remaking. However, even for social reconstructionists, some constancies of present day culture need to be preserved, for example, the Bill of Rights. But, "it does not follow that reinforcement of traditional patterns of life and culture is the chief task of the school."[3]

Behavioral Experimentalism: The Nature of Reality

For behavioral experimentalists, reality is a nonmetaphysical world of experience in harmony with nature. Since experience and reason based on experience are the only sources of reliable knowledge, people are unable to gain any true knowledge in regard to a supernatural, trans-empirical world. As behavioral experimentalists see it, metaphysical ontological problems involving out-thereness have been explored and found unyielding to inquiry. So, for them, the whole realm of nature, just as we experience it, is the way things really are.

In place of an absolutistic conception of a permanently fixed, final, ultimate reality that is stable and uniform; reality, for behavioral experimentalists, consists of attributes of a world with the lid off, marked by change, novelty, and an evolving flux that reaches its highest level in the development of human society. The world, then, is not sitting out there in a state of being. Rather, it is in a dynamic process of *becoming* within an open-ended universe.

Behavioral experimentalists hold a theory of mind and nature that rejects all dualisms, such as that of classical realism, and any reductionistic materialism, such as that of logical empiricism. The world of reality is one, not two. Within their *refined naturalism*, nature is a process, not a substance or law, and all of nature is characterized by *emergent evolution*. For behavioral experimentalists, existence has a completely naturalistic, nontheistic, nonmystical character, and nature is something that can be used for human purposes. The world that we live in is all we have, and everyday experience is where all thinking begins. "The opinion which is fated to be ultimately agreed to by all who investigate, is what we mean by the truth, and the object represented in this opinion is the real."[4] Since humankind's conception of reality, resulting from careful empirical inquiry, is as close to reality as we can hope to get, we may call this experienced world reality.

Behavioral experimentalists think that within the process of emergent evolution there has been a continuity of mind with the biological order of existence and a continuity of living things with the physical order of reality; in other words, humankind has evolved mentally and morally as well as biologically. Thus, they reject any historical dualistic interpretation of humankind and nature.[5] The unqualified acceptance of the continuity of the human, organic, and physical orders of existence is accompanied by a strong emphasis upon the intellectual and moral attributes of human beings. The concept *mind* also is anchored within the historical theory of emergent evolution of natural events.

Behavioral Experimentalism: The Nature of Human Motivation

For behavioral experimentalists, human beings are bio-social organisms behaving in serial alternating reaction with the physical-social environment. Humankind is an emergent within a natural evolutionary process. There is a continuity of lower and higher forms of life, and a continuity of mind with the biological order of existence. "The human or psychical level emerged as more complex behaviors appeared within the psycho-physical level, just as this intermediate level of living things developed as a result of an unique organization of chemico-physical energies."[6] The mental attributes of humankind have developed out of the simpler biological behavior of the other organic forms.

A newborn human organism becomes a minded organism through its participation in the world of objects. This world is one in which things and processes have become discriminated, identified, and classified in terms of their behavioral potentialities. Motivation is the urge to act that results from an organism's prior stimulation. In keeping with the evolutionary interpretation of the genesis of mind, people's nature is both biological and social. It is also fundamentally changeable.

The Meaning and Levels of Behavior

Human conduct cannot be adequately explained by exclusive use of physical and biological categories of existence. So the psychological orientation within this philosophical position is a *social behaviorism* that to a significant degree harmonizes with the behavioristic approaches to psychology.[7]

Behavior can occur on either a physical, a psycho-physical or animate, or a psychic-social level. The psychic-social level emerged as more complex behaviors have appeared within the psycho-physical level. Traits of both physical and psycho-physical levels necessarily pervade the human level of behavior. So, to be human, is to be physical, organic, and social.

When functioning on a psychic-social level, humankind is not a machine that responds automatically. Instead, its responses can be delayed and can reflect the organism's comprehension of the situation, which occurs within the flow of human experience. Our conceptual apparatus and function is not a direct reflection of the nature and structure of the world, but the result of an interaction, worked out in an evolutionary manner, between the world and our perceptual equipment accompanied by our needs and interests.

Within social behaviorism, "Human behavior is intrinsically selective in nature because responses are to the qualities of things, and what these qualities signify for the future."[8] So, behavior is not merely a succession of discrete reactions to external stimuli. Instead, it is an *organized pattern* of *acts* in which anticipated outcomes condition responses to things that are immediately given. Behavior then is a unified response involving both the organism and the environment. Preliminary and anticipatory responses are made possible through the use of symbols and language.

The Nature of Experience
"A significant unit of behavior has a beginning, a middle, and an end. It originates in a feeling and sense of a tensional or disturbed relationship with surroundings, it continues through the adjustive acts that seek to relieve the tension, it culminates in the establishment of a satisfying, functioning relationship."[9] This three-stage historical process characterizes human experience, which is basically adjustive in nature. Experience includes all that we do, think, and feel, taking the world as we find it. It is most of all a process of acting, doing, and living and our knowledge is incidental to this process. Human beings live both in, and by means of, the environment and are motivated to action because of their loss of integration with their environment. They do or act, they next undergo or feel, and they then change their behavior. The life process is intrinsically a process of adjustment. "In sensory relations with the world, we are actively engaged in a give-and-take with the world; we are doing things to the world and/or objects at the same time that they are doing things to us, impressing us or stimulating us."[10] Behavioral experimentalists call this organism-environment alternating reaction process interaction. But interaction, so defined, has a sharply different meaning from that of the cognitive-field position of simultaneous mutual interaction of a person and his psychological environment (SMI) (see Chapter 9, page 194).

Emergence of Mind and Self
It is communion, made possible by the use of language and other symbols, that has raised humankind to the level of mind and self, above the order of other animals. The human being alone is a talking animal.

> It is as the sentient life of the psycho-physical creature is articulated and made determinate and self-conscious through this participation in the language, the history, the knowledge, and the

practical and fine arts of a society that mind develops in the individual. This social nature of the person has profound implications for our view of educational psychology, for a primary purpose of educational psychology should be to discover how the
organic needs and drives and potentialities of the newborn acquire the determinate interests, patterns, and values they actually
assume as a result of their interaction with the ways of life and
thought of their particular society.[11]

So a self is inherently social in nature. A biological organism becomes a self through its participation in the ways of life and thought
of a community.[12] First there is biological birth and physiological
growth and development. Second there is acquisition of language to
communicate meanings with others, and then there is emergence of
selfhood. So, mind—self-conscious, responsible, reflective, and creative—appears within the natural history of conduct.

Behavioral Experimentalism: The Nature and Source of Truth and Knowledge

For behavioral experimentalists, knowledge or truth consists of hy-
pothesized patterns of facts that work successfully; they test out when
exposed to the rigors of scientific tests. Truth is tentative, not absolute;
it is gained through social experience. It is tested by persons first doing
or acting and then undergoing the results of their behaviors. Knowledge must be capable of being demonstrated to any impartial qualified
observer; it is at all times public. One's knowing so and so means that
one is prepared to demonstrate it. Truth is tested, not by correspondence to absolute reality or by mere internal consistency, but by its
consequences.

Behavioral experimentalists look to experience as the most dependable source of reliable knowledge, and they confine their interests to
analysis and description of experience as it relates to conduct and
knowledge. For them, human experience is not a mysterious process
by which an inner psychic agency or substance seeks to know and to
interact with a world that is external and alien to its own functions.
Neither is it a spectator's report on a given, fixed reality waiting to be
uncovered. Instead, it is a form of adjustive behaving. *Experience*, be-
haviorally defined, is given the lead role in the acquisition of truth. It
is the name for a transactive relationship; one does something to some
thing then that thing responds by doing something to one. It is a serial
alternating reaction, first of the environment to the organism, then of
the organism to the environment. So defined, results of experience are
publicly available and testable, so they are warranted truths.

Since, "Experience is as close as we can get to the 'name' of reality,"[13] human knowledge is characterized by movement and change. So, whatever knowledge is possible is temporary and tentative in character. Accordingly, in place of asserting the existence of absolute truth, "We are driven back . . . upon the finite limitations of human knowing and are required to settle for 'truth' with a lower-case t . . . ."[14] Truth always becomes known in a circumstance of *use*. Hence it is never sought for its own sake. So, behavioral experimentalists customarily either place or imply the word *tentative* before the word *truth* to designate an idea that will serve as truth until something better comes along.[15]

The ultimate test of truth is whether the hunch or hypothesis that is tried out and acted upon really works. Does it explain the situation, rationalize the disparate phenomena that have been observed, or solve the problem? In the degree that a hypothesis performs this duty it is said to be true.

Intelligence, the ability to achieve truth or knowledge, is a dynamic term that signifies not a substantive entity of mental "stuff" but an activity, process, or form of behavior. Intelligence, "operating in quite human ways in relation to quite human problems, will give the answers that are needed to bring the newly born infant to maturity."[16] It "is a characteristic of those actions in which given things are used as signs of future conditions or consequences, and in which present things are turned into means for the achievement of these anticipated consequences."[17]

Behavioral Experimentalism: The Nature and Source of Human Values

Since behavioral experimentalists have little interest in metaphysics, they place great emphasis upon the nature and source of functional values and truths. For them, their emphasis upon earthly consequences of human activity is scientific method as applied to moral questions; the theories of knowledge and values are joined. Moral science, however, differs from physical science in that its experiments must be extended over longer stretches of history and they are less deliberately manageable. But, people should test their values in the same way that they test their truths. An effective method of inquiry should apply, without any abrupt break, to both scientific and valuational problems.

Values are human-made principles measured by the scope and intensity of public consequences in terms of public tastes. "The scope and intensity of public consequence are what help us to measure the morality or immorality of the act."[18] While public standards of goodness and beauty are by no means absolute or unchanging, they are given a status superior to the private standard of any individual. Whereas a socialized approach to life and learning is highly valued, private intuitions of an individual in regard to self-evident values are shrugged off as useless. Societies should construct their own values without transcendental assistance.

Behavioral experimentalists oppose any idea of a universal moral law, which is to be discovered from the essential nature of the cosmos and humanity. They repudiate the entire thesis that people must search for ultimate and changeless values in some reality outside, and beyond the control, of human beings. For them, there are no supernatural eternal values. However, an experimental, scientific study of values goes against the long tradition of absolutistic, rationalistic, intuistic, and authoritarian system of establishing them.

This position, like existentialism, reaffirms the ancient Greek dictum that "man is the measure of all things." But, unlike existentialism, it emphasizes that humankind is a social animal. Its adherents strive to make the human condition more humane by alleviating, in every way possible, humankind's inhumanity to people and by submitting all moral values to the test of human experiences. All values are appraised in the context of their functional social utility. What works, however, is not merely what works for me, but what works for all people.

People get security, not from values that have been handed down to them, but by developing a method for dealing with the problems that they confront. Rather than bringing answers out of the past and imposing them on present problems, people should exercise their ability to achieve answers to problems and difficulties as they arise. They, however, should not operate arbitrarily, ignoring the past. Instead, their values, their knowledge, and their experience should be changed, not haphazardly, but through being directed by human intelligence.

Values emerge within the stresses and strains and hopes and aspirations of everyday life. When refined, they become ideals to serve people effectively until they are either replaced or reconstructed in the interests of humankind. The heritage of democratic, reflective social structures and values provides that which is best for the most people. This heritage is built on faith in the capacity of human intelligence to enable people to enjoy the fruits of cooperative experience.

There are two kinds of values: ethical values and aesthetic values. A synonym for ethics is morals, and these values are established standards of conduct. Ethics, then, deals with moral conduct, what people do. Whatever works for both society and the individuals who compose it is good. This contrasts with absolutistic positions that whatever is Good works. For example, defensible standards of sexual conduct are those that contribute to the welfare of society and its individual members. They are not authoritarian dictums passed down from absolutistic sources. Since a people's ethics are established experimentally, there are no patterns of conduct that are always good and none that are always bad; ethics are situational in nature.

> In fine, the human organism is so constructed that there is a vital continuity—or carryover—from one experience to another. Thus through learning habits and attitudes develop—character is found. Character may be defined as a structure of more or less permanent and integrated modes of interacting with the world of things and persons.[19]

Aesthetic tastes as well as moral judgments are grounded in public experience. Works of art are ultimately tested in the marketplace of public judgment. The purpose of art is to communicate, not to behold and depict ultimate reality. Artists have new insights, feelings, and experiences and attempt to share their experience with others. In this way, art becomes an instrument for the elevation and improvement of human experience.

In contrast with absolutistic philosophies, which place aesthetic determinants in objective standards that are beyond the ken of human experience, behavioral experimentalists see all aesthetic judgment resting upon what we respond to in our world. Whether a Beethoven symphony is beautiful, depends upon how people feel when they hear it.

Behavioral Experimentalism: The Purpose of Education

The purpose of education, for behavioral experimentalists, is to give learners experience in effective experiencing so as to develop fundamental intellectual and moral dispositions in students in the form of desired behavior patterns toward nature and other people. So, education is primarily a social undertaking that involves interpreting, perpetuating, and improving the prevailing social system for succeeding generations. "An adequate theory of education will include concepts of a cause-effect relation between deliberately planned experiences and the learning that results, while at the same time viewing the student as being capable of responsible choice."[20]

The aim of education is this-worldly, flexible, practical, democratic, and scientific. Questions regarding a transcendental deity and people's final end are of little significance. Instead, concerns are with work, politics, human relationships, and better living. Adherents of this position have wedded their naturalistic explanation of thought, life, and society to a spirit of reform of a social order constructed by human beings. They have rejected the notion that a belief in a supernatural deity is essential to the acceptance of the brotherhood of people and the fundamentals of democratic living. For them, *spiritual* means a high order human engagement; it does not involve a deity, angels, the devil, original sin, or immortal souls.

Some specific goals of education, for behavioral experimentalists, are as follows:[21]

1. To develop a world view devoid of all dualisms that separate humankind from nature, spirit from flesh, purpose from mechanism, and morals from the conditions of living.

2. To promote the integration of the development of human values and intelligence through furthering a rich appreciation of the forms and qualities of things in their connection with one another as a positive resource for the development of intellectual powers.

3. To promote the primary mode of experiencing, which involves feeling, doing, and undergoing; and learning from that which is done, suffered, and enjoyed.

4. To emphasize dealing with both things and words. An educational program that emphasizes things and not words is as defective as one that emphasizes words and not things.

5. To give students a balance of primary experience and their learning through the use of literary materials.

6. To develop in students the ability to preserve a characteristic pattern of activity through a process of continuous adjustment with surroundings.

7. To help biological organisms become selves, which are inherently social in nature, through their participation in the ways of life and thought of a community that includes language, history, knowledge, and practical and fine arts.

8. To develop the kinds of persons who will be responsible citizens in a democratic society, not obedient, submissive subjects of an autocratic leadership who carry out the functions that are imposed upon them.

To achieve these goals, teaching-learning situations should be replicas of a problem-filled world, and teachers should serve as managers or directors of the learning process. Students are to learn the desired dispositions or behaviors by doing things or behaving in the desired manner. The socialization of students is emphasized along with their intellectual development. Education should consist of life itself, not a preparation for living. Instead of teaching traditional formal subject matter, teachers should substitute study of specific problem areas such as transportation, communication, and city planning. Through such study, education would take an active role in social change, which is the very vehicle of human progress and fulfillment. In the teaching-learning process, there should be shared analysis and evaluation of what a community does and undergoes. There is an intrinsic connection between freedom of thought and inquiry and the maintenance of a society that is cooperatively controlled in the interest of the good life of all its members.

Behavioral Experimentalism: The Nature of the Learning Process

Behavioral experimentalists employ a theory of humankind, mind, and nature that rejects both the dualism of classical rationalism or idealism and the reductionism of materialism. (Reductionism means that all realities, including biological and psychological ones, are reduced to material properties undergoing change of motion in space.) For behavioral experimentalists, a learner is neither a trained nor an unfolding mind, but a thinking do-er who needs a conditioned intelligence, and a person's level of humanity is measured by the intelligent functioning of his outward behavior. Adherents of this philosophy take seriously Darwin's statement, "There is no fundamental difference between man and the higher animals in their mental functions."[22] So, for them, humanity is continuous with other aspects of nature. There is an essential continuity among all animal species. Behavioral tendencies, including learning, are generally similar throughout the animal kingdom. Hence, conclusions drawn from experimentation with lower animals are equally applicable to human beings. The origin of people's rational power can be traced to simpler types of *adjustive behavior* found in lower animals. The *mind* of a learner, then, is not a special entity or substance, but a distinctive kind of adjustive social behavior.

Social Behaviorism and Learning

Behavioral experimentalism is group oriented. Hence, it has placed a major emphasis upon behavioristic social psychology and sociology. Accordingly, its adherents often have identified their psychological approach to learning as social behaviorism. They have emphasized the social reinforcement of behaviors through the use of serial adaptive responses. They have thought that experimental problem solving, the highest kind of learning, is performed best in social situations. Experimentally oriented learners, to be effective in group behavior, need to be socially attuned to the motivations and capacities of others. Since individual minds are products of society, learning should proceed in a social context; "it is in social and collectivized experiencing that we can come to some highly effective working truths."[23] Hence, "it is through participation in this cultural world with its 'charged and weighed stimuli' that an individual acquires in a few years the meanings which it took his social group many generations of effort, suffering, failure, dis-

covery, and invention to develop. It is the possession and the use of
these meanings which gives human behavior its distinctive intellectual
character."[24]

The Meaning of Learning
The term *learning* is an intellectual construct to account for, or explain,
certain changes in behavior. Human behavior is caused by events that
precede it, and it can be studied and, in ever-increasing measure, be
predicted. A scientific study of human behavior, then, can give humankind an understanding of its learning process.

"The term *learning* may . . . be applied to any process within which
potential stimuli become meaningful, change meaning, are discriminated with respect to possible meaning, and the like."[25] So, learning is
a matter of conditioning meanings, which are the building blocks of
education. "Patterns of meaning can be changed or extended in many
ways, ranging from a simple [passive] reorganization by classical conditioning to a highly creative [active] reconstruction by extended reflective activity."[26] "To attach meaning to an object, event, or situation is
to treat it as a stimulus."[27]

Within its social context, learning is a dynamic process of an organism's growth through the reconstruction of its existing behaviors and
attitudes. An organism's growth means the increase of its intelligence
in the management of life's problematic situations. Thus, there is psy-
chophysical activity of organisms within which, "The disturbed equilibrium of the physical level manifests itself as *need* in the behavior of the
living thing."[28] Accordingly, effort is the property of a homeostatic behavior that is moving toward a satisfying adjustive relationship between the organism and its environment. (Biological homeostasis is an
organism's natural tendency to seek an adjustive balance between itself
and its environment.) So, learning is modification of the forms of living
through organism-environment interaction, "the organism is modified
by that which it encounters, suffers, and enjoys."[29]

Learning: The Reconstruction of Behavioral Experience
For behavioral experimentalists, *experience* is the name for the interactive relationship, of doing-and-undergoing, that is moved to the center
of the stage and given the lead role in epistemology.[30] Being actively
engaged in a give and take with the world, people are constantly doing
things to the world and its objects at the same time that the objects are
doing something to the people involved. Just as in physical engineering we dam a stream and nature responds with water power, so people
do things to the world and the world in response does things to them.

It is within the context of adjustive acts that learning occurs. "The
behavior of the organism is modified as it begins to connect that which

it undergoes with that which it does. Attitudes of expectation are thus developed, and the living form begins to respond to things in terms of what they denote in the way of eventual satisfactions and dissatisfactions. It is through these experiences with environmental conditions that habits develop."[31] Meaning denotes action and expectation. "It is essentially behavioral in character, but the behavior is transactional; that is, it involves interactions of human beings with the environments in which their lives are implicated."[32] The meaning of a thing is determined by the responses it evokes.

Experience, then, is primarily a doing and undergoing involving the organism and the environment, through which the organism's behavior is modified. But, the environment does not adjust to the individual organism; adaptation is always the act of an organism in response to certain stimulation. While the adaptation is conditioned by the environment, the initiative always comes from the organism. Hence, in dealing with its environment, an organism is both *passively* conditioned by its environment and *actively* relating itself to its environment.

Experience includes all that people do, think, and feel. It includes reflection as well as action, feeling as well as knowing, speculating as well as seeing and touching. But, it does not include any transempirical components of reality; those intellectually out of reach of a human biological organism. Experience then, is the recurrent interaction between a biological organism and the things that surround it. Human thinking, self-consciousness, and planned actions are really secondary reflections of specific, observable responses elicited by specific stimulations. "Learning is thus inescapably behavioral in nature. . . ."[33]

Learning and Thinking
Thinking is a type of experience that is derived from learning and from which it gets both its content and its relevance. To repeat, learning is the process of doing or acting then suffering or enjoying the results. Thinking, like learning, is a biological process as are seeing and breathing. "It is within the matrix of these organic-environmental adjustments or transactions that thinking originates."[34]

Thinking is not blind trial and error action; it is action guided by ideas. It denotes an organism's becoming conscious of its own conditions and problems, and consciously striving to deal with them through action guided by an inference, idea, or hypothesis. Within this process, an idea is a plan of action to be undertaken, a hypothesis to be tested by its consequences, and "In man, nature becomes conscious of its own on-going processes. . . ."[35]

The pattern of scientific, experimental inquiry provides the pattern for all significant reflective thought. "A reflective act is an act patterned to deal with some determinate situation of difficulty. Ideas can become general because we encounter many conditions that are so similar that essentially the same response can be made to them."[36]

We know things by receiving impressions from reality, which we then convert into guesses or hypotheses of what is true, then verifying them by trying them out on reality to see how they work. We act on the world, then we receive the reaction of the world; we receive the consequences of our behavior. "This endless progression, this open-ended series of doing-undergoing-doing-undergoing, etc., is the process by which Experimentalists engage in epistemological (knowledge gaining) activity. It is what they call 'reflective thinking'."[37]

Behavioral Experimentalism: The Nature of the Teaching Process

Behavioral experimentalism has been a mainstream application and implementation of Dewey's pragmatic philosophy to principles of education. Adherents of this position have developed curriculums centered on projects and activities, and have generally promoted social reforms through education. They have used a scientific approach to tackle social and economic problems. Since they consider education to have no constant base other than change, they seek reliable knowledge only from actions or behaviors that are relevant to the solution of genuine problems. Adherents of this philosophy think that people should be scientifically oriented as behavioral problem-solvers confronting and resolving the problematic situations with which human life is filled. They generally have opposed having students acquire specific habits through drill in discrete units of manual and verbal behavior.

Teachers select and direct students' experiences through arousing interest in problems that promote appropriate experiences. In the promotion of desired student experiences, they emphasize the importance and use of class communication and group dynamics. Their students learn by *doing*, by solving society-oriented problems. Teachers aim to replace regimented, standardized, routine, and artificial teaching with dynamic teaching that reaches all the children of all the people. They recognize that all kinds of experience educate, but they desire to promote those kinds of experience that are highly educative. They place social living at the heart of the educative process. Instruction is based on the general notion that "we learn what we live."

Teachers want active schools and active students, but they replace chance activity with activity that leads to genuine knowledge and fruitful understanding. Such knowledge and understanding consists of warranted beliefs; they are the offspring of one's doings or behaviors. The crucial test of learning is whether students develop the ability to respond to actual life circumstances with enriched meaning and increased power of control over their environment. "We educate a child and nature responds with certain changes in behavior."[38] To quote Professor Kilpatrick, one of the leading behavioral experimentalists, "We learn what we live. . . . We learn our responses, only our responses, and all our responses; we learn each as we accept it to live by, and we learn it in the degree we accept it."[39]

Teachers as Directors of Learning

Since teaching is essentially a social undertaking, "the teacher must be a director of a social, corporate enterprise, maintaining harmony and morale, provoking from each member of the group full power of participation, and serving as manager of the learning project so that genuine growth takes place in the group and in each individual."[40]

The educative process should begin with learners' identification of their own interests, curiosities, and concerns. But, somehow, the learners must be awakened to their scholastic needs through a process that is centered on the learners themselves. Habits are best developed as the product of significant, purposeful undertakings. In their development of morals, teachers are to:

> Select, then, the moral dispositions you wish the children to have, not only in their thoughts but in their overt conduct. Then contrive real, lifelike situations where those dispositions may be tested at the youngsters' level of experience, where they can recognize through the living of a situation that there are alternate solutions to moral problems and that some alternatives are better than others, because they lead to better consequences.[41]

Teachers as Research Project Directors

Since a person's level of humanity is measured by his outward behavior, a significant idea is, in essence, a plan of action or an hypothesis to be tested by its consequences when applied to actual existences. The development of this power to connect what we do with what we undergo is what education is all about. Students learn subject matter content in the process of using it to solve problems or answer questions. In this way, they use their knowledge and through using it learn.

For behavioral experimentalists, "the *project* method is the learner's version of the research scholar's *scientific* method."[42] A project is a problem that usually is suggested by the instructor. For instance, a class studies what kind of grass should be planted on the athletic field. In so doing, students learn facts of botany, soil structure, drainage, etc. Future Farmers have their animal projects through which they learn principles of animal feeding, marketing, finance, etc. Thus, their experimentation consists of *learning by doing*. The purpose of projects is to develop problem solvers who are scientifically oriented to the continuing task of confronting and resolving the problematic situations with which contemporary life is filled. "Character may be defined as a structure of more or less permanent and integrated modes of interacting with the world of things and persons."[43]

In the teaching process, many teachers who adhere to behavioral experimentalism encourage students to find their own positions in regard to issues, while carefully concealing their positions. They conduct their teaching in the third person so as to make subject matters really object matters. They discourage assertions of personal, subjective views on anything thus making scientific inquiry the primary aim of education. Hence, they promote an uncoerced community of inquiry conducted in light of public consequences.

The Subject Matter Emphasis of Behavioral Experimentalism

The educational aims of behavioral experimentalists have centered upon gaining knowledge for use, as opposed to purely intellectual studies taken for their own sake. Education should be so organized that students are not confined to learning from books, but also have the opportunity to learn through direct interaction with the world of things and persons. For these experimentalists, social studies are of primary importance. But, they should be centered upon things to find out, not memories to be absorbed. Behavioral experimentalists would also offer most conventional courses, but within a changed perspective and purpose.

Adherents of this position have thought that a curriculum should consist of a series of problems to be solved, involving serious contents of the world, rather than a set of subjects to be learned. So, they have tended to invert curriculums from centering on subject matter to centering on *life situations*. For example, they often have belittled courses in history because all that one can do with history is to learn about it; nothing can be done to change it. They would replace pure chronological history with courses in citizenship, social living, and the problems of democracy. Since the social studies are closest to the unsettled and indeterminate features of the world, they should be elevated to a position of primary importance in the life of the young. When taught, traditional subjects should be related to the concept of mankind as a problem-solving animal concerned with control over his environment. The study of geography should begin with the geography of the neighborhood then gradually expand to larger geographic entities: community, state, region, nation, continent, and globe. "A primary principle of the 'activity' curriculum is that we learn *how to think* as we learn how to control experimentally our interactions with the environment."[44] Whether a particular art or science is to be taught is a negotiable matter, to be determined in light of the culture's own ethic.

Footnotes

[1]George S. Counts, *Dare the School Build a New Social Order* (New York: John Day, 1932).

[2]See Peter F. Carbone, Jr., *The Social and Educational Thought of Harold Rugg* (Durham, N. C.: Duke University Press, 1977).

[3]Theodore Brameld, "A Reconstructionist's View of Education," in *Philosophies of Education*, ed. Philip H. Phenix (New York: Wiley 1961), p. 109.

[4]John L. Childs, *American Pragmatism and Education: An Interpretation and Criticism* (New York: Henry Holt and Company, Inc., 1956), p. 44. Reprinted by permission of Holt, Rinehart and Winston.

[5]Ibid., see p. 77.

[6]Ibid., p. 82.

[7]Ibid., see pp. 78–79.

[8]Ibid., p. 67.

[9]Ibid., p. 194.

[10]J. Donald Butler, *Four Philosophers and Their Practice in Education and Religion*, 3rd ed. (New York: Harper & Row, 1968), p. 379.

[11]Childs, *American Pragmatism and Education*, p. 103.

[12]See Marie E. Wirsing, *Teaching and Philosophy: A Synthesis* (New York: Houghton Mifflin, 1972), p. 191.

[13]Van Cleve Morris and Young Pai, *Philosophy and the American School*, 2nd ed. (Boston: Houghton Mifflin, 1976), p. 145.

[14]Ibid., p. 107.

[15]Ibid., p. 147.

[16]H. Gordon Hullfish, "An Experimentalist View of Education," in *Philosophies of Education*, ed. Philip H. Phenix (New York: Wiley, 1961).

[17]Childs, *American Pragmatism and Education*, p. 67.

[18]Morris and Pai, *Philosophy and the American School*, p. 252.

[19]Childs, *American Pragmatism and Education*, p. 110.

[20]H. Gordon Hullfish and Philip G. Smith, *Reflective Thinking: The Method of Education* (New York: Dodd, Mead, 1961), p. 177.

[21]See Childs, *American Pragmatism and Education*, pp. 100–104.

[22]Charles Darwin, *The Descent of Man* (New York: Appleton, 1920), p. 66.

[23]Morris and Pai, *Philosophy and the American School*, p. 161.

[24]Childs, *American Pragmatism and Education*, p. 100.

[25]Hullfish and Smith, *Reflective Thinking: The Method of Education*, p. 180.

[26]Ibid., p. 181.

[27]Ibid., p. 179.

[28]Childs, *American Pragmatism and Education*, p. 89.

[29]Ibid., p. 89.

[30]See Morris and Pai, *Philosophy and the American School*, p. 147.

[31]Childs, *American Pragmatism and Education*, pp. 57–58.

[32]Ibid., p. 47.

[33]Ibid., p. 194.

[34]Ibid., p. 57.

[35]Ibid., p. 66.

[36]Ibid., p. 47.

[37]Morris and Pai, *Philosophy and the American School*, p. 148.

[38]Ibid., p. 65.

[39]William H. Kilpatrick, *Philosophy of Education* (New York: Macmillan, 1951), p. 244.

[40]Morris and Pai, *Philosophy and the American School*, pp. 196–197.

[41]Ibid., p. 282.

[42]Ibid., p. 190.

[43]Childs, *American Pragmatism and Education*, p. 110.

[44]Ibid., p. 24.

BIBLIOGRAPHY

Brameld, Theodore. *Patterns of Educational Philosophy.* New York: Holt, Rinehart and Winston, 1971.

Brown, Bob Burton. *The Experimental Mind in Education.* New York: Harper & Row, 1968.

Carbone, Peter F., Jr. *The Social and Educational Thought of Harold Rugg.* Durham, N.C.: Duke University Press, 1977.

Childs, John L. *Education and Morals.* New York: Appleton, 1950.

Childs, John L. *American Pragmatism and Education: An Interpretation and Criticism.* New York: Henry Holt and Company, Inc., 1956.

Counts, George S. *Dare the School Build a New Social Order.* New York: John Day, 1932.

Cremin, Lawrence A. *The Transformation of the School.* New York: Knopf, 1961.

Darwin, Charles. *The Descent of Man.* New York: Appleton, 1920.

Dewey, John. *The Public and Its Problems.* New York: Holt, 1927.

Dewey, John. *Art as Experience.* New York: Putnam, 1958.

Dupuis, Adrian M., and Norberg, Robert. *Philosophy and Education.* 3rd ed. Beverly Hills, Calif.: Benzinger, Bruce and Glencoe, 1973.

Dykhuizen, George. *The Life and Mind of John Dewey.* Carbondale and Edwardsville, Ill.: Southern Illinois University Press, 1973.

Hook, Sidney. *Philosophy and Public Policy.* Carbondale and Edwardsville, Ill.: Southern Illinois University Press, 1980.

Hullfish, H. Gordon, and Smith, Philip G. *Reflective Thinking: The Method of Education.* New York: Dodd, Mead, 1961.

Kilpatrick, William H., ed. *The Educational Frontier.* New York: Appleton, 1933.

Morris, Van Cleve, and Pai, Young. *Philosophy and the American School.* Boston: Houghton Mifflin, 1976.

Neff, Frederick C. *Philosophy and American Education.* New York: Center for Applied Research in Education, 1966.

Phenix, Philip H., ed. *Philosophies of Education.* New York: Wiley, 1961.

Pratte, Richard. *Contemporary Theories of Education.* Scranton, Pa.: Intext Educational Publishers, 1971.

Raup, R. Bruce, et al. *The Improvement of Practical Intelligence.* New York: Harper & Row, 1950.

Schilpp, Paul A., ed. *The Philosophy of John Dewey.* Evanston, Ill.: Northwestern University Press, 1939.

Shermis, S. Samuel. *Philosophic Foundations of Education.* New York: American Book, 1967.

Wynne, John P. *Theories of Education.* New York: Harper & Row, 1963.

Chapter 9
Cognitive-Field Experimentalism, a Positive-Relativistic Educational Philosophy

Cognitive-field experimentalism is a unique contemporary version of an indigenous American educational philosophy that has been identified as the experimentalist or pragmatic position. (The other leading version is behavioral experimentalism described in Chapter 8.) This philosophy is an attempt to fulfill the need for an educational philosophy that is implemented by a systematic scientific psychology: cognitive-field psychology.

John Dewey recognized that he had not provided an integrated systematic psychological system to implement his otherwise well-rounded educational philosophy. At age eighty he wrote, "Although I have said that I regard psychology as indispensible for sound philosophizing at the present juncture, I have failed to develop in a systematic way my underlying psychological principles."[1] In 1955, Professor Childs surveyed the then existent systematic psychologies, ranging from those centered upon active unfoldment of personalities to those centered upon conditioning of passive organisms, and wrote, "All the foregoing theories of education suffer because they are grounded in inadequate conceptions of behavior and mind."[2]

Cognitive-field experimentalism, like other systematic educational philosophies, is a basic outlook that colors the thoughts, ideals, and actions of its adherents. However, this is a philosophy more concerned with the methods and outlooks of dealing with the problems of humankind than the abstractions that often concern philosophers as such. Accordingly, it is neither a speculative pursuit nor a method of detached analysis, but a systematic outlook that provides a foundation for a program of living. Its adherents construe educational philosophy as the study of such an outlook as it relates to teaching and learning.

Like behavioral experimentalism, cognitive-field experimentalism emphasizes the use of a scientific outlook and reflective thinking. But, cognitive-field psychology gives it a significantly different meaning from that of behavioral experimentalism. Whereas behavioral experimentalism gives primacy to the social behavior of humankind as it has evolved historically, cognitive-field experimentalism centers upon involvements of individuals and the understandings gained as they live their lives in contemporary situations. Also, cognitive-field experimentalism emphasizes the immanent purposive nature of human behavior much more than does behavioral experimentalism. (Purposiveness of behavior will be thoroughly examined later in this chapter.)

This educational philosophy is a contemporary representation of the *pragmatic* position that has extended from William James and John Dewey through thinkers such as Boyd H. Bode, Ernest E. Bayles, and George R. Geiger. However, the tenets of cognitive-field experimentalism are not in complete accord with the ideas of any one of these able leaders.

The principle sources of the psychology with which this educational philosophy is implemented have been the works of Kurt Lewin, Gordon W. Allport, Morton Deutsch, Sigmund Koch, Rollo May, Donald S. Snygg, Edward C. Tolman, and Herbert F. Wright. Contemporary scholars whose research supports various aspects of this position include Albert Bandura, Jerome S. Bruner, Richard de Charms, Edward L. Deci, Norman S. Endler, Fritz Heider, David Magnusson, Walter Mischel, and Bernard Weiner.[3]

Cognitive-field experimentalism is a *positive-relativistic* outlook. A central idea of *relativism* is that an object derives its qualities from the total situation, which includes its surroundings as well as itself. No object has meaning apart from its context, and a thing, event, or idea derives its qualities or meaning through its perceived relationships with other things, events, or ideas. Thus, the way we perceive any object or event is colored by the total perceptual situation, and we deal with objects relationally rather than as things in themselves.

It might appear that, if relativism were a valid concept, a person could never make a definitive statement about anything. However, this is not an insurmountable problem. In order to view a thing relativistically, one simply determines a convenient point of reference. Such relatively fixed points of references are *relatively absolute*. The word *absolute*, so used, as an adjective, means no more than that the point of reference is one of relative fixity or stability. The noun *absolute*, in contrast, connotes an existence outside of any context.

The term *positive* differentiates positive relativism from nihilism, a negative relativism. Nihilism, or nothing-ism, means that life is meaningless and useless. Since nihilists make their relativism absolute, they hold a pessimistic outlook that denies the possibility of any genuine basis for truth and moral principles. Positive relativism, in contrast with nihilistic pessimism, is melioristic. (Melior is the Latin word for better.) *Meliorism* is an emergent synthesis arising from the contrast of two opposing positions: pessimism and optimism. It implies that there is little basis for the assumption that matters are inevitably getting either better and better or worse and worse. But, since conditions can be improved through enhanced learning, we should constantly try to make them better.[4]

It is important to note that cognitive field experimentalists do not deny the existence or even the subsistence (abstract, eternal existence) of absolutes. Instead, they define reality and truth relativistically and assert no position in regard to beliefs concerning absolute existences. The functional application of a concept, not its metaphysical roots, is the criterion of its truth and value. One is being positive-relativistic in his thinking when, being uninfluenced by his commitment to any absolutes, through the use of his human intelligence one endeavors either to improve conditions or to develop something better to take their place and does so by means of a creative intelligence instead of a commitment to an absolute ideal. Hence, the goals and ends of an individual's thought and behavior are to be found within the possibilities of the present situation projected into the future; they are in no sense final and absolute.

Cognitive-field experimentalism functions as an *emergent synthesis* that transcends many of the difficulties underlying other positions and provides a philosophical basis for a set of educational practices that both reflect a knowledge of pertinent scientific evidence and are adequate and consistent. Its adherents take into account the contributions of other philosophical positions and strive to develop an emergent synthesis from these various lines of thought rather than form an eclectic compromise that could take the form of a hodgepodge. Whereas one forms an eclectic compromise by selecting aspects of opposing theories and taking a position somewhere between them, one forms an emergent synthesis by selecting and modifying knowledge from incompatible positions, adding new thinking as needed, and developing a new position that seems internally consistent yet more adequate than its precursors.

Cognitive-Field Experimentalism: The Nature of Reality

Cognitive-field experimentalists approach reality as positive relativists. Hence, they describe reality, but not existence, in psychological terms instead of objective physical terms. Accordingly, reality obtains a functional meaning through use of the concept *perceptual interaction*, which is the key to understanding this educational philosophy. Perceptual interaction, experimentally and situationally defined, is the process of making sense of what persons gain through their senses. Accordingly, their reality consists of what they *make of* that which they gain through their senses. (This concept is expanded on pages 192–193.)

Positive relativists carefully avoid the use of any and all forms of absolutes. The term *absolute* is derived from the Latin *absolvere*, which means to set free. Accordingly, the *noun* absolute refers to something that exists independent of human perception, valuation, and cognition and is not dependent upon anything beyond itself. When a thing or idea is absolute, it is both unlimited and independent of its context. So when one asserts the absolute nature of a thing or concept, one declares that it is free from conditional or mental limitations. Some philosophically absolute realities that may be held to exist are mind, truth, intelligence, beauty, and goodness. However, any of these concepts may also be construed relativistically.

Since cognitive-field experimentalism has emerged as a constructive, positive reaction against the absolutistic ways that have characterized many facets of thinking throughout recorded history, it is not negativistic in any manner or degree. It is neither atheistic, agnostic, or skeptical. Atheism is an absolutistic doctrine that there is no deity. Agnosticism is the belief that the existence or form of God or Ultimate Reality is unknowable. However, unlike atheism, it does not assert that there is no God. Skepticism centers upon uncertainty or doubt in regard to any knowledge of reality.

Cognitive-field experimentalists, then, are neutral but not antagonistic toward any reality except that which can be dealt with through critical intellectual activity in the form of problem solving, scientific method, and reflective thinking. So they emphasize critical intellectual activity as opposed to speculative, metaphysical formulation. But they do not belittle students' *beliefs* so long as they are recognized to be beliefs.

Positive relativism is based upon the premise that ultimate metaphysical reality as a thing-in-itself, if it exists, is unknowable through perceptual means though not necessarily beyond belief. Consequently, positive relativists see little point in concerning themselves with attempts at the observation of ultimate existences as things-in-themselves. Nevertheless, their purpose is not to destroy the ability and desire to speculate about the nature of absolutes, rather to recognize the limitations of such activity. Thus, students may believe what they will about absolute existences, so long as their beliefs do not impede their acquisition and use of scientific, reflective knowledge; knowledge tested by its functional consequences.

A Supposed World of Commonality

Adherents of cognitive-field experimentalism distinguish reality from existence. Without denying the independent existence of objects, or even of other people's ideas, they insist that each person interprets his or her world in such a way as to form a meaningful personal pattern; and that this interpretation of his or her world is the reality upon which each person acts. However, they also recognize that a generalized concept of a *supposed* physical-social world provides an experiential ground for individuals' perceptions of their respective experienced worlds. Accordingly, whereas they recognize that each person acts as if there exists a sort of physical-social world within which he or she lives, they also assume that any perception of a physical-social world will be colored by the purposes and experiences of the observer and by the procedures used in perceiving that world. This does not mean, however, that a person literally creates his or her world. Rather, in any field (science, social relations, morality, even religion) each individual makes, not the world, but a personal notion of the world.

So people operate in relation to a supposed common sense world of commonality that provides raw material for individual perceptions. But a perceptual world is always an individual one. A supposed world of commonality is one accepted as such, or in other words, it is one thought probable. In summary, whereas the common world is a supposed one, one's perceptual world is a predictive or prognostic one. Whereas a supposed world provides nonpsychological foreign hulls of life spaces, perceptual worlds are life spaces, insights into which provide guides for intelligent actions. (See pages 175–178, for a treatment of life spaces.)

Metaphysical Neutrality

In developing a philosophy appropriate and highly pertinent to public education, cognitive-field experimentalists stay neutral on the question of whether or not there is a supernatural or transcendental metaphysical existence. They simply note that persons size up their perceived worlds as they find them in a way that makes things fall into a pattern, and that a perceived world is something significantly different from one accepted as a matter of absolute commitment. Consequently, they emphasize that, in a pluralistic nation committed to religious freedom and separation of church and state, public schools and nonparochial private educational institutions should be truly secular institutions. Accordingly, they neither ridicule nor reject supernaturalism and transcendental teleology; they merely consider them not pertinent to the educational job at hand. Whenever they are serving in their unique capacity, teachers in nonparochial institutions should promote critical intellectual activity, not metaphysical formulations. Accordingly, they, as teachers, should restrict themselves to *secular* functions.

Secular is derived from the Latin word *saeculum*, which means finite time. Thus, secular matters are those belonging to the present, empirical world as contrasted with *nonsecular* matters, which relate to an eternal, metaphysical world. Whereas what people have done or are doing about religion is a secular matter, religions as such are nonsecular. The historical fact that certain peoples have believed in the immortality of souls is a secular concept, but the immortality of souls is a nonsecular one. Its restricting its studies to secular matters means that a school should not raise those scientifically unanswerable metaphysical questions about which humankind has been, is now, and will continue to be concerned. However, it should study the nature of such questions and the history of their introduction into the thinking of humanity.

In keeping with the first amendment of the United States Constitution, which provides for the separation of church and state, a teacher in a public school should not appear either to favor or disfavor any student's metaphysical or nonsecular beliefs. Teachers should assume a neutral stance in relation to all nonsecular commitments. In this way, educators would adhere to the dictum, as stated by Justice Frankfurter, that "no religion shall either receive the state's support or incur its hostility."[5]

The need for confinement of educational activities to secular matters in no way implies that teachers should exclude the study of moral values from their classrooms. Instead, they should promote the historical study of various ideological foundations of morality, and emphasize that in all classroom deliberations a secular basis for morality should be sought. Since secularly developed values have an empirical basis, they should be given an importance equal to that of any other subject matter. However, it should be left to students' home and other nonschool relationships to develop metaphysical sanctions for the value systems that may be fostered at school.

Cognitive-Field Experimentalism: The Nature of Human Motivation

Cognitive-field experimentalists think of people as neutral-interactive purposive persons in simultaneous mutual interaction (SMI) with their psychological environments. They approach the study of human motivation with the conviction that any human being, in keeping with that person's attained level of development and understanding, does the best that he or she knows how for whatever he conceives himself to be. This means that humankind manifests *situational choice;* that is, at any time unit of one's continuous series of life spaces, a person may to a significant extent choose the way to turn.

The concept *situational choice* is an emergent synthesis arising from the conflict between the ideas of *transcendental free will* and a *mechanistic determinism*. (See the Glossary for descriptions of free will and determinism.) Cognitive-field experimentalists think that human beings make real choices, but they do not identify with either side of the free will-determinism argument. They simply mean that "every intelligent act involves selection of certain things as means to other things as their consequences."[6] At a point in a situation when a choice is involved, a person really decides which way to go. So, intelligent human action is taken to be immanently purposive, and it is best interpreted in light of the goals it is designed to achieve.

The purposiveness of cognitive-field experimentalism, then, is immanent in (operating within) not transcendental to (extending beyond) the world of experience; it prevails in work-a-day life situations. When a child or youth is behaving purposively, that person is pursuing goals in light of his or her insights; the person is behaving intelligently. The goal or goals toward which the individual strives psychologically exist in that individual's present life space. The essence of a goal is in what is expected or hoped for, not in what finally happens. Although the goal may be reached in the future, or never reached at all, we are affected now by that goal, as a psychological fact. For example, a student's goal to become a teacher is a goal toward teaching as presently viewed, which may be a far cry from teaching as it will eventually be experienced.

Cognitive-Field Psychology and Life Space

It is its psychological implementation that makes cognitive-field experimentalism distinctly different from behavioral experimentalism.[7] The purpose of cognitive-field psychology is to formulate tested relationships that predict the behavior of individuals in specific psychological situations. In order to understand and predict such behavior, one must consider a person and his psychological environment as a pattern of interdependent facts and functions. One starts with a model of a person and the surrounding world as it is pertinent to that person. Learning modifies the person's world as represented by the model.

Life space, the psychological model, contains the individual person, the goals that are sought, negative goals to be avoided, the barriers between person and goals that restrict his psychological movement toward them, and the paths (potential and actual) to those goals. Psychological paths are ways of achieving goals. All psychological events (acting, thinking, learning, hoping, dreaming) are mutual functions of a whole made up of coexisting facts that constitute a life space; not isolated properties of the individual or the environment. A life space represents, not physical objects as such, but functional and symbolic relationships. Hence, it includes presently perceived objects and memories, myths, art, anticipation, and religion. The life-space model provides a pattern for thinking, as contrasted with a picture of an absolute existence.

The life-space concept is a scientific formulation used to express what is possible and impossible in the life of a person and to anticipate what is likely to occur. It represents the total pattern of factors or influences that affect an individual's behavior at a certain moment or a longer unit of time. Hence, it includes the person, the person's psychological environment, the person's insights and goals, and their dynamic interrelations. A child, as it develops, lives through a more or less continuous and overlapping series of life spaces. Each life space of a moment or longer duration contains a *person* and the person's *psychological environment* of that unit of time; both are surrounded by a non-psychological foreign hull. (See Figure 2.)

Psychological Person.   Cognitive-field psychologists place one's person at the center of one's psychological field. A *person* is that body or configuration of matters with which one identifies oneself, of which one takes care, and to which one gives one's allegiance. So defined, it is not a fixed quantity or a static thing. It is achieved, as contrasted with being inherently possessed. One's person may include one's body, speech, thoughts, home and family, church, property, and social roles.

Under no circumstances is a psychological person considered either a biological organism or a mystical substantive self, or a combination of the two. A person is not limited to mind or body, nor is it a mind and body. Rather, a person is a purposive behaving self that is the

Figure 2. Life space, the psychological model.

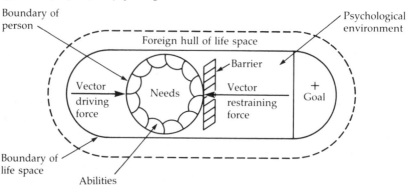

From Morris L. Bigge, *Learning Theories for Teachers,* 3rd ed. (New York: Harper & Row, 1976), p. 195. Reprinted by permission.

center of abilities and needs; it is what a child means when it says "I"
or "me." The concept person may be considered synonymous with
self. Whereas teachers more often think of Billy Smith and Sally An-
derson as persons, Billy and Sally, when thinking of themselves, are
more likely to use the term self.

It is within the personal-social living of an individual that a person
emerges and continues to change throughout life. It may be said that
the basic human need is for preservation and enhancement of this
emergent self or person. One even owns a loyal dog in order to enhance and give constancy to one's psychological person.

Psychological Environment.   A unique psychological environment
envelops a person. It includes all the things, functions, and relationships that, at a given time, surround the person and mean something
to that person as well as their meanings. It is that which a person
makes of aspects of the physical and social environment. It includes
everything in which, toward which, or away from which the person
can make psychological movement; can do anything about.

A person's psychological environment, then, contains that part of
the physical and social environment with which he or she is psychologically engaged at a specific moment or longer expansion of time because it is relevant to the person's purposes at that time. Such an environment is not an undifferentiated medium in which a person is
immersed. It consists of objects and events, not a sum total of optical,
acoustical, and tactile sensations. So construed, a person and his psychological environment are neither independent nor dependent but interdependent variables.

An individual's perceptions of his or her person and environment
consists of *regions* and *subregions* that are distinguishable, functional
parts of a life space. These functional regions are psychologically significant presently existing, remembered, or contemplated conditions,
places, things, and activities defined functionally as parts of a life
space. Regions may consist of personalities, objects, and events; conceptions of aspects of oneself; specific activities; states of being; and
membership in groups or classes of people.

Foreign Hull.   A life space, consisting of a person and his psychological environment, is always surrounded by a nonpsychological foreign hull, which is composed of those aspects of the person's physical
and social environment that are observable by the one studying that
person, but that, within the unit of time under consideration, have no
significance for the person being studied; they are outside the person's
psychological environment. Since the content of a foreign hull has
physical-social but not psychological reality, its physical and social con-

ditions both provide and limit the variety of a person's possible life spaces. Anything that appears to be in a person's physical environment, but of which he or she is completely oblivious, is in the foreign hull of that person's life space. However, anything with which the person interacts in any way, either positively or negatively, is no longer in his foreign hull but in that person's life space proper.

A person, the person's psychological environment, and the foreign hull of that person's life space are represented by concentric figures. A person is within the psychological environment and both are within the foreign hull. Nonpsychological factors observed only by an outsider can at the next moment become psychological ones for the person being studied. There can be movement both ways through the boundary of a person or a life space or through any of their regions. For an aspect of the physical world to influence the intelligent behavior of a person, it must be moved from a foreign hull into the person's life space through interaction with it. (Psychological interaction is explained on pages 192–193.)

The Principle of Contemporaneity

Contemporaneity means literally all at one time. A psychological field or life space is a construct of such nature that it contains everything psychological that is taking place in relation to a specific person at a given time. The unit of time viewed microscopically is a moment; but macroscopically it may cover hours or even weeks. Whatever the length of time, everything is going on at once, that is the meaning of *field*.

The principle of contemporaneity means that psychological events are determined by conditions at the time behavior occurs. One cannot derive behavior from either the future or the past as such. Since neither past nor future events now exist, they cannot, as such, have any effect on the present. Thus, influence of a future can only be anticipatory, and effects of a past can only be indirect. Nevertheless, through the continuity of life spaces, past psychological fields do have their trace, or residue, in a present field that influences a person's behavior. *Trace* is a region or condition of a present life space that has similarity to a characteristic of earlier life spaces; it means that there is some similarity between regions of succeeding life spaces.

In order to understand a person's present personality structure, it is often convenient and perhaps necessary to inquire into the individual's personal history. But such inquiry is merely a means of knowing the present structure of his life space. A person's psychological field that exists at a given time contains, as well as the environment of the present, the views of the individual about the future and the past. But, any psychological past or psychological future is a simultaneous part of a psychological field existing at a given time.

An individual's views about the past, as about the rest of the physical and social world, are often incorrect; nevertheless, they constitute a significant psychological past in that person's own life space. Furthermore, the goals of an individual as a psychological fact lie in the present, and they too constitute essential regions of his life space. The contents of the goals may lie in the future, and they may never occur, but the nature of an expectation is not dependent upon the event coming to pass. If a warrior were brave in order that in the future he would go to the happy hunting ground, whether or not a future happy hunting ground actually exists would have no bearing on his bravery. His happy hunting ground is a goal region of his contemporaneous life space.

Personal Needs and Environmental Values

Within cognitive-field psychology, one's motivation develops through one's differentiating one's life space into regions and subregions (functional objects and activities) and simultaneously cognitively structuring the regions and subregions by grasping some of their meaningful relationships. As new regions and subregions emerge, they also are to some degree structured cognitively; that is, they are made meaningful in line with the person's purposes. Since motivation is goal oriented, it centers upon personal needs and correlative environmental values. Motivation occurs, not because of past experience or conditioning, but as an aspect of a current psychological situation. It arises when one perceives an inadequacy, disharmony, or inconsistency in one's values, outlooks, attitudes, or actions. Thus, it takes the form of needs.

Needs. A psychological need is a self-centered hunger that motivates a person to work toward a goal or avoid or seek relief from a negative goal. Needs, then, are central regions of a person. But, a need does not in itself cause behavior; part of the environment, a perplexing or goal factor, must also be operative for a psychological need to exist. When perplexed, a person feels a necessity to do something but has no good idea of what to do; the person has a need even though no definite goal has yet been formulated in relation to it. In a psychological situation needs and goals, although not identical, are closely interrelated. Accordingly, a person's purposive behavior may be described either as attempts to reach goals or as attempts to satisfy needs. Goal achievement and need satisfaction are accomplished through the same process of intelligent action. Behavior in a specific situation usually stems from a combination of several needs; it is a derived need. During one's lifetime a person's needs constantly change. Nevertheless, many of one's needs and other features of one's successive life spaces remain approximately the same over long periods of time. This latter tendency involves a *continuity* of life spaces. There are, however, periods of crisis in a person's life when quick and striking changes in needs occur, even in those needs for which a high level of continuity had been established.

Valences.   The imperative or challenging aspects of an environment are its *valences*. Valences make the regions of an environment either attractive or repulsive; valences are either positive or negative. The valence of an object or activity usually arises from the object as a means of, or barrier in the way of, satisfying a need. Thus, the valences of environmental objects and the needs of a person are correlative, and the valences of factors of one's environment determine the direction of a person's psychological movement. An individual's person-centered needs and abilities parallel that individual's environment-centered goals and valences. But to speak of needs as centered in the person and of goals and valences as centered in the environment does not mean that they are located in these respective places. They are located in a situation or life space; in both person and environment. Centeredness merely indicates a closer identity with one than the other.

Any statement about needs involves positive and negative valences. For example, an increase in the intensity of a need (for instance, the need for recreation) leads to an increase in the positive valence of certain activities (going to the movies, reading a book) and an increase in the negative valence of certain other activities (doing hard work).

The particular objects or activities that bear valences, and the strengths of their valences, are quite different for a baby, a kindergartner, an adolescent, and an adult. A child's insistence on independence in some activity indicates that the activity has taken on a definite valence and that a part of the child's goals has become the enhancement of the child's self. A boy of three trying to jump down a step may refuse help. The step, to him, has a definite valence. Unless he reaches certain results by his own effort, he will not be content. This is evidence of emergence of a psychological self.

Cognitive-Field Experimentalism: The Nature and Source of Truth and Knowledge

The positive-relativistic orientation of cognitive-field experimentalism implies that truth or knowledge is a matter of human interpretation rather than a literal description of an absolute world. When we assume that objects have to be dealt with relationally, rather than as things-in-themselves, a distinctive method of defining truth or knowledge is required, as is an equally distinctive process of arriving at it.

When considering their truth-value system, cognitive-field experimentalists think with Dewey that "the aims and ideals that move us are generated through imagination. But they are not made out of imaginary stuff. They are [human creations] made out of the hard stuff of the world of physical and social experience."[8] Accordingly, humankind derives a general scheme of experimental truth and values through experience itself, not from universal principles that have a cosmic origin and sanction.

The positive relativism of cognitive-field experimentalism involves humankind creating truth, not merely finding and reporting it. Cognitive-field experimentalists substitute the fruits of human interactive experience for any a priori, presumptive intuitions or operations of pure reason that would have absolute, nonempirical truth as their object. For how can a person know what he or she would know if it were possible to know what one is by nature unequipped to know?

Nature of Truth or Knowledge

Truth consists of insights developed and held by human beings using human methods. It is an open-ended product of an open-ended system of thought. So defined, it is not based upon eternal and universal principles. It is human-made, and human beings will change it as needed. This does not mean that truth is unimportant or ephemeral. It does mean that it evolves as human experience develops.

Truths, then, are warranted assertibilities established through empirical, experimental study. They are not inherent in ideas or objects, but are that which befalls ideas in the process of being tested in life situations. Facts become knowledge when they are judged to be relevant to the solution of problems, and such judgment is tested in the crucible of experience. This does not mean that truth has no objective standard and that it always varies from person to person, group to group, and time to time. In fact, many truths have been so adequately tested that we may safely treat them as if they were certainties. However, the appropriate definition of certainty is "something in which I have tremendous faith."[9] Hence, we talk, act, and live as if we were completely confident in the reality of an existent universe, an out-thereness, simply because it is immensely advantageous for us to do so.

Since relativists regard truth as tentative and instrumental (not final), they refrain from making dogmatic statements about the nature of humanity and the universe. Rather, a statement is considered true because of its usefulness: its accuracy in prediction and the agreement of people competent in its area to the possible consequences of acting on it. It should be emphasized that a relativistic definition of truths in no way discounts their value.

The Source of Truth and Knowledge
Cognitive-field experimentalists' approach to the achievement of knowledge is prospective, not retrospective. Predictable outcomes in given situations, not logical roots or historical origins as such, are what count most. Consequently, they seek not historic circumstances but insights into contemporary experiences: life spaces. Such insights are meanings that may be considered rules for action; and meanings, at their best, are insights abstracted and generalized so as to fit most any occasion. The meaning of a statement lies in the difference it makes in purposeful operations. Hence, a statement that describes matters also prescribes how they may be applied in future situations.[10]

When truth is conceived relativistically, verification is truth making, not truth finding. Even the axioms of mathematics are postulated creations of human thought. To research scholars, facts are *taken* not *given*. They are constructed from controlled observations guided by hypotheses and theories. Interpretation of the acquisition of knowledge is a description of the way problems are actually solved by scientific and reflective means; "there is but one sure road of access to truth— the road of patient, cooperative inquiry operating by means of observation, experiment, record and controlled reflection."[11] The basic objective in inquiry is not a report on some preexistent, absolute reality, but the development of instruments whereby people may more effectually find their way about in the world.

In the process of creating truth human beings develop and use, not exact pictures of an absolute reality, but conceptual models. A good conceptual model is a *cognitive map* that enhances our capacity for finding our way about in the world.[12] Since any hypothesis is regarded as true that most successfully explains the pertinent facts or data, or solves the problem at hand, the worth of a model consists in its aid to prediction. Models should be made as comprehensive in scope as possible. However, even in the same general area of study, different models may be more usable for different purposes. For instance, when one plans and makes a short trip, one uses a flat map; when the trip is much longer, one uses a globe; and when one is a geographer attempting an exact mathematical measurement of the earth, one's model is an oblate spheroid.

Our actions are based on the confidence we hold in our models, the range of which may extend from mere likelihood to certainty. However certainty, experimentally defined, means extreme confidence, not absolute surety. There are scientific truths upon which we would stake very, very great odds. Nevertheless, we should not assume any of these to be absolute. Since the number of trials testing any truth is finite, scientific or reflective prediction or probability is likewise finite.

Everyone cannot check everything from scratch. Nevertheless, it is hazardous to accept any purported truth that cannot be verified experimentally. In our use of models, we must give credence to the observations and findings of others who are competent in their fields of study. But, we should critically examine any conclusion, to the extent of our ability, to make sure that it is implicit in the pertinent data that are available. Relationships that are called *universals* are thoughts tested by their consequences and ultimately agreed upon by a community of competent knowers. Scientific study does not establish absolute inevitability, but only relative frequency and probability. Objectivity in science means being public, not being absolute. So, no special privilege need be accorded authority or tradition. The essence of a scientific outlook is devotion to empirical experimentation in a world in which there are no final truths. Free inquiry, after the pattern of scientific procedure, is the most reliable road to dependable truth.

The measuring sticks or criteria of scientific truth may be encompassed under the headings of adequacy and harmony in light of obtainable data. According to the principle of adequacy, all known pertinent facts must be taken into consideration. No fact may be ignored, no matter how unpalatable it might seem. A conclusion, to be properly scientific, must harmonize all the data; that is, it must make the data add up. If a single pertinent fact seems to be contradictory, if it remains unexplained, then the conclusion is not to be trusted.

Cognitive-field experimentalists do not think of science as consisting of a hierarchy: physics, chemistry, and biology at the top; psychology and education at the bottom. For them, each science is an area for empirical inquiry in its own right. Taking their positive relativism seriously, they advocate cooperation among all scientific endeavors, but do not concede that any area of science should be restricted by the specific laws, principles, concepts, and definitions of a sister science. They recognize that humankind may be studied in physical, biological, or psychological dimensions, and they in no way disparage the physical or biological study of Homo sapiens. However, they insist that to understand the human learning processes we must center our efforts on the psychological dimension. Accordingly, psychology and education should benefit from the results of scientific inquiry conducted in all areas, but they need not be bound by the constructs of any one of them.

Cognitive-field experimentalists extend their relativistic, open-ended outlook to embrace all intellectual and valuational matters. Thus, they leave the way open for empirical verification of hypotheses that have previously been supported only by intuitive feelings or dogmatic beliefs, provided the hypotheses are stated in such a way as to be susceptible of empirical verification.

Cognitive-Field Experimentalism: The Nature and Source of Human Values

Values, for cognitive field experimentalists, are instrumental, not ultimate or final, and humankind is the originator, conservator, and changer of its values. What count are the foreseeable consequences of a proposed line of conduct, as they bear on human relations. Values center upon preservation and enhancement of selves both individually and collectively, and there is no necessary conflict between the two. Enhancement of individuals and enhancement of the groups to which they belong are complementary processes.[13]

Simply stated, values consist of what we prize or are willing to settle for. However, immediate likings, enjoyments, or desires are not in themselves values. But, they do provide problematic material for the construction of values. Likings are often associated with values, but they become values only when they are judgmentally approved; some become ends to be sought, whereas others are ends to be rejected.

Joining of Truths and Values

Through an understanding of a cognitive-field experimentalist interpretation of experience and reality within which intellectual and emotional factors are interwoven, truth and value acquire a joint meaning that gives a continuity of cognitive and evaluational functions. Accordingly, ethical and artistic values, like intellectual ones, are warranted assertibilities resulting from inquiry and reflection. Thus, there is no sharp cleavage between the problems of science and the problems of values. All worthy ideas or propositions are instruments for human service and progress whose use may be established through reflective processes.

Values Within Cognitive-Field Psychology

Cognitive-field psychology treats human values in terms of needs and valences. A *need* develops through one's interaction with one's psychological environment. It is a state of a person that influences one's behavior toward a goal. A *valence* is an imperative environmental fact in that it is a property of a region or functional part of one's environment that either draws the person psychologically toward it or repels the person away from it. As contrasted with needs, which are person-oriented, valences are focused on environment. When a girl has a strong need for a bicycle, the valence of a bicycle is high. So valence and value are synonymous concepts.

The Source of Values

Since truth and values are instrumental not final, they are exposed to the continuous test of human experience. The appropriateness of an act is dependent, not on an absolute standard, but upon the individual and group purposes and foresights involved in it. Through intelligent valuation, the means by which we make a living is transformed into ways of making a life that is worth the living. Valuation, then, does not involve an escape to something beyond experience, but is concerned with people making the most and best possible growth through both personal and social experience. And growth is upward improvement from where they now are, not progress toward some ultimate, absolute perfection that transcends the work-a-day world.

Cognitive-field experimentalism is melioristic in regard to values as well as knowledge. *Meliorism* signifies the outlook that matters can be constantly improved through learning, so we always should strive to make them better. Progress, then, is most dependably achieved through our extension of the significance of ourselves and our environments as we experience them. *Better* is a more worthy concept than *best*; it is better to travel than to arrive. Ends in view, when reached, become means in a continuing experiential process. Growth, traveling, cuts across any discontinuity of ends and means; it is not a means to any ultimate or final end. Moreover, we may grow upward from where we now are without an ultimate target toward which we are reaching.

Morality and values, as developed in public schools, should be independent of any specific theological foundation. However, this does not mean that a student's interlacing of values and theology should be belittled by the school but that the students and teacher should approach valuation using the tools of human intelligence and invention.

Although one does the best one knows how for whatever one thinks one is, through holding an inadequate conception of the personal-social nature of human beings one may unwittingly injure oneself. Overemphasis upon individualism can be pushed to the point where it actually discounts the dignity and worth of individuals; human beings are cultural as well as purposive and intelligent. Accordingly, the idea of absolute autonomy of individuals is a completely inadequate guideline for the direction of human affairs. The course of the cognitive structures of a person's life spaces, which are in continuous psychological movement, can be predicted accurately only in relation to the personal-social environment within which it proceeds.

The same general pattern of inquiry, though not necessarily the same methods and techniques, followed in the resolution of conflicts of knowledge in scientific disciplines can and should be used to establish effective value judgments. Everything, including values, should be judged by its consequences in and on human experience. Values, arise within the stream of experience, and there is an aspect of value in every experience from that of loving someone to that of gaining an understanding of the most abstract mathematical formula. All conduct that is not either blindly impulsive or mechanically routine involves valuation. "The problem of valuation is thus closely associated with the problem of the structure of the sciences of *human* activities and *human* relations."[14]

Although experimentalists have no single criterion of value, they in no way endorse moral anarchy. It is not a case of anything goes. Some values really have validity. Furthermore, values are not equally acceptable, but their degree of acceptability is not determined by resorting to an absolutistic source. A moral life involves something other than a continuous state of contentment. It implies involvement and even perplexity, and it entails a process of living within which persons effectually rework or reconstruct both themselves and their environment so as to reach goals that they consider important in light of their purposes.

Since cognitive-field experimentalists do not evaluate attitudes and action on a metaphysical basis, they consider them valuable or virtuous when they reflect (1) confidence in the continued development of truth through directed, cooperative human endeavor; (2) devotion to experimental study in an open-ended universe; (3) pursuance, even against obstacles, of activities in behalf of ideal ends because of the conviction of their general and enduring value; (4) expansion and enrichment of ideals and application of the ideals to actual life and growth; and (5) development of richer selves in terms of insights, goals, ideals, and interests that provide a pattern of objectives for the improvement of personal-social living.

Observation of these criteria of value would mean commitment to a democratic way of life. However, the commitment would be of such nature that it does not elevate democracy to the position of an absolute. Instead, democracy would represent the best insights that human beings have, to date, about what is required for the fullest development of individuals and society. The distinctive characteristic that prevents it from becoming absolute is the inherent principle that whenever human insight is improved, human standards will vary accordingly. As intellectual development proceeds, such variation could come to replace the very principles of democracy with something better. In their broader sense, democratic principles apply to all phases of human activity. They entail a continuous extension of common interests and purposes among people, despite their differences, as they construct a way to a better life.

Cognitive-Field Experimentalism: The Purpose of Education

A democratic society has a unique culture, and a basic problem of education involves its proper relationship to that type of culture. *Culture* means the established way of life or the social heritage of a people. It consists of all the socially transmitted results of human experience through which a group of people conduct its way of life. It includes customs, knowledge, morals, ideals, and standards and the institutions through which they are manifested.

The Appropriate Relationship of Education to the Culture

There are three basically different and conflicting attitudes in regard to education's proper function in preserving and improving the culture: We may envision its performing the functions of a cultural architect, a conservator of the culture, or a democratic leader in development of citizens' insights pertinent to amending the culture. Education that performs the functions of a cultural architect provides the ideas and directives for renovating the culture in line with the thinking of educational experts in regard to what the culture should be like. This position is often identified as *social reconstructionism.* Obviously, it is an autocratic or authoritarian approach to education. As a conservator of the culture, education serves communities by perpetuating them in their existing forms. It preserves traditional knowledge, beliefs, attitudes, and values. This, too, is an autocratic, authoritarian approach to education.

Cognitive-field experimentalists think that education should provide democratic leadership in development of citizens' insights pertinent to amending the culture. Education should promote a study of the prevailing aspects of existing cultures, but always with the purpose of helping students develop insights pertinent to amending them; that is, changing them for the better. The ideal role of educators in a democracy is neither to change cultures in a revolutionary way nor to conserve them in their present forms. Instead, educators should help students examine their cultures, see the contradictions and confusions within them, and find ways of progressively refining them.

When the subject matter under study is some aspect of the culture, the primary purpose of the investigation should be neither to change it nor to preserve it, but to appraise it and strengthen its viability through finding ways to improve it as it is being transmitted to new generations. Accordingly, an attempt is made to uncover contradictions and conflicts in a culture and to determine possible ways of resolving them. The ultimate hope of democratic educators is that the culture will be progressively refined by a citizenry that has learned the habit of studying problems in a reflective, democratic manner. So education should foster social change, but help to keep it orderly and constructive.

A teacher, as a democratic leader, need not discard all personal preferences. Like either a social reconstructionist or a conservator of culture, the teacher too holds certain ideas in preference to others. However, the method of teaching, unlike that of either a social reconstructionist or a conservator of culture, is the method of democracy. In a very real sense, teacher and students together strive to gain more adequate insights for building a better culture.

Social and technological changes are now sweeping the world at such a rate that almost any specific fact or procedure taught today is likely to be obsolescent even before learners complete their formal education. Consequently, a more serviceable goal for education than the mere accumulation of facts and behaviors is the creative discovery by the students of worthy concepts and generalizations, and the development of thinking processes and cooperative learning skills. In this way, the achievement of significant learning by students has much in common with the resolution of social issues by a democratic society.

The Appropriate Relationship of Educators to Students
In their relationships with students, educators may be either authoritarian, anarchic, or democratic. In authoritarian situations teachers exercise firm, centralized control. They closely direct the actions of their students. They do the planning for the classes and issue the directions. They tell students what to think as well as what to do. In anarchic situations, teachers and other professional personnel do not lead the students in any manner. They are present, they might answer questions, but essentially students are permitted to follow their own initiative. They decide what they will do and when they will do it.[15]

In the *democratic learning situation* advocated by cognitive-field experimentalists, the teacher plays the role of a democratic group leader. Within such a situation, the principal business of education, learning, is promoted through teacher-student cooperative endeavor. The teacher's chief purpose is to lead students in the study of significant problems in a specific area. Such study presupposes interchange of evidence and insights, give-and-take, and respect for one another's ideas. In a democratic classroom, ideas are subject to vigorous criticism from both student and teacher. In this way both students and teacher learn through reconstructing their life spaces so as to give them more meaning. Although a teacher may be an authority on a subject, and should be to teach it best, the situation is so arranged that students are encouraged to think for themselves in the interest of their long-sighted well-being. To think means to arrive at an effective conclusion based upon a substantial amount of checkable empirical evidence.

In its deeper meaning, democratic education is a process of helping students in the formation of fundamental intellectual-emotional dispositions toward the world, including their fellow humankind. In other words, education "is that reconstruction or reorganization of experience which adds to the meaning of experience, and which increases ability to direct the course of subsequent experience."[16] Teaching, then, should be pointed toward experiences that assist students in making their outlooks more adequate and more harmonious and thereby more serviceable as guides for actions. Accordingly, it should be more exploratory than explanatory and more provocative than evocative. That is, it should teach people how to think more than what to think. It should strive to produce partisans, but be nonpartisan in the achievement of this task. It behooves a nation that is straining in democratic directions to maintain democratic relationships between teachers and students. Furthermore, evidence now available suggests that students probably learn more effectively in a democratic classroom than in one that is either authoritarian or highly permissive.[17]

Democracy and Freedom

The definition of democracy often has consisted of a compromise position that combined aspects of both autocracy and anarchy. Accordingly, democracy often has been taken to mean liberty or license for anyone to do as he pleased, provided those freedoms did not interfere with his neighbors' freedoms. In this way democracy acquired a negative meaning.

Cognitive-field experimentalists conceive modern functional democracy, not as a compromise, but as an emergent social structure that acquired its meaning through people's understanding of both autocracy and anarchy, their rising above them, and their formulating a new synthesis to replace the earlier compromise. Whereas autocracy implies *unequal freedom* and anarchy is characterized by *unlimited freedom*, democracy entails *equally limited* freedom. As a third-grader stated after his class had been discussing democratic ideas, "Then it is not what you will let me do or what I will let me do, but what we will let us do."

Cognitive-Field Experimentalism: The Nature of the Learning Process

It is in its treatment of the learning process that cognitive-field experimentalism differs most from behavioral experimentalism. Cognitive-field psychology has its deepest roots in field psychology.[18] It also has some roots in Gestalt psychology, but it is significantly different from the Gestalt position in that it has lost any Gestaltist idealistic orientation. The basic principle of cognitive-field psychology is that, in keeping with his level of development and understanding, each person does the best that each knows how for whatever that person thinks he or she is; that is, the person is *immanently purposive*.[19]

The constructs and methodology of *cognitive-field psychology* provide an experimentalist philosophy with an advantageous instrument with which to establish warranted assertibilities not absolute truths concerning human learning. (Warranted assertibilities are propositions affirmed by checkable evidence.) Whereas behavioristic psychologies have emphasized overt behavior, cognitive-field psychology concerns itself with outward behavior only insofar as it may provide clues to what is transpiring psychologically, that is, in accordance with the logic of a growing mind or intelligence. Since learning is an enduring change in knowledge, skills, attitudes, or values, it may or may not be reflected in changes in overt behavior. One does not learn by doing except when the doing contributes to a change in one's cognitive structure or understanding. Learning occurs through, and results from, experience; however, "mere activity does not constitute experience."[20] For an activity to be experience, it must feed into a realization of the consequences that accompany it.

To be psychological in pursuits, a cognitive-field oriented teacher must look at the world through the eyes of the learner. To describe a situation psychologically, the teacher must describe that which confronts the individual under study. A person's learning cannot be ascertained merely through direct observation; it must be inferred through observation and study of the person's total situation, which is a *life space* or *psychological field*.

Learning: A Change in Insight or Cognitive Structure
According to cognitive-field psychology, a child or youth in a learning situation is not unfolding according to nature, neither is he or she being passively conditioned to respond in a desired manner. Rather, at one's level of maturity and comprehension, one is differentiating and restructuring oneself and one's psychological environment; one is gaining or changing one's insights. *Insight*, concisely defined, is a basic sense of or feeling for relationships. Thus, it is a meaning or discernment. A generalized insight is an understanding. Although there is nothing about the term insight that requires it to be right in any absolute sense, it is a grasp of a situation that often goes deeper than words. So, insight into a situation is its meaning. Meaning, so used, denotes that to which an object or idea points or what it signifies. The insights of persons are not equated with their consciousness or awareness or their ability to describe them verbally. Instead, the essence of insight is a sense of or feeling for the pattern in a life situation. The total pattern of insights constitutes the cognitive structure of a person's life space.

Learning, then, is a process whereby, through interactive experience, persons gain new insights or understandings, or reconstruct old ones, regarding themselves and their environment. They change the cognitive structures of their life spaces so as to make them more serviceable for future guidance. Insights or cognitive structure are answers to questions concerning such matters as how something is constructed, what is related to what, what one belongs to, how one does something, of what good a thing or an action is, and what one should be doing. They may be preverbal, verbal, or nonverbal. One may gain an insight before one has words to express it, one may have a complete and exact verbalization involving some degree of insight, or an insight may be achieved with no verbalization accompanying it.

Insights may be deeply discerning or they may be shallow. They may serve as dependable guides for action or they may prove ruinous. It is an insightful process when a ball player gets a feel for the correct swing of his bat, when a little child discovers how to dress herself, when a youth learns to drive an automobile, when a child gets the idea of multiplication, perhaps through addition, or when a college student learns how to "read" Shakespeare.

A completely new situation would be cognitively unstructured. A person would have no knowledge of what would lead or point to what. Thus, at that moment the person's behavior would be completely random. (This is the position of a rat when it is first placed in a "problem box.") However, rarely, if ever, does a person function in a completely unstructured situation. More often people find themselves in situations that are inadequately or inharmoniously structured. This means that they have problems and need to extend their learning, that is, to change the cognitive structures of their life spaces.

A person changes the cognitive structure of his or her life spaces through *cognitive differentiation, generalization,* and *restructurization* of its respective regions. A region is a functionally distinguishable part of a life space; it is the psychological meaning of a remembered, a contemplated, or a presently existing object or activity. Respective regions of a life space may include one's conceptions of aspects of one's self, specific activities such as working and eating, states of being such as feeling frightened or secure, membership in groups and classes, and one's perceptions of personalities, objects, and events.

Cognitive Differentiation.   Cognitive differentiation is the process within which regions are subdivided into smaller regions. In differentiation, relatively vague and unstructured regions of a life space become cognitively structured and more specific. Thus, the person comes to see differences within what was previously thought to be the parts of a thing. Differentiation, then, means discerning more specific aspects of one's environment and oneself. Through cognitive learning one differentiates (1) oneself or one's person from the environment, (2) different aspects of one's person and environment from each other, (3) a psychological past and future from the present, and (4) imaginative levels of reality from the concrete reality of one's life space.

Cognitive Generalization.   Cognitive generalization is a process in which a generic idea or concept is formulated through discerning the common characteristics of a number of individual cases and identifying the cases as a class of ideas or objects. Thus, one identifies similarities among aspects of oneself or one's environment that had previously seemed quite different. A generalization arises through categorization of subregions into a unified region of a person's life space.

Although in common usage generalization is the opposite of differentiation, psychologically they complement each other. When learning that cats, dogs, horses, and birds are animals a child is generalizing. Then through a combination of differentiation and generalization, the child may divide the physical world into vegetable, animal, and mineral classes.

Cognitive Restructurization.   One not only differentiates and generalizes one's life space into new regions but simultaneously cognitively restructures regions of one's life space. One changes the meanings of its respective regions in relationship to oneself and to each other. Thusly, a person discovers significant new relationships between some aspects of his or her life space and nonrelationships between others previously considered related. Within the process of restructurization, one defines or redefines directions in one's life space; that is, one learns what actions will lead to which results. This is done through perception of significant relationships of different functional regions of a personal life space. Restructurization, then, consists of separating certain regions that had been connected and connecting certain regions that had been separated.

Psychological Processes That Characterize the Learning Process
Cognitive-field theorists think that four concurrent psychological processes transpire in the life of a person within which learning occurs: interaction of a person and his psychological environment within each life space; continuity of succeeding life spaces; differentiation in the person's time perspective; and changes in the person's concrete-imaginative levels of reality.

Interaction Within Each Life Space.   *Interaction* is the psychological process within which one makes something of one's person and psychological environment. Perceptual interaction, for cognitive-field psychologists, is an interrelationship between a person and that person's psychological environment. The person psychologically reaches into the environment, encounters some aspect of it, and brings that into a personal relationship. As a simultaneous part of the encounter, the person realizes the consequences of the entire process. (See the Glossary for a more technical definition.)

In a life space, the person and the person's psychological environment are in simultaneous mutual interaction (SMI) and are interdependent. Each depends upon the other for its nature and functions; it is impossible to treat one adequately without also treating the other. Accordingly, one's person is definitive of one's environment and likewise one's environment is definitive of oneself.

Continuity of Succeeding Life Spaces.   Since each life space covers only a limited expanse of time, an individual lives through a continuous series of overlapping life spaces that have much in common but seldom if ever are identical. Thus, life spaces are characterized by continuity of both the individual's successive persons and psychological environments. Since we can anticipate some degree of similarity and continuity in life spaces as the experiences of one moment shade into those of the next, for practical procedures, we may assume a duration of life spaces for periods longer than a moment, perhaps a class period, a week, or a month.

Within a series of overlapping life spaces, a person's life is a continuity of psychological tensions, locomotions, and new equilibriums. When there is an increase of tension in one part of a life space relative to the rest of the system, disequilibrium occurs. A person experiencing this state attempts to return to equilibrium, so psychic energy is expended; the person engages in psychological activity. Being intelligent and purposive, the person constantly expands and restructures the person's life space to some degree. Consequently, new disequilibriums continuously emerge.[21]

Permeability is a prime characteristic of the boundaries of aspects of a life space and their regions. There can be movement both ways through the boundary of a person or a psychological environment or through the boundaries of any of their regions. In succeeding life spaces, aspects of one's person may move into future environmental regions of one's life space or even into its foreign hull, and vice versa. Only the inner stratum of self (needs) remains relatively stable, although it too may change drastically over periods of time, as when a person changes religious faiths.

Differentiation in a Person's Time Perspective.   The basic idea of cognitive-field psychology is that everyone lives in the present. A person can't really live in either the physical past or future. In other words, one lives when one lives, which is right now. So, psychologically speaking, the past is past-present, the future is future-present, and the present is present-present. The past-present consists of what we ordinarily call memories, and the future-present consists of what we ordinarily call anticipations or expectations.

During development, an enlargement of a person's time perspective occurs; a psychological past and future become more significant. A small child lives very much in the present. A child's time perspective includes only an immediate past and an immediate future. However, as one matures, one's time perspective tends to expand. Thus, anticipations of more remote future events and growing memories of past events come to influence one's present behavior. But, the only past with which a person can deal is what he or she thinks happened in the past. Likewise, the only future that can influence a person now is the person's anticipation of a future that he or she thinks may eventuate.

A person's present life situation contains *traces*, or memories, of past incidents, but all of these are part of the present situation or life space. The past can be of present significance only through the operation of factors in the present that are identified as past. Anticipation of a future also occurs in the present; it is how one envisions the future, not what will actually happen, that counts in the present. If a child is good on Monday in order to get a star on Friday, whether or not the star is actually received on Friday has nothing to do with the child's behavior on the previous Monday. Anticipation of the star is the child's motivation for good behavior on Monday.

Changes in Concrete-Imaginative Levels of Reality.   Normal human development carries with it not only an enlargement of time perspective but also an increased differentiation of the concrete-imaginative dimensions of one's life space. As used in cognitive-field psychology, imaginative processes are symbolic thinking, wishing, dreaming, imagining, and kindred practices.

A young child does not clearly distinguish imaginative objects from concrete facts, wishes from goals, or hopes from expectations. Then, as a person grows older, he or she tends to make sharper distinctions between concrete and imaginative reality. True, fantasy in the form of wishful thinking is common in adults. However, adults generally are better able to distinguish imaginative processes from concrete experience.

Relation of Concrete-Imaginative Levels to Time Dimensions of a Life Space.   Two salient characteristics of a life space within any given unit of time are the level of concrete-imaginative reality at which the person is operating, and the degree to which the individual's life space encompasses a psychological past and future. There is a direct relationship between the respective concrete-imaginative levels of reality and the degree of time-binding that pervades the life space of a person at a given time. At the level of concrete facts, immediate goals, and practical expectations, a life space contains only an incipient past and future; they are just beginning to be. Thus, concrete reality is to be found mainly in the present moment. But, as a person's life space assumes more imaginative dimensions, time-binding functions become increasingly extended and significant until, at an extremely imaginative level, the person's entire life space may be centered on either a psychological past or future.

Imaginative levels of reality range from more expectations and their means of fulfillment to hallucinations that give rise to extreme guilts and fears. Aspirations, wishes, imagination, symbolic thought, creativity, fancy, fantasy, dreams, and nightmares may be found on levels between the two extremes, ranging from concrete reality to extremely imaginative reality. In the psychological past, these take the form of memory, pride, innocence, error, fault, sin, and guilt. In the psychological future, they embrace goals, hopes, anticipations, conjectures, fabrications, visions, fears, and despair.

Figure 3 symbolically depicts the interrelationship of the concrete-imaginative dimension and the time perspective of a person's life

Figure 3. Concrete-imaginative levels of a life space as related to its psychological past and future.

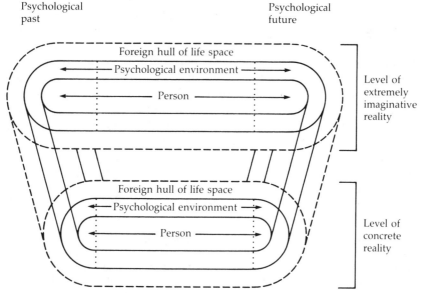

From Morris L. Bigge, *Learning Theories for Teachers*, 3rd ed. (New York: Harper & Row, 1976), p. 232. Reprinted by permission.

space. The figure should be interpreted to signify not merely two but numerous levels of reality, which may range from life on a purely biological level to one of complete absorption in fantasy. The figure illustrates both the concrete-imaginative and the time-binding dimensions of a life space. Think of the figure as three-dimensional. Its lower and upper bases represent extreme levels of concrete and imaginative reality. The part of the figure to the left of the vertical lefthand dotted line represents the person's psychological past, the part to the right of the vertical righthand dotted line represents his psychological future. Notice that, when the person is operating on an extreme level of concrete reality, there is very little psychological past or future in his life. The person is little concerned with either yesterday or tomorrow; the person simply lives each day as it comes. But, as a person functions on more imaginative levels, his or her psychological past and future also become more salient aspects of his or her life space. Thus, whereas on the level of concrete reality a psychological past and future hold a relatively minor significance, as a person operates on more imaginative levels the time dimensions of his or her life space become more and more important.

Cognitive-Field Experimentalism: The Nature of the Teaching Process

Cognitive-field experimentalism, as it relates directly to the teaching process, portrays learning as a process through which persons gain or change their insights, outlooks, or thought patterns. Persons learn through differentiating, generalizing, and restructuring their persons and their psychological environments in such way as to acquire new or changed insights, understandings, discernments, or meanings concerning them. Thereby they achieve changes in motivation, group belongingness, time perspective, and ideology. Learning involves persons' purposive development of more adequate insights or understandings; the extension of knowledge and discovery; the fashioning of artistic creations; the promotion of ties that hold people together in mutual aid and affection; and the expansion of areas of common goals and purposes through the harmonization of thoughts and interests. Through learning so conceived, knowledge becomes a power that may be used experimentally for the benefit of individuals and all humankind.

The Teacher
Teachers, with a cognitive-field orientation, see their unique function as that of implementing serviceable insights of students so that they may become more adequate and harmonious personalities; that is, to

become more intelligent. Hence, the teachers constantly try to involve their students in real problem situations that produce personal tensions. However, they do not cater to every student whim. Rather, they prompt students to rethink their goals and discard those that are trivial or whimsical. Teaching, then, is identified with teacher-student research in the area concerned. What is learned is not a set of behaviors as such, but insights regarding students' behavioral potentials and the behaviors that may be expected from other things and people.

In order to teach other persons in a significant way, a teacher should have sympathetic understanding of students as people and should develop an accurate idea of what is actually transpiring in the life spaces of those students. To understand students and their cognitive worlds, a teacher needs to develop a sort of disciplined naiveté, in order to see each student's person and environment as the student sees them. A teacher must think, "If I were Jack's age and had his psychological environment and a system of insights and values similar to his, what would I be trying to do and why would I be trying to do it?"

A teacher should have an extensive and varied background of knowledge and should be alert to the attitudes and outlooks students are developing. The teacher's ideal should be to promote an atmosphere that fosters maximum insightful growth. This requires the ability to judge which attitudes or insights are conducive, and which are detrimental, to continued growth.

Advocates of cognitive-field experimentalism think that a teacher should teach; neither baby-sit nor dictate. A baby-sitter performs a custodial function but teaches little; a dictator imposes the right answers. A teacher, in contrast with both, should perform a democratic teaching role in a process of student-teacher mutual inquiry. Teaching for insight or understanding can be either reflective or nonreflective, but democratic teaching should strive toward reflective procedures.

The Reflective Teaching Process

Reflective teaching, then, is problem-centered. The presence of genuine problems that students feel a need to solve distinguishes reflective from nonreflective teaching. The atmosphere is one of mutual inquiry, teacher-student and student-student, within which genuine problems are developed and solved. At the outset of a study, a real question develops for which students have no adequate answer. Through working cooperatively, the students and teacher develop what is for them a new or more adequate solution. Although performing a unique function in relation to a group of students, the teacher remains a part of the group as its members participate in the learning process.

When reflective teaching and learning are successful, students emerge with an enlarged store of tested generalized insights and an enhanced ability to develop and solve problems on their own. When students learn reflectively, they make genuine discoveries. But, to discover something, a student need not invent it, only explore a matter in such a way as to make more sense of it. Students continue to acquire traditional learnings, but they acquire them as verifying or substantiating data. Hence, teachers in no way disparage the importance of subject matter, although they think that students should invest knowledge with significant meanings.

Reflective teaching involves problem-raising and problem-solving. After aiding students in raising a problem, the teacher then helps them investigate it until the best possible answer is found. Problem-solving consists of formulating hypotheses and testing them with all available pertinent evidence. Facts are gathered in profusion, but teachers make no attempt to encourage fact learning or fact recall as such. Problems that make for ideal classroom study involve situations that are difficult enough to be challenging, yet simple enough that most students in a class will be able to cast and test hypotheses leading to a solution.

Development of a Problem.   To have a problem, a person must have a personal goal or goals and must find it impossible to reach that goal quickly and directly. A student may not achieve the goal readily, because he or she sees no open path to it or because there are two or more competing paths, or two or more competing goals, and the student cannot decide which to pursue. These are the familiar no-path or forked-path situations described by John Dewey.[22]

Cognitive-field concept may be effectively used to express the basic elements of a problematic situation. Either there is a goal region in a person's life space that has a positive valence, and there is a barrier between the person and the region of positive valence, or there are several conflicting goal regions provoking simultaneous psychological movement. These two types of situations are barrier or no-path situations and conflicting goal situations and are shown in Figure 4.

Conflicting-goal situations lend themselves best to reflective or problem-centered teaching. In a Type I situation, one has two conflicting goals or two psychologically opposite regions of one's life space, both with positive valences. (When positive goal regions are psychologically opposite both cannot be achieved at the same time.) In the illustration of Type I, vector vb represents a psychological force equal to the valence of region b, and vector va represents a force equal to the valence of region a. In a Type II situation, one is faced with two psychologically opposite significant regions of one's life space, each having a negative valence; one wants to escape both, but this is impossible. In a Type III situation, a region of positive valence and a region of negative valence are in the same psychological direction from one; they are functionally similar or perhaps identical but movement toward one requires move-

Figure 4. Field-conflict situations.

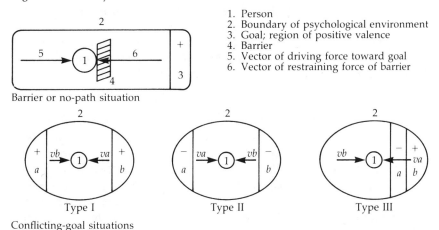

1. Person
2. Boundary of psychological environment
3. Goal; region of positive valence
4. Barrier
5. Vector of driving force toward goal
6. Vector of restraining force of barrier

Barrier or no-path situation

Type I   Type II   Type III

Conflicting-goal situations

From Morris L. Bigge, *Learning Theories for Teachers*, 3rd ed. (New York: Harper & Row, 1976), p. 349. Reprinted by permission.

ment away from the other. The direction of movement is determined by the relative strength of the pertinent psychological forces at the time of movement.

Superficially, Type I and Type II situations appear much alike; however, they are crucially different. Quite often, whether a conflict situation is Type I or Type II depends largely upon the individual's interpretation of the situation. A person in a Type II situation is like a ball being pushed from opposite directions by two sticks; once it gives a little, it flies off to the side, out of the picture. A person in such a situation is trying to escape two opposite negative driving forces and is likely to become completely frustrated and, like the ball, leave the field. Psychologically the person flees from the scene or becomes irrationally aggressive, that is, engages in either *flight* or *fight*. This means that the person suddenly moves from a relatively concrete level of his life space to an extremely imaginative level. In a Type I situation, like a ball being pulled in opposite directions, a person usually will stay in the field, that is, remain engaged with the problem and try to resolve the conflict at the level of reality at which it is met. The person is attracted to two goals, both with positive valences. The goal toward which the person moves is the one with the higher value or valence.

Since Type II situations (two opposite negative goals) give rise to frustrations, they should be avoided in teaching procedures. In contrast, Type I situations (two opposite positive goals) involve and perplex but do not frustrate students, so they should be sought.

A Type III conflict situation develops when a person contemplates violating one of the basic mores of his society, especially if it is for the first time. The person wants to perform the tabooed act and simultaneously wants not to do it; thus the act has both positive and negative valences. The person involved might perceive the taboo not as a negative goal region but a barrier between him and the positive goal region. In this event, the barrier would have a negative valence that must be counteracted by the strongest positive valence of the act, if it is to be performed.

Solution of a Problem.   Helping students develop problems is only one aspect of reflective teaching. The other four aspects are involved in solution of the problem.[23] Problem solving consists of formulating and testing hypotheses. We should emphasize here that the five parts of reflective thinking, teaching, and learning are *aspects*, not *steps*. They seldom are followed in a consecutive orderly fashion. They may develop in any order or any or all of the aspects may develop concurrently. Reflective processes commonly are characterized by confusion, hesitation, and irregularity.

Formulation and testing of hypotheses should be conducted in an atmosphere that resembles a scientific laboratory as far as possible. The same open-minded and objective attitudes that characterize any scientific investigation should prevail. Hence, the teacher's role should be analogous to that of a head scientist in a laboratory; the teacher should help students construct hypotheses, then assist them in testing them out.

Formulation of Hypotheses, considered guesses or hunches, constitutes the second aspect of reflective learning. *Deducing the logical implications of the hypotheses* constitutes the third. Often, the two aspects are so intermingled that it is difficult to distinguish one from the other. In reflective teaching, students are encouraged to formulate as many hypotheses as possible in regard to what might resolve the discrepancies or inadequacies in thought that have been exposed. Simultaneously, they are urged to deduce as many of the logical implications of each hypothesis as they can muster.

In *testing hypotheses*, the fourth aspect, students are encouraged to examine the hypotheses in the light of all obtainable, pertinent evidence. Problem-centered study may encompass a variety of evidence-seeking activities including the use of individual and group research, home study, field trips, and guest speakers. It may also involve considerable explanation and illustration by the teacher. An informal lecture can be a highly useful tool both for providing data for students' consideration and for instigating and promoting further reflection.

The fifth aspect of reflective teaching-learning, *drawing conclusions*, is perhaps the most difficult aspect of a teacher's endeavor to promote reflective learning through reflective teaching. However, the basic, guiding principle is that the teacher and students should strive to achieve a consensus on the conclusion, unanimity being the ideal. But even though representing a minority of one person, no student should be coerced in any way to alter a position to conform with that of the group consensus or the majority.

A conclusion may involve either reacceptance of the idea originally brought under question, modification of the idea, or formulation of a substitute idea. The important concern is that students push their thinking further than it had gone before. They need not arrive at an answer that has been preconceived by the teacher. Teaching for reflection is provocative, rather than evocative. Reaffirmation of the idea that the teacher had earlier induced students to doubt is quite acceptable, provided that in the course of their study the students come to understand the idea better and to have a better grasp of the evidence pertinent to it.[24]

The Subject Matter Emphasis of Cognitive-Field Experimentalism

The key to improvement of present and future learning, for cognitive-field experimentalists, is the reconstruction of teaching-learning processes and materials so as to prepare people for the vocational and cultural world of both today and tomorrow, but to accomplish this in such a way as to enhance the intellectual insights and moral values germane to each life and vocation. Hence, there should be no sharp distinction between liberal and vocational studies.

Adherents of this educational philosophy think that education should promote the learning of traditional subject matter in a nontraditional manner. For them, worthy traditional subject matter encompasses the arts, sciences, and humanities. The essential characteristics of reflective teaching have enough flexibility to be employed in all school subjects, including those which seem on the surface to be rather cut-and-dried. Problem-centered teaching emerges whenever a teacher, through adroit questioning and statements induces students to doubt that which they now accept, then helps them analyze critically the issues that have arisen. Opportunities regularly appear in most conventional subjects for a teacher to operate in this manner. Passages in a textbook, assertions made by students, a news story, or a motion picture or television show may serve as a springboard for creation of problems. Problem-centered teaching grows more from a unique relationship between teacher and students than from any different nature of formal course materials.

Some courses and some types of course organization, however, lend themselves more readily to reflective teaching than do others. A course, whose subject matter is not narrowly prescribed is probably a better tool than is a narrow course. This difference, however, is not inherent in the nature of the subject matter as such but lies in the frame of reference within which the subject matter customarily is treated. There is a growing body of evidence that every subject-matter area on every level has been and is being taught reflectively, at least by some teachers. The reflection-level can become the prevailing mode of teaching and learning, provided teachers and students become convinced that it is the most advantageous level on which to operate, and teachers know their subjects. "Dewey expects of teachers . . . that they know their subject matters almost as experts know them. . . ."[25]

A course in which problem-centered teaching is used cannot be bound rigidly to a textbook. Since, real problems are psychological in nature, data used in solving them are rarely organized in the same logical pattern as textbooks and courses of study. The *logical organization* of a book simply does not usually coincide with the *psychological growth* of intellects. Hence, courses should be allowed to cut across subject matter lines whenever such deviation makes sense in terms of the particular problems being studied. Determination of which subjects, or which topics within a subject, should be handled as problems cannot be made without reference to a specific teaching situation. In each case, a teacher should reckon with the maturity and experiential background of students, community attitudes, his or her personal preparation and skill, and the anticipated consequences of having a class delve deeply into the subject.

Through application of cognitive-field experimentalism, with its emphasis upon reflective teaching and learning, traditional learnings continue to be acquired, but now they are acquired as verifying or substantiating data. Learned competencies are abilities, that is, understandings or generalized insights, which enable learners to exercise enhanced recognitions, anticipations, predictions, distinctions, and verifications as intellectually warranted assertibilities, relativistic truths, established through empirical, experimental study.

Footnotes

[1] John Dewey, "Experience, Knowing and Value: A Rejoinder," in Paul Schilpp, ed., *The Philosophy of John Dewey* (Evanston, Ill.: Northwestern University Press, 1939), p. 554.

[2] John L. Childs, *American Pragmatism and Education: An Interpretation and Criticism* (New York: Henry Holt and Company, Inc., 1956), p. 80. Reprinted by permission of Holt, Rinehart and Winston.

[3] See Norman S. Endler and David Magnusson, *Interactional Psychology and Personality*, (Washington, D.C.: Hemisphere Publishing Corporation, 1976), especially Chapter 1, "Personality and Person By Situation Interactions."

[4] See John Dewey, *Reconstruction In Philosophy* (New York: Mentor Books, 1950), p. 142.

[5]See Sam Ducker, *The Public Schools and Religion* (New York: Harper & Row, Publishers, 1966), p. 78.

[6]John Dewey, *Logic: The Theory of Inquiry* (New York: Holt, Rinehart and Winston, Inc., 1938), p. 460.

[7]See Morris L. Bigge, *Learning Theories for Teachers*, 4th ed. (New York: Harper & Row, 1982), pp. 169–227 for development of cognitive-field psychology and the meaning of life space.

[8]John Dewey, *A Common Faith* (New Haven, Conn.: Yale University Press, 1934), p. 49.

[9]Hugh Skilling, "An Operational View," *American Scientists*, 52, no. 4 (December 1964): p. 309A.

[10]See Ernest E. Bayles, *Pragmatism in Education* (New York: Harper & Row, 1966), for expansion of the source and meaning of truth.

[11]William Van Orman Quine, *From a Logical Point of View* (Cambridge, Mass.: Harvard University Press, 1953), p. 79.

[12]See Colleen S. Decker and T. Frank Saunders, *A Model For Models* (Tucson, Ariz.: C. S. Decker and T. F. Saunders, 1976).

[13]See John Dewey, *The Public and Its Problems* (New York: Henry Holt, 1927), p. 191.

[14]John Dewey, *Theory of Valuation* (Chicago: The University of Chicago Press, 1939), p. 3.

[15]See Jurgen Herbst, "The Anti-School—Some Reflections on Teaching," *Educational Theory*, 18, no. 1 (Winter 1968): p. 22.

[16]John Dewey, *Democracy and Education* (New York: The Macmillan Company, 1916), p. 89.

[17]See Ernest E. Bayles, *Democratic Educational Theory* (New York: Harper & Row, 1960), Chapter 1, "Experiments with Reflective Teaching."

[18]See Kurt Lewin, *Field Theory in Social Science,* edited by Dorwin Cartwright (New York: Harper & Brothers, 1951).

[19]See Albert Bandura, "Behavior Theory and the Models of Man," *American Psychologist*, 29 (December 1974): 859–869.

[20]John Dewey, *Democracy and Education*, p. 163.

[21]See Edward L. Deci, *Intrinsic Motivation* (New York: Plenum Press, 1975), p. 162.

[22]See Morris L. Bigge and Maurice P. Hunt, *Psychological Foundations of Education*, 3rd ed. (New York: Harper & Row, 1980), p. 93.

[23]See Morris L. Bigge, *Learning Theories for Teachers*, pp. 311–341 for expansion of these techniques.

[24]Morris L. Bigge and Maurice P. Hunt, *Psychological Foundations of Education.* Pages 482–485 describe teaching at the fifth-grade level through reflective means. Pages 500–509 develop reflective teaching of the meaning of race. Pages 517–519 report an actual unit that was used in teaching a high school English class reflectively.

[25]Joe R. Burnett, "Whatever Happened to John Dewey?", *Teachers College Record*, 81, no. 2 (Winter 1979): 196.

BIBLIOGRAPHY

Bandura, Albert. *Social Learning Theory*. Englewood Cliffs, N.J.: Prentice-Hall, 1977.

Bateman, Grant, William Lieurance, Agnes Manney, and Curtis Osburn. *Helping Children Think*. Tri-University Project in Elementary Education. New York: New York University Press, 1968.

Bayles, Ernest E. *Pragmatism in Education*. New York: Harper & Row, Publishers, 1966.

Bayles, Ernest E., and Hood, Bruce L. *Growth of American Educational Thought and Practice*. New York: Harper & Row, 1966.

Bigge, Morris L. *Positive Relativism: An Emergent Educational Philosophy*. New York: Harper & Row, Publishers, 1971.

Bigge, Morris L. *Learning Theories for Teachers*, 4th ed. New York: Harper & Row, Publishers, 1982.

Bigge, Morris L., and Hunt, Maurice P. *Psychological Foundations of Education*, 3rd ed. New York: Harper & Row, 1980.

Brown, Bob Burton. *The Experimental Mind in Education*. New York: Harper & Row, 1968.

Brunner, Jerome S., et al. *Studies in Cognitive Growth*. New York: John Wiley & Sons, Inc., 1966.

Burnett, Joe. R. "Whatever Happened to John Dewey?" *Teachers College Record*, 81, no. 2 (Winter 1979): 192–210.

Dewey, John. *Reconstruction in Philosophy*. New York: Mentor Books, 1950, originally published by Henry Holt, 1920.

Dewey, John. *Human Nature and Conduct*. New York: Holt, Rinehart and Winston, Inc., 1922.

Dewey, John. *Art as Experience*. New York: Capricorn Books, 1958; originally published by G. P. Putnam's Sons, 1934.

Dewey, John. *Experience and Education*. New York: The Macmillan Company, 1938.

Dewey, John. *Theory of Valuation*. Chicago: The University of Chicago Press, 1939.

Endler, Norman S., and Magnusson, David. *Interactional Psychology and Personality*. Washington, D. C.: Hemisphere Publishing Corporation, 1976.

Feinberg, Walter. *Reason and Rhetoric: The Intellectual Foundations of 20th Century Liberal Educational Policy*. New York: John Wiley & Sons, 1975.

Frank, Philipp. *Relativity—A Richer Truth*. Boston: Beacon Press, 1950.

Hook, Sidney. *Education and the Taming of Power*. LaSalle, Ill.: Open Court Publishing, 1973, especially Chapters 5 and 6 on Dewey's ideology.

Hullfish, H. Gordon, and Smith, Philip G. *Reflective Thinking: The Method of Education.* New York: Dodd, Mead & Company, 1951.

Hunt, Maurice P., and Metcalf, Laurence E. *Teaching High School Social Studies,* 2nd ed. New York: Harper & Row, Publishers, 1968.

Jelinek, James John, ed. *Philosophy of Education in Cultural Perspective.* Tempe, Ariz.: Far Western Philosophy of Education Society, 1977, especially Chapters 2, 7, 21, 24, 30, 32, 38, and 46.

Jones, Richard M. *Fantasy and Feeling in Education.* New York: New York University Press, 1968.

Kuhn, Thomas S., *The Structure of Scientific Revolutions,* 2nd ed., Chicago: The University of Chicago Press, 1970.

May, Rollo. *Psychology and the Human Dilemma.* New York: Van Nostrand Reinhold Company, 1967.

Metcalf, Laurence E., "Research on Teaching the Social Studies," in N. L. Gage, ed. *Handbook of Research on Teaching.* Chicago: Rand McNally & Co., 1963.

Meyer, Agnes E. *Education for a New Morality.* New York: The Macmillan Company, 1957.

Mischel, Walter. "The Self as the Person: A Cognitive Social Learning View," in Abraham Wandersman, Paul J. Poppen, and David F. Hicks, eds. *Humanism and Behaviorism: Dialogue and Growth.* Oxford: Pergamon, 1976, pp. 145–156.

Neff, Frederick C. *Philosophy and American Education.* New York: Center for Applied Research in Education, 1966, Chapter 4.

Reid, Louis Arnaud. *Philosophy and Education.* New York: Random House, Inc., 1962.

Robinson, Daniel N. *Systems of Modern Psychology.* New York: Columbia University Press, 1979, especially pages 174–186 and 211–214.

Shargel, Emanuel I. "John Dewey and The School As a Special Environment," in *Philosophy of Education 1980, Proceedings of the Thirty-Sixth Annual Meeting of the Philosophy of Education Society,* edited by C. J. B. Macmillan. Normal, Ill.: Philosophy of Education Society, 1981.

Shermis, S. Samuel. *Philosophic Foundation of Education.* New York: American Book Company, 1967.

Weiner, Bernard. *Achievement, Motivation and Attribution Theory.* Morristown, N.J.: General Learning Corporation, 1974.

Wertheimer, Max. *Productive Thinking,* enlarged edition edited by Michael Wertheimer. New York: Harper & Row, 1959.

Glossary

Absolute. Something free from, and independent of, human perception, cognition, and valuation; it is both unlimited and independent of its context.

Abstraction. The process of extracting certain qualities of a thing without altering its shape or other qualities; say, taking the color from a piece of cloth or the hardness from iron.

Accidents (vs essence). The sensory experienced characteristics of objects.

Adequacy. The careful consideration of all pertinent information available within a philosophy and its tenets.

Aesthetics. Study of creation, value, and experience of art and beauty.

Agnosticism. The doctrine that the existence or form of God or Ultimate Reality is unknowable.

Analytic philosophy. A school of philosophy concerned with criticizing, analyzing, and clarifying the meanings of words, concepts, and ideas; it centers upon formal analysis and definition of language and usage of logical grammar; and looks behind the sciences to analyze the concepts and methods that they use; also called linguistic analysis, verbal analysis.

A posteriori (vs *a priori*). (From: what comes after.) Knowledge stated in empirically verifiable propositions; inductive, synthetic knowledge based upon, and not prior to, experience.

Apperception. A psychological mentalistic process in which new ideas relate themselves to a store of old ones within one's mind.

A priori (vs *a posteriori*). (From: what comes before.) Deductive knowledge based on principles that are self evident apart from observation or experience; independently of sensory experience, an *a* *priori* proposition is necessarily true or false based on purely logical or semantic grounds.

Atheism. The doctrine that there is no deity or God.

Axiology. A general theory of value: what is good and beautiful; primary concepts are ought, duty, right, and wrong.

Behavior (behaviorism). Any actual, potentially measurable movement of or within a biological organism.

Behavior (cognitive-field psychology). Any psychological change in a life space; a change that is in accordance with a growing intelligence.

Behavioral experimentalism. A school of pragmatic educational philosophy that is implemented by behavioristic psychology; it combines realistic assumptions with idealistic goals.

Behaviorism. A psychological position that assumes that people are neutral-passive biological organisms whose behaviors are determined by their genetic patterns and the physical environments that impinge upon and stimulate them; adherents reject introspection; any organism responds according to its genetic pattern and prior conditioning.

Behaviorism, social. A behavioristic experimentalist psychology that emphasizes social reinforcement of behavior through use of serial adaptive responses in social situations.

Cause, final. That which is the end or purpose of a process: a completed house.

Cause, first. The supreme cause of existents, which is the divine mind of the Deity.

Christian idealism. (See idealism.)

Classical realism. A philosophic position that holds that both physical things and ideas exist in their own right (realism) and both are underpinned by ideas that are forever relevant (classical); also called lay neo-Thomism, rational realism.

Cognitive-field experimentalism. A school of pragmatic educational philosophy that is implemented by cognitive-field psychology; an emergent synthesis from earlier conflicting positions.

Cognitive-field psychology. An interpersonal, social psychology that integrates biological, personal, and social factors; it centers upon persons interacting with their psychological environments.

Cognitive process (vs behavioral process). (From: to know.) A process through which people gain understanding of themselves and their respective environments so as to guide their relationships with their environments.

Cognitive structure of a life space. A person and the environment as known by the specific person; insight, understanding, or discernment of meanings of aspects of one's life space.

Concept. A generalized idea or common meaning that is abstracted from experiences; the rule for usage of a given term.

Concrete-imaginative levels of reality (cognitive-field experimentalism). The operation level of one's life space, located somewhere between a level of biological subsistence and a level marked by symbolic thinking, wishing, dreaming, imagining, and kindred processes.

Conditioning. Formation of stimulus-response sequential relations that result in an enduring change in either a pattern of behavior or the likelihood of a response of an organism.

Conditioning, classical. Conditioning that occurs without reinforcement; stimulus substitution.

Conditioning, instrumental. Conditioning that occurs through reinforcements, i.e., increasing the probability of a behavior through reduction of an organic need or satisfaction of a drive stimulus; response modification.

Construct. A generalized, invented idea or concept not directly observable but formed from related, observable data to correlate a broad range of such data.

Contemporaneity (cognitive-field psychology). (From: all at one time.) The idea of everything that is psychological occurring at once.

Cosmology. Problem of the origin and structure of the universe and the nature of being.

Cosmos. The ordered and arranged world or universe.

Culture. The established way of life or social heritage of a group of people; it includes customs, morals, ideals, and standards and the institutions through which they are manifested as they are transmitted socially from generation to generation.

Dasein (existentialism). (From: existence or being in the world.) The sort of being that applies to humankind, a consciousness of conscious Being, the fundamental happening within human experience.

Deism. The position that God transcends, but is in no way immanent in, nature; God created the universe with its natural laws but remains apart from it.

Determinism. The view that human behavior is caused and controlled by previous chains of causes and effects; every event has prior causes, and all human acts result from some combination of reflexes, stimuli, sensations, feelings, associations, and habits that form their antecedent causes.

Dichotomy. The division into two mutually exclusive groups or ideas.

Divine Grace. Unmerited Godly assistance given to people for their regeneration or sanctification; its achievement comprises the highest level of contemplation.

Dualism. The philosophical idea that reality is composed of two basically different kinds of fundamental substances, mind and matter, that cannot be reduced to one another.

Dualistic theism. Philosophic position that recognizes both a supernatural and a natural order of being.

Eclecticism. The practice of selecting aspects of conflicting outlooks and combining them into a mosaic type of position.

Eclectic compromise (vs emergent synthesis). A mosaic-like position achieved by selectively borrowing aspects of opposing outlooks or theories without recognizing their basic contradictions with one another and using them as they appear appropriate to situations that arise.

Emergent. Something novel that appears in the course of evolution of ideas; not an intermediate position.

Emergent synthesis (vs eclectic compromise). A relatively new systematic outlook achieved by selecting and modifying existent knowledge from incompatible positions, adding new thinking, and developing a new position that is both internally consistent and more adequate than its precursors.

Empiricism (vs rationalism). The philosophic position that the basic source of knowledge is sensory experience and perhaps introspection, but not reason, intuition, or speculation.

Entelechy. A genuinely real nonmaterial vital force or principle that is responsible for life and growth.

Epistemology. The area of philosophical theory on the nature and source of knowledge: what can we know and how do we know it?

Essence (vs accidents). The absolute forms of things; the intrinsic nature that makes each thing what it is.

Eternal verities. Everlasting truths.

Evocative education (vs provocative education). Education that calls forth in students the right thoughts and behaviors.

Existentialism. A nonrational school of philosophy that stresses both the uniqueness and absolute freedom of each individual: "existence precedes essence"; humankind is actively creative; emphasizes feeling of anxiety and satiation of needs; also called phenomenological philosophy, psychedelic humanism.

Existential moments (existentialism). The time at which one awakens to one's own existence in such a nature that moral choice is recognized as inescapable.

Experimentalism. The philosophical outlook that considers truths to be the results of scientific inquiry measured in terms of predictive accuracy and satisfactory consequences.

Facticity. A scientific mode of knowing centered on the view that objects, in existing, simply exist as they are in themselves; an object is just what it appears to be and no more; being-in-itself.

Field, psychological. A life space; a situation within which a person, that person's psychological environment, and the interaction between that person and that environment are viewed as occurring all at once.

Foreign hull (cognitive-field experimentalism). Aspects of an organism's physical-social environment that are observable to others but which at that moment have no significance for the person being studied; complex of nonpsychological factors surrounding a life space.

Free will (vs determinism). The power within oneself of genuine self-determining choice in regard to moral principles; the will is endowed with capacity to discern ultimate good from ultimate bad.

Gestalt. A form, pattern, or configuration plus whatever comprises the configuration.

Harmony. The integration of all, or at least most, pertinent information into a reasonably consistent overall pattern.

Hedonism. The doctrine that the principal good in life is pursuit of physical pleasure.

Homeostasis, biological. An organism's tendency to move toward equilibrium both within itself and between itself and its environment and to maintain its normalcy against both internal and external disrupting agencies.

Homeostasis, psychological (cognitive-field experimentalism). The tendency and efforts to develop new equilibriums between a person's self and that person's psychological environment throughout a continuous series of life spaces.

Hypothesis. A considered guess or hunch in regard to which some pertinent data are available; a trial answer to be tested.

Idea (Plato). The universal essential form of a category that underpins a class of existent things that make it up: the bookness of all books, say.

Idealism. The philosophical school that asserts that basic reality is mental: it consists of ideas, thoughts, minds, or substantive selves, and not of matter; idea-ism; also called Christian idealism.

Insight (cognitive-field experimentalism). The basic sense of, or feeling for, relationships in a life situation; a meaning or discernment; a generalized insight is an understanding.

Interaction (cognitive-field experimentalism). A perceptual encounter within which one structures oneself and one's environment in terms of the relevance of their various regions or aspects to definition and pursuit of goals; a cognitive experiential process within which a person, psychologically, simultaneously reaches out to his or her environment, encounters some aspects of it, brings those aspects into relationship with himself, makes something of those aspects, acts in relation to what he or she makes of them, and realizes the consequences of the entire process; also called perceptual interaction.

Intuition. Direct apprehension of knowledge without either conscious reasoning or sense perception; formation of a direct relation between the mind and some article of knowledge.

Lay neo-Thomism (see classical-realism).

Learning, explanatory-understanding level. Students acquiring teacher-given relationships between generalized principles or rules and the facts that support each and the uses to which the relationships or principles may be applied.

Learning, exploratory understanding level (see learning, reflective).

Learning, memory level. Either rote verbal or behavioral storage of factual materials for future recall or manifestation.

Learning, reflective. The careful, critical examination of an article of knowledge in light of the testable evidence that supports it and the further conclusions toward which it points; the exploratorily process of gaining understandings through reconstructing one's life spaces so as both to add meaning to one's life and to increase one's abilities, individually and in cooperation with others, to direct the course and content of one's future life spaces; also called exploratory understanding level learning.

Life space (cognitive-field experimentalism). A model of a total psychological situation, which consists of a person, the psychological environment, and the regions or aspects of each; a series of one's life spaces pictures what is possibly in one's life and what is likely to occur.

Linguistic analysis (see analytic philosophy).

Logical empiricism. The philosophic position that exalts empirical science over metaphysics; its adherents consider the unique task of philosophy to be analysis of logical relations between propositions and definitions of terms; previously called logical positivism.

Logical positivism (see logical empiricism).

Meliorism. (From: betterism.) The view that matters are open to constant improvement through human learning and endeavor; contrasts with optimism and pessimism.

Metaphysics. (From: after physics.) The view that a reality exists beyond the observable world and is conceived to be transcendental to humankind's sensory experience; includes ontology (being), cosmology (order in being), and teleology (purpose of being).

Monism. The view that there is only one kind of fundamental reality: mind, matter, God, or something else.

Natural moral law (vs positive-governmental law). The view that universally valid rules exist that are discoverable by intuition and reason alone; also called a higher law.

Naturalism (vs supernaturalism). The view that the world of experience is the whole of reality; everything, being, and action is a part of Nature.

Nihilism. The view that nothing truly has any value.

Noetic being. The view that things have absolute existences as forms, and minds have the capacity to apprehend them.

Nominalism (vs realism). The view that a universal concept, such as dog or humankind, is merely a common name for objects of a given description; generalized terms are only composite names for particulars, not names for genuinely real existent universals.

Nonsecular (vs secular). A concern with matters that relate to a supernatural, metaphysical world of reality, and which are not measurable in terms of physical space and time.

Normativism. The philosophic school concerned with construction and evaluation of basic outlooks concerning values.

Noumena (vs phenomena). A world independent of human perception that consists of things known by the mind rather than by the senses.

Ontology. A concern with the nature of being of Being: a transcendental, independent, and absolute existence.

Operant (behaviorism). The set of acts that constitutes an organism's behavior and is controlled by the stimuli that follow the behavior.

Original sin. The view that all people, at birth, have a common innate tendency toward evil or badness.

Pantheism (all is God vs all is God's). The view that God is immanent in, not transcendent to, Nature; God and the universe are one and the same.

Paradigm. A basic pattern or way of looking at matters.

Perception. The more or less complex image of a thing provided through the senses, intellect, memory, and imagination.

Perceptual interaction (see interaction).

Person (cognitive-field experimentalism). That configuration of matters with which an individual identifies himself, takes care of, and gives allegiance to what one makes of all the features that one thinks of or deals with as one's own, including one's organism.

Phenomena (vs noumena). The aspects of a perceived world of experience.

Phenomenological philosophy (see existentialism).

Positive relativism. The philosophic school that defines reality and truth in a relativistic, constructive fashion and asserts no position in regard to absolute existence; its adherents assert the availability of instrumental truth and reality and affirm the feasibility of a body of constructive knowledge.

Pragmatism. The philosophic school that extends experimental inquiry to all realms of human experience and intellectual activity; emphasizes democratic values and procedures; a form of empiricism that includes both behavioral and cognitive-field experimentalism.

Predestination (vs historical determinism). The view that all events in the lives of human beings have been decreed from the beginning of time by a sovereign God.

Proposition. A declarative sentence that consists of a subject, which represents a thing, process, event, or concept; a predicate, which states something about the subject; and a middle term such as is, which connects the subject and the predicate. Propositions may consist of synthetic statements about characteristics of the physical world that are derived from observed facts or of logical, analytical statements of the relations of either the terms of propositions or of the propositions themselves in terms of either logic or pure mathematics.

Provocative education (vs evocative education). The view that education centers upon teaching students how to think, using facts, as opposed to teaching them merely facts and behaviors.

Psychedelic humanism (see existentialism).

Psychological (vs logical). In harmony with the logic of a growing mind or intelligence.

Psychological environment (cognitive-field experimentalism). Things, functions, and relationships that, at a given time, surround a person and have meaning for the person.

Purpose, immanent. The view that one pursues the best that one knows how for the welfare of whatever one conceives oneself to be.

Purpose, transcendental. The view of a purpose that is over and beyond that which is pursued in human experience; the plan and goal of a Deity.

Quiddity (Aristotle). The essence or basic whatness of a thing.

Rationalism (vs empiricism). The philosophic position that views the basic source of knowledge as reason; minds have the power to know truths independently of experience.

Rational realism (see classical realism).

Realism (vs idealism). The philosophic view that objects received by our senses really exist independent of any human knowledge and that people's knowledge of them in no way alters the nature of their being.

Realism (vs nominalism). The philosophic view that universal concepts, for which composite class terms stand, have a genuine, absolute existence quite independent of its representatives that appear to the sense; there is a concept of chairness of which this chair is a representative.

Realism, naive. The common sense view of a world of natural matters; uncritical acceptance of reality of objects perceived through the senses.

Reality, ultimate The conception that the absolute nature of matters can be glimpsed by the intellectual apprehensions of sages and prophets, scholars and poets, and ártists and theologians.

Reconstruction of experience (cognitive-field experimentalism). One's grasping significant relationships of regions of one's life space so as to add to its meaning and to increase one's ability to direct the course and contents of one's future life spaces.

Reflexive thought (philosophical analysis). The process of thinking turned back on itself; thinking about thinking.

Regions of a life space (cognitive-field experimentalism). Psychologically significant conditions, places, things, and activities defined functionally as aspects of one's life space.

Relatively absolute (cognitive-field experimentalism). The concept of a state of being taken as a relatively fixed, stable point of reference that is a functional arbitrary standard contrived by humankind but susceptible to future change.

Respondent (behaviorism). A behavior that is brought on by a preceding stimulus.

Secular (vs nonsecular). (From: finite time.) Matters belonging to the present empirically experienced world, thus measurable in terms of time and space.

Self actualization (existentialism). One's making oneself and in the process developing a self-directed intuitive self-awareness.

Situational choice (vs free will and determinism). The view that, at any juncture in one's life, one may to some extent choose the way one will turn next.

Simultaneous mutual interaction or SMI (vs sequential cause and effect). The concurrent situational relationships of a person and aspects of the person's psychological environment.

Skepticism. The view that doubts the abilty to know about what really exists or whether it can be known.

Solipsism. The view that, since nothing exists outside one's mind, I alone exist.

Speculative philosophy. A type of philosophy that is concerned with the way matters really are; its adherents make considered guesses or speculations about the absolute nature of the cosmos, or universe, and the people in it.

Subsistence (idealism). The view of a supernatural superexistence that provides the basis and patterns for earthly existences.

Substance. That which is genuinely real in the deepest sense; it exists in and of itself.

Supposed world (cognitive-field experimentalism). The concept of a commonly accepted world of commonality, which provides physical-social raw materials for people's perceptions; it provides foreign hulls of life spaces.

Syllogism. A deductive reasoning device to test the logic of a statement or proposition through formal rules of logic.

Synthetic a priori propositions. Statements of metaphysical principles arrived at through intuition or inspiration, but in a way to imply that they are based upon induction from empirical evidence, for example, reality is mental.

Tautology. (From: saying the same thing.) An analytic statement that, because of its logical form, is true by definition; for example, a quadruped has four legs.

Teleology. The view that the universe is supernaturally endowed with purpose.

Theism. The view that God created humankind with a human nature, consisting of a material body and an immortal soul, and that God both transcends, and is immanent in, Nature.

Transcendental. Existing beyond the world of observable objects.

Understanding. A generalized insight on discernment in the form of a concept, rule, theory, or law.

Valences (cognitive-field experimentalism). Properties of regions of a life space that attract or repel one; imperative environmental positive or negative characteristics; values.

Value, absolute. The view that value is justified independently of any reference to human needs, interests, or ideals.

Value, instrumental. The view that something has value because of its individual and social usefulness; a normative standard acquired through reflective empirical inquiry.

Value, intrinsic. The view that a thing has value for itself alone, regardless of its usefulness.

Variables, dependent. Actions or movements caused by preceding independent variables; effects.

Variables, independent. The causes of actions or movements.

Variables, interdependent (cognitive-field experimentalism). Qualities of the regions or aspects of a life space so characterized that the meaning of each depends upon the meanings of all the others.

Verbal analysis (see analytic philosophy).

Verification principle (logical empiricism). The view that something is meaningful if and only if it either can be proven empirically, through use of the senses, or it is an analytic tautology of logic or mathematics.

Verifiability criterion (logical empiricism). The analysis of the meaning of a statement based upon either analytic or empirically tested proofs.

Warranted assertibility. An insight or understanding that emerges from reflective inquiry and is judged by its consequences in and on human experience.

REFERENCES

Grooten, J., and Steenberger, G. Jo. *New Encyclopedia of Philosophy,*
    New York: Philosophical Library, 1972.

Lacey, A. R. *A Dictionary of Philosophy.* London: Routledge & Kegan
    Paul, 1976.

Runes, Dagobert D. *Dictionary of Philosophy.* Totowa, N.J.: Littlefield
    Adams & Co., 1960.

Titus, Harold H. *Living Issues in Philosophy,* 5th ed. New York: Van
    Nostrand Reinhold, 1970.

Webster's Third New International Dictionary. Springfield, Mass.: G. & C.
    Merriam, 1961.

Index